CHRISTOLOGY AND GLOBAL ETHICS

Christology and Global Ethics

Encountering the Poor in a Pluralist Reality

Alexandre A. Martins

Paulist Press
New York / Mahwah, NJ

Cover photo by byMALENS/Pexels.com
Cover design by Joe Gallagher
Book design by by Lynn Else

Library of Congress Cataloging-in-Publication Data
Names: Martins, Alexandre Andrade, author.
Title: Christology and global ethics : encountering the poor in a pluralist reality / Alexandre A. Martins
Description: New York ; Mahwah, NJ : Paulist Press, [2023] | Includes bibliographical references and index. | Summary: "This comprehensive approach to Christology combines the Bible, theology, and ethics, and presents a dynamic understanding of faith in Jesus that embodies it ethically in reality"—Provided by publisher.
Identifiers: LCCN 2023010488 (print) | LCCN 2023010489 (ebook) | ISBN 9780809156245 (paperback) | ISBN 9780809187850 (ebook)
Subjects: LCSH: Jesus Christ—Person and offices. | Globalization—Moral and ethical aspects. | Poor—Health and hygiene. | Liberation theology. | Cultural pluralism. | World health. | Health services accessibility—Moral and ethical aspects.
Classification: LCC BT203 .M3345 2023 (print) | LCC BT203 (ebook) | DDC 232—dc23/eng/20230710
LC record available at https://lccn.loc.gov/2023010488
LC ebook record available at https://lccn.loc.gov/2023010489

ISBN 978-0-8091-5624-5 (paperback)
ISBN 978-0-8091-8785-0 (e-book)

Published by Paulist Press
997 Macarthur Boulevard
Mahwah, New Jesey 07430
www.paulistpress.com

Printed and bound in the
United States of America

To Dante, Santiago, and Sydney,
who taught me the meaning of love and the joy of living

Contents

Foreword

The Spirit: An Intervention

Much depends on Luke 4:16–30 in Alexandre A. Martins's *Christology and Global Ethics*.

In the introduction, he calls it not only this book's "central biblical text," but also adds that he has made an existential choice to live his life based on this proclamation of Jesus. The text grounds his entire life project. Being asked to do a foreword to this stunning work, I cannot but pause here with the text.

Three insights frame my reflections on the text that serve to prompt the reader's engagement: what precedes it, what it is, and what follows it.

BEFORE

Luke begins chapter 4 by reminding us of Jesus's baptism, where "the Holy Spirit descended upon him" (Luke 3:22). The first verse tells us, "Jesus, full of the Holy Spirit, returned from the Jordan and was led by the Spirit in the wilderness." The Spirit dwells in Jesus and leads him.

Jesus is tempted after forty days of prayer and fasting. He is "famished" (Luke 4:2), dare we say, exhausted. Precisely when he is more vulnerable than we have seen him, the temptations begin. In Luke, these temptations ascend in their seriousness, each one becoming more problematic than the last, the final one tempting a preemptive death escape before the ministry begins.

At the end, Jesus emerges victorious, stronger than ever. He returns to Galilee "with the power of the Spirit" (Luke 4:14). A quick report of Jesus's entry into Galilee follows, but he goes to his famed hometown, which the guileless Nathaniel has described with a quip twenty centuries ago: "Can anything good come out of Nazareth?" (John 1:46).

Jesus enters the temple. He takes his place at the scrolls and reads what he is given:

> The Spirit of the Lord is upon me,
> because he has anointed me
> to bring good news to the poor. (Luke 4:18)

From the baptism to the desert, through the temptations and back to his own hometown, the Spirit has animated Jesus every step of the way.

What precedes everything leading up to the visit in Nazareth is the Spirit's agency.

DURING

Seen in this light, the pericope is not simply a foundational announcement; it is an intervention. Lest the Nazarenes try to domesticate Jesus's proclamation, he emphasizes its prophetic worth. He makes the text provocative. Today, we would call it an intervention, a moment that needs to be reckoned with.

In his own exegetical treatment of the text in the second chapter, called "Anointed to Evangelize the Poor," Martins highlights the intervention as the definitive act of identifying "The Poor as the Privileged Recipients of the Gospel," and its effect as meaning, "liberating from the shackles of social exploitation."

This is the release of captives.

AFTER

In recent years, the term *parrhesia* has been highlighted. It signifies bold, uncompromising speech. The term is used over thirty times in the New Testament. John uses it to describe when Jesus is speaking directly or plainly, both with his disciples (see John 11:14; 16:25, 29) as well as to the world (see John 18:20), and Mark uses it when Jesus first speaks openly about his passion (Mark 8:32).

Parrhesia is a way of speaking freely, unhesitatingly, directly, plainly, no-holds-barred. Luke uses it only in the Acts of the Apostles. The instances are curious: being "filled with the Holy Spirit" (Acts 2:4); and Peter uses it in his first speech at the Pentecost (Acts 2:29). Then, in Acts 4, Peter and John are arrested for boldly proclaiming Jesus, but after their release, they pray to the Lord that they speak with boldness, and we are told that their prayers are answered—they "were all filled with the Holy Spirit and spoke the word of God with boldness" (Acts 4:31). Luke makes the same description of Paul (see Acts 28:31) in proclaiming Christ boldly in Rome. In fact, Paul describes himself often with parrhesia (see Phil 1:20; 2 Cor 3:12; 7:4).

Luke does not use the word in Jesus's inaugural proclamation, but his style is the prototype for all subsequent preaching. The unhesitating boldness of being inspired and led by the Spirit that Jesus realizes is named and imitated in the post-Pentecost accounts of the preaching of the twelve and Paul.

The sign of the Spirit is parrhesia. It's the mark of the master and the disciple. It's the definitive mark of Jesus's first proclamation, spoken to the poor, breaking the shackles of captivity. It is the sign that "today this scripture has been fulfilled in your hearing" (Luke 4:21).

Martins could not have picked a better point of departure for his work on Christology and global ethics.

James F. Keenan, SJ
Canisius Professor
Boston College

Acknowledgments

Writing a book is a long, reflective process, full of emotions, excitement, and joy, but also distress, lament, and frustration. However, I never felt lonely while working on this book. For me, writing a book is an experience of encounter—encountering faces, names, voices, and realities. All those I encountered—from immanent and transcendent realities, near and distant faces, companions in the daily life and partners in a dream—contributed to the development of this book. Although my name is on the cover, this book is not a result of a solitary work of a reflective mind but rather the result of many meaningful encounters throughout the years and across continents. Thank you all for being partners on this journey.

A blank page always fascinates me. Perhaps, when I see a blank page—on a day when I can look at it for a long time, contemplating meaningful encounters—is a wonderful experience of freedom and gratitude. A blank page can empower and motivate me, as a mystical manifestation of something spiritual that can become material and transmittable to others.

This feeling of empowerment and welcome is due to the many people who have contributed to the person I am today, especially my education that creates my ability of analytical reflection, systematization of thought, and literary transmission. I am grateful to all those, beginning with my humble parents, who never reached middle school, as well as to my teachers and professors, and to the rural workers, the proletarians, the suffering people, the indigenous, the poor and the marginalized, my friends, current colleagues, my wife and children, and the Mother Earth.

More specifically, I am thankful for the development of this project. It began with my *amada* wife, Sydney, who supports me in every moment of my life and, for this project, had to work hard taking care of our twin children, Dante and Santiago, so that I could focus on my writing. Thank you to my dear friend and academic and existential mentor, Jim Keenan, for opening new doors for me and writing a foreword. I am grateful for the support of the leadership teams of the Catholic Theological Ethics in the World Church, including Andrea Vicini, Kristen Heyer, Shaji George Kochuthara, Antonio Autiero, Toussaint Kafarhire, Suzanne Mulligan, Mathew Illathuparampil, and Toni Ross; and to the Brazilian Society of Moral Theology, including Mário Marcelo, Marta Luzie, André Boccato, Moésio Pereira, Ronaldo Zacharias, and Maria Inês. I am also very thankful for the support and work of Paul McMahon, editor at Paulist Press. It was delightful working with him from the beginning to the end of this project. My thanks go to Paulist Press for believing in this project and publishing its result. Thanks also to Silas Hasselbrook for helping me in revising parts of the manuscript; to Margaret Guider, who generously discussed this project at its initial phase; to Bryan Massingale, who offered great insights in the development of my thought; and to M. Therese Lysaught for her effort in promoting new voices from Latin America. I also want to express my gratuity to the Albert Gnaegi Center for Health Care Ethics at Saint Louis University and its director, Jason Eberl, for the support through its Hübet Mäder Chair of Health Care Ethics Fellowship 2021–22, and to Marquette University's Theology Department, College of Nursing, and Center for Research and Innovation that provided support for this project. In addition, thanks go to my Marquette colleagues Deirdre Dempsey, Irfan Omar, Kate Ward, Conor Kelly, John Thiede, Joseph Ogbonnaya, Andrew Kim, Therese Schnable, and Christine Schindler, from whom I have learned, through joyful moments of conversation, about ethics and global health.

Finally, my thanks go to the Pachamama for all you provide for us to live well on this planet. Forgive us for our lack of care and tenderness.

Amém, Axé, Saravá, Awerê…!

Introduction

Christology is a core discipline in Christian theology. It is not an exaggeration, metaphorically speaking, to suggest that *Christology is the heart of theology*. The significance that Christology has for systematic theology also extends to the Catholic Church's moral teaching, to the historical journey of the faithful and those who theologically examine this experience of faith. God reveals the transcendence in the journeying of people, who are gathered in community by the Holy Spirit through a personal encounter with Jesus Christ.

Considering the significance of Christology for theology and for the life of Christian communities, this book presents Luke 4:16–30 as its central biblical text. The justification for this approach is based on an existential choice that I have made to live a life centered in a commitment to Jesus's project, a life committed to the poor and to their struggle for liberation and the opportunity to flourish with dignity. Therefore, the approach to Christology of this book is based on a perspective of liberation theology advanced by the Gospel of Luke. Consequently, this study of the mystery of Jesus is presented from the perspective of the experience of the poor in Latin America in dialogue with Luke 4.

In the United States, liberation theology is often seen as a specialized theological discipline in and of itself, but this conception can lead to a limitation in understanding, especially when it comes to recognizing the scope of liberation theology as *a new way of doing theology*, as suggested by Gustavo Gutiérrez, Leonardo Boff, Ivone Gebara, and many other Latin American liberation theologians. In this new way of doing theology, a theologian develops his or her reflection about faith from a concrete experience of a community that embodies this faith in a historical journey. In doing theology, a liberation theologian begins from the experience of a community that is marked by oppression and engaged in a struggle for liberation that is grounded in faith. Therefore, liberation theology, understood as a new way of doing theology, poses a challenge to every theological field of study from systematics to ethics, to biblical studies, to the history of Christianity. My objective in this book is to demonstrate its particular significance for the theological discipline of Christology. In doing so, I offer a christological foundation for theological ethics with local and global relevance. Conscious of the fact that it is precisely in the reality of life that a community of Jesus's followers experiences its faith, I come to recognize how the mystery of God reveals itself in human history. This historical interaction between God and the people is a foundational source for doing theology in the way we come to understand traditional Catholic sources of revelation—Scriptures, Magisterium, and Tradition—and their ethical implications.

This work requires a clear *theological locus*, where faith is experienced, ethically embodied, and theologically developed. Hence, I present a Christology that is rooted in Latin America, and which, from this locus and to it, is considered as a gift to the reality of the faithful where God manifests the trinitarian love. This reality is marked by poverty, oppression, injustice, and violence contradicting the gospel that impact the historical journey of most Latin American faith communities. However, this context is not only a place where the ugliness of suffering and injustice is manifested, but also a place of encounter where great strength and cultural beauty are reflected in the lives of diverse communities of faith, love, and hope.

In taking account of this reality, while looking directly at the faces and experiences of the poor, this book develops a Christology that presents the poor as the privileged recipients of the good news. Respecting the cultural diversity of Christian traditions, this christological account emerges from liberating ways that Catholic communities have expressed their experience of faith, embodying through discipleship their adherence to Jesus in a particular social context that requires freedom from oppression. Hence, following the Latin American liberation theology that began to be articulated in the 1960s, I suggest a personification of Jesus Christ who is on the side of the poor and the oppressed, an incarnate God who respects local cultures in a healthy process of inculturation, and who provides spiritual strength in a historical pilgrimage toward a life with full dignity.

In many aspects, this christological study is an introduction to Latin American Christology and liberating ethics and, thus, an introduction to a method of liberation theology to be used in all theological disciplines. In doing so, this account differentiates itself from many books on liberation theology that tend to treat this new way of doing theology as a theological discipline. Using a liberating methodology, this Christology is based upon Luke 4:16–30, when Jesus begins his public ministry by reading a text of the Prophet Isaiah in the synagogue. By focusing on this biblical passage, I present a method of articulating and living liberation theology through joining oppressed communities as a way of reading Scripture, teaching theology, and transforming unjust social contexts. Furthermore, such a reading the biblical text reveals the mystery of God and the mission of Jesus's disciples by stressing a profound depth of interaction with the concrete historical experiences of communities and their struggles for liberation; so as to demonstrate a harmonic circular relationship between Scripture and the experience of a community in history.

In Luke 4:16–30, the poor are presented as the privileged recipients of the gospel message. This New Testament pericope points to a search for understanding the joint mission of the Word and the Spirit in communion with the Father, revealing the trinitarian mystery of God. At the same time, the Lukan text suggests that the Church's mission is to continue the work of Jesus in history, under the guidance of the Holy Spirit. Thus, Luke 4 allows us to realize the action of Jesus in history guided by the Spirit; the same Spirit who empowers the Church to continue the ministry of Jesus throughout history.

As one considers this biblical experience of encountering Jesus and his historical ministry, it is possible to develop a theological perspective in which one can visualize Jesus Christ encountering the suffering reality of Latin American people and announcing, through his disciples, the good news to the poor. This encounter occurs in a particular context, in which Jesus Christ acquires the facial features of these people, guiding them through a commitment to the historical construction of a new reality that manifests the presence of God's kingdom.

Although this christological account has an introductory aspect, it provides a contemporary original analysis of an experience of encounter with Jesus Christ within a reality where a community marked by poverty embodies its faith. Therefore, I offer a theological text that resonates in the lives of Latin American people and those communities around the world that face similar struggles for liberation. This provides an equilibrium between the Christ of faith and Jesus's historical revelation as an incarnate God who walks with his people in history.

Here, the objective is to present a christological account from Luke 4:16–30, in which we can understand Jesus's mission of bringing the good news to the poor, the implications of this text for theological studies, and its significance for the Latin American reality and other contexts marked by poverty and oppression. Within this goal, I develop an exegetic-hermeneutic study of Luke 4 to comprehend the text and context, considering the situation of the historical community out of which the Lukan corpus was written and the audience that constituted the first recipients of the text. I argue that announcing the gospel of liberation (the good news) to the poor was a central part of Jesus's ministry and that it is essential for the historical journey of the Church, responsible for continuing Jesus's mission in history assisted by the Holy Spirit.

The Lukan text offers resources for expanding this textual analysis to a systematic theological reflection, in which to create the conditions for a dialogue between the Church's Tradition and the theological work produced in Latin America. Thus, I address the theology of the joint mission of the Word and the Spirit in communion with the Father, relating this theology to important topics from theological anthropology, ecclesiology, ethics, and liturgy. This effort demonstrates the comprehensive and integral aspect of Catholic theology as a harmonic corpus where divisions into subdisciplines are better understood and unified. Luke 4:16–30 reveals a pivotal event, offering a Christology that unifies all interconnected aspects of Christian life and the Church's mission.

In summary, I present a Christology incarnated in the reality of people who have experienced Jesus Christ in their context, a Christology that shines light on the Latin American challenges of poverty and, as such, serves as a resource for the pastoral ministry of the Catholic Church.

This book is divided into six chapters. Parts of the book originally appeared in an introduction to Latin American Christology that was published in Brazil. These chapters (currently, chapters 2, 3, and 4) were revised and updated. Four other chapters were added (1, 5, 6, and 7). The first chapter focuses on theological method, reflecting on the liberationist way of doing theology. It aims to prepare the reader—unfamiliar with contextual theology informed by this method—for the following chapters, which apply this method. The ensuing four chapters shape a harmonic christological account beginning with a biblical and historical analysis of Luke 4:16–30. This is followed by a systematic theological reflection that focuses on ethical and ecclesial aspects, and their pastoral applications. Considering the tradition of the Catholic Church, chapters 3 and 4 take account of the Latin American *chão* (ground) as the place (theological locus) from which this Christology arises and, at the same time, this *chão* is the reality that this study seeks to engage in to create and sustain a dialogue with the poor and other historically oppressed social groups. Finally, the last three chapters address global issues in health care from a theological, christological perspective, developed from my work in theological bioethics and global health. These chapters consider the mission of Jesus and the Church in a globalized world, looking at the specific field of health care because of the Catholic Church's historical engagement in serving the sick and the poor around the world.

In more detail, the first chapter articulates a methodology of doing theology informed by the many ways of knowing and meaning by those who are usually dismissed as agents able to offer any contribution to academic theology. In this chapter, the theological method is grounded in the historical experience of marginalized communities of faith and advanced through contemplation and dialogue. Consequently, I demonstrate how contemplation and dialogue sustain a methodological framework for doing theology that emerges from hermeneutical mediations (interlocutors in dialogue) through which the incarnate God (Jesus) is manifested in the immanent reality where the ethical implications for a community of faith are made evident.

The second chapter presents an exegetical study of Luke 4:16–30 to understand who the poor are in the biblical narrative, and why

Jesus affirms that they are the privileged recipients of the gospel message. The main goal of this chapter is to provide a closer look at Jesus's ministry as it is presented by the New Testament, particularly in the Gospel of Luke. Moreover, this chapter examines the understanding of poverty in the Gospel and its relationship with Isaiah 61:1–2, an Old Testament passage read by Jesus in the synagogue, and its link to the concept of integral liberation.

From this Lukan text, the third chapter addresses questions related to announcing the good news to the poor within the Catholic tradition. We examine texts from the Church fathers and from the Church's magisterium, leading to what I call the Latin American tradition and its emphasis on the preferential option for the poor from a liberating reading of scriptural texts. Then I explore an area of systematic theology that deals with the joint mission of the Word and the Spirit that pervades all of Jesus's ministry as well as the Church's life and its action in history, along with the eschatology of communion with the Father, revealing that the joint mission of the Word and the Spirit is an expression of the trinitarian mystery.

The Lukan text is the main source for the theological themes presented in this book. They spring from the exercise of listening and welcoming the Word of God manifested in the Bible and its encounter with the poor in their reality. Therefore, this theological account originates with Jesus's encounter with the poor and is framed in terms of a Christology incarnated in the reality and culture of the poor, because they are privileged recipients of the gospel message understood as the good news of liberation.

The fourth chapter analyzes the continuity of Jesus's mission as carried forth by his community of disciples and missionaries. The faith community, that is, the Church as people of God, continues Jesus's mission in history by announcing the gospel to the poor under the assistance of the Holy Spirit and an ongoing listening to God's Word. The Holy Spirit is the one who animated and guided Jesus during his life and continues doing the same with Jesus's disciples throughout history. This is the historical life of the Church.

The Holy Spirit is a dynamic strength in the disciple's life in history and a guiding force toward a transcendent experience, beyond history, that points to the resurrection. Hence, I propose a Church community committed to Jesus's project of the historical liberation of the poor firmly grounded in the hope of the resurrection. In this chapter, we examine the relationship between Christology and the poor in their cultural diversity and historical struggles for liberation from oppression within the context of Latin America. Jesus goes forth to encounter those who are the most vulnerable and those who are experiencing suffering. This is a Christology of inculturation by the action of the Holy Spirit who renews all things *from below*. As a result, the christological account in this chapter stresses pastoral aspects of the ministry of Jesus's disciples and the practical implications that inform how that faith is celebrated in an existential liturgy, committed to the historical construction of a reality that reflects the kingdom of God. The dynamism of the Holy Spirit and the historical experience of encounter with Jesus in the community strengthen theological discourse and praxis by allowing theology to engage in many areas of human existence and of social organization. The last three chapters exemplify this dynamism and strength.

Grounded on the Lukan text studied earlier, chapter 5 outlines how this narrative shows the centrality of the sick, who are also poor and oppressed, in Jesus's mission led by the Holy Spirit. I argue that care for the sick, the oppressed, and the poor are essential parts of the mission of Jesus's followers, also guided by the Holy Spirit. The promotion of health and well-being is an effort that needs to combine medical care for the sick and action to build justice. This is done by liberating the oppressed and joining them in a process of liberation from their poverty to attain the common good.

Chapter 6 addresses the challenge of global health governance from theological insights from the Gospel and Catholic social teaching. Many actors and leaders of global health and their initiatives in middle- and low-income countries embody a top-down approach of health-care delivery and strategies of health promotion among the poor. In addition, some of these promoters of global health stress the need of a centralized model of global health governance to address challenges and, in doing so, they perpetuate a top-down approach. Considering the voices of the poor and their wisdom, I argue for a different model of global health, with a bottom-up approach and a decentralized governance that begins with and from the leadership of the poor. Consequently, the poor are global health agents and not passive recipients of international aid.

Considering the global context of injustice in accessing health care and how this situation contradicts the project that Jesus of

Nazareth clearly revealed in Luke 4, the last chapter focuses on end-of-life experiences marked by poverty and oppression. By focusing on the narratives and stories of unjust deaths caused by social vulnerability and lack of health care, this chapter presents a tragic reality that challenges established ways of addressing end-of-life issues in global health, in dialogue with marginalized communities, while challenged by Pope Francis's invitation to listen and learn from those at the bottom of society, such as the poor and indigenous people.

Ultimately, the goal of this book is to offer resources for Christian communities that seek to understand their faith better and to discover ways of living out the teaching of Jesus more fully. In other words, my dream is that it will reach faith communities, reading groups, and introductory theological studies in churches and Catholic schools. How will this happen? Answering this question is the challenge that I present to every reader. I suggest each reader to dialogue with me by engaging the ideas presented in this book while considering the context of each community and what affects those who are the most vulnerable, particularly the poor and the sick. My invitation is to think critically and seek to encounter a Christology that is incarnated in each reality. I am only presenting one experience of doing Christology, incarnated in the impoverished and pluralistic reality of Latin America, the context of my faith community. I urge each reader to dialogue with their respective reality, the local challenges, and the beauty of every cultural way of embodying the christological faith.

Finding ways of dialogue within the context of diverse communal experiences is my greatest aspiration. This is an ambitious dream, but we can dream together because every theological reflection should aim at contributing to the historical ministry of the Church to promote liberation, justice, and human dignity while encountering Jesus Christ. In addition, this book offers a modest proposal for scholarly theological discussion, particularly about Christology and theological ethics, in our ongoing effort to grow in our faith and our understanding of Jesus's teaching and in our discipleship.

Finally, I wrote most of this book while I was in Latin America, most of the time in Brazil. Consequently, most of the books and articles I read for this work were in Portuguese and Spanish. Many of them have translations into English. Hence, I found quotes used and references in the English translations, whenever possible. When I was unable to find the exact reference in the English edition, I offered my translation, indicated the Portuguese or Spanish versions I used, and when available, added the English edition in the final bibliography.

1

A Theological Method from the Knowledge of the Forgotten

Narratives are at the center of people's historical experiences of transcendent realities. Narratives not only give expression to these experiences with a variety of styles and languages, often full of metaphors and mysteries, but they also help other people and communities that encounter these narratives to have their own experiences of the transcendent. This is what one finds in biblical texts that are narratives of people who experienced God within their own historical contexts. Throughout history, individuals and communities in their particular contexts have read these narratives in order to find God and to have their own personal and communal encounters with the transcendent, with an incarnate God within human history. Argentinian biblical scholar Joaquim Severino Croatto says that these narratives possess a reserve-of-meanings (*reserva-de-significados*) because they are always acquiring new meanings from the individuals and communities that read and reread them. With each new contact, these texts become relevant within new contexts and struggles.[1]

Narratives reveal an experience of faith that a community has with God who is present in its history. The transcendent—that the Christian tradition names God, as Aquinas does (ST I, q. 13, a. 1), or Trinity, Father, Jesus Christ, and Holy Spirit—is present in the immanent reality. Theology is an effort, always imperfect, to understand this experience of God's revelation, as "accepted by faith," a conviction that carries the seal of grand masters of theology, such as Thomas Aquinas:

> Although those things which are beyond man's knowledge may not be sought for by man through his reason, nevertheless, once they are revealed by God, they must be accepted by faith. Hence the sacred text continues, "For many things are shown to thee above the understanding of man" (Sirach 3:25). And in this, the sacred science consists. (ST I, q. 1, a. 1)

As a systematic intellectual effort to understand the experience of God, abstract accounts and discussions about the mystery of God became a dominant feature in the discipline and development of Christian theology. Scholasticism was the apogee of this way of doing theology philosophically. As a result, many theological accounts were quite distant from the historical experiences of communities, leading many theologians to consider that the only authentic theologies were those that dealt with universals. In the twentieth and twenty-first centuries, contextual theologies, such as liberation theology, were dismissed by some passionate defenders of this abstract way of doing theology.[2] One of their reasons for this marginalization was what they perceived to be the lack of universality in these contextual theological accounts. Contemporary critics of contextual theologies forget, or intentionally ignore, that this *supposed* universality of "noncontextual" accounts were created in Europe by Europeans who possessed a European worldview that was grounded in Hellenistic philosophy and culture. They were not universal. Indeed, they gave expression to a contextual understanding of God's experience.

There exists a colonizing mentality in Christian theology. This fact helps us to understand why any attempt to advance new ways of doing theology, most of which have emerged outside of the European context, are judged to be secondary, inferior, or not really theology at all. While this is not the subject of this essay,[3] it is important to note that a colonizing mentality dismisses anything that does not come from the so-called top, where the theological status quo is preserved with its supposed universality. Strangely, the very biblical narratives that serve as foundational resources for the creation of this theological status quo deal directly with the experience of a God who liberates an oppressed people fleeing slavery (Exodus) and an incarnate God who becomes human in order to share in the historical reality of the poor and marginalized, dying on a cross as a nobody. Moreover, those who enjoy this theological status quo did not develop their understanding of the mystery of God based on an ahistorical reality, protected from any particularity created by local circumstances, a specific geographic location, or a specific language. As far as I know, they did not develop a systematization of theology from heaven, using an angelical language.

It is important to recognize that the theological status quo is also contextual. It exists because of political, economic, and colonial powers among others. This status quo has little to do with theology or the experience of God. To be clear, I am not dismissing this theology. It is part of the Christian theological tradition and, as such, is a foundation for any new way of doing theology. For example, one of the factors that made liberation theology possible was its foundation in the theological tradition since the first centuries of Christianity, but another foundation was the encounter between this tradition and the reality of the people, particularly the poor and oppressed who experience God in their historical struggles. Because of this encounter, new meanings and new theological reflections emerged, expanding the understanding of their experience of God, a transcendent reality in the immanent practice of a faith community. Therefore, these experiences generate narratives from the lowest strata of societies and the margins of the theological status quo.

This essay offers a methodological account of doing theology from the historical experience of marginalized communities of faith. Particularly, I speak from a Latin American context—Brazil, to be specific. I stress the need for an interdisciplinary theological method, in which the experience of the poor and oppressed, their narratives and voices, have a contribution to make to our systematic and imperfect attempts to understand the mystery of God. As a reflection on the faith experience of a community, theology cannot be detached from the living faith and historical challenges faced by a community, such as socioeconomic injustices and all forms of oppression. The historicity of an experience of faith requires certain tools that are necessary when examining the reality in which a community experiences God. Such instruments are needed to cross the boundaries of the academic discipline of theology. Hence, there is a need for dialogue with other disciplines, such as the social and natural sciences, for it is through such dialogue that opportunities can be created to offer occasions for contemplation to communities where theological reflection becomes an Exodus, that is, a liberating experience of historical and eschatological salvation.

CONTEMPLATION AND DIALOGUE

Understood as an academic discipline, theology is a second act led by members of a faith community who develop a systematic reflection on the experience of faith (the first act).[4] Even when, as an academic discipline, it serves itself and its own scholarly progress, theology depends on the faith embodied by people who believe in the transcendent. In Christian theology, professional theology originates from within a community of believers, who share a vocation to serve the Church as theologians. Therefore, when theology emerges from the community of faith, it serves as a reflection on the faith of which the theologian is an adherent, and it then returns to the same community as a gift for the faithful so that they may grow in their belief and in the ways that this faith is embodied in the world.

Theological reflection or studies do not simply arise from the creative mind of a theologian, but rather from an experience of contemplation of the transcendent and its ramifications in the life of a community of people who share the same faith. Any authentic theological method cannot be far from this experience. As an insider, a professional theologian lives out an intellectual and ecclesial vocation of serving the Christian community. This does not exclude the objectivity and rigor while theological accounts are developed. However, the objectivity of methods cannot make a theologian an outsider; otherwise, he or she runs the risk of blurring the boundaries between theology and the sociology of religion, an important discipline and necessary partner when doing theology. At the same time, it cannot replace the theological service of helping a community of believers to understand their experience and to grow in their relationship with the transcendent and the ethical implications this relationship entails.[5]

Theology arises from the experience of faith. In the Christian faith, everything begins with an encounter that changes people's lives; this is the first act: an encounter with Jesus Christ. The New Testament tradition shows it clearly. The Gospel narratives and other New Testament texts were written later, after a transformative encounter with the risen Jesus, when the first communities felt the necessity of understanding their experiences and transmitted them to others. All primitive communities experienced Jesus and told his story, but all of them expressed their faith differently because they encountered an incarnate God within their own context and struggle, where Jesus became real for them. Although the four Gospel narratives have similarities and present the story of the same main character, they are different because they provide an experience of a living God in diverse contexts with specific challenges to address.

There is no revelation outside of history and the limitations created by time and space. Although the truth of God is transcendent and ahistorical, the manifestation of the truth is in the history of a community that experiences and believes in this transcendent truth. As the Vatican II Dogmatic Constitution *Dei Verbum* affirms, "This plan of revelation is realized by deeds and words having an inner unity: the deeds wrought by God in the history of salvation manifest and conform the teaching and realities signified by words, while the words proclaim the deeds and clarify the mystery contained in their" (no. 2).

There is a dialogical interaction between the Word of God and the realities where this Word is experienced. In a circular relationship, the Word signifies realities, and these realities confirm a teaching by helping the people of God to understand the Word and its significance for a historical community. It is a dynamic movement of existential meaning and historical impact aminated by the Holy Spirt. Thus, theological reflection occurs in this dynamism of a transcendent faith manifested in the creatureliness of the human history of Jesus's disciples. Therefore, theology emerges as the outcome of contemplation and dialogue within a community that is expansive in its engagement of the world and its challenges. Let us understand the ways in which this expansion of contemplation and dialogue is a key for theological method.

Contemplation

Faith in Jesus begins with an encounter, a contemplation of the truth that challenges us to change our life. This encounter raises questions. We see this occurring with St. Paul: "Now as he was going along and approaching Damascus, suddenly a light from heaven flashed around him. He fell to the ground, and then he heard a voice saying to him, 'Saul, Saul, why do you persecute me?' He asked, 'Who are you, Lord?' The reply came, 'I am Jesus, whom you are persecuting'" (Acts 9:3–5). Paul did not understand this encounter at the moment it occurred. He could not see. Later, he understood it as a gift of faith: "I did not receive it from a human source, nor was I taught it, but I received it through a revelation of Jesus Christ" (Gal 1:12). Then Paul added, "When God, who had set me apart before I was born and called me through his grace, was pleased to reveal his Son to me, so that I might proclaim him among the gentiles" (Gal 1:15–16). When Paul reflected about this experience and its practical existential implications, he began to do theology. So, he understood that faith in Jesus was about freedom, one of the main topics of his letter to the Galatians, and that the Law could not prevent Gentiles who encountered Jesus from experiencing the incarnate God within their own context.

At the Council of Jerusalem, Paul challenged leaders in that faith community, particularly Peter and James, to reflect on the faith and to consider that the encounter with Jesus is a grace that is not restricted to those who are circumcised. What makes people followers of Jesus is their faith, and the burden of circumcision should not be imposed on a Gentile who encounters Jesus (Acts 15:19–20). As a member of the community and a theologian, Paul saw God's revelation in the history of a people who witnessed the gospel and then developed a theology that was given back to the community that inspired it, thereby helping the community to grow in its understanding of faith.

In the encyclical *Deus Caritas Est*, Pope Benedict XVI stresses the centrality of an encounter with Jesus for faith, a contemplation that becomes the source for Christian life and theology: "Being Christian is not the result of an ethical choice or a lofty idea, but the encounter with an event, a person, which gives life a new horizon and a decisive direction" (no. 1). The encounter with Jesus is an experience of God's love (*agape*) who is incarnated in history, the foundation of Church's liturgical and ethical practices. Benedict XVI continues, "Faith, worship and *ethos* are interwoven as a single reality which takes shape in our encounter with God's *agape*" (no. 14). This leads us to reflect on those who are marginalized, like the Gentiles in Paul's context, and the poor and oppressed in our own contexts.[6] Amid the marginalized, Jesus's disciples recognize God's love in history. "Love of God and love of neighbor have become one: in the least of the brethren we find Jesus himself, and in Jesus we find God" (no. 15). Therefore, the reality where God's love is experienced and embodied as love for the other who suffers is a theological locus.[7] Every theology is attached to the historicity of Christian experience, even the theological reflection developed in Western culture of the Global North.[8]

Every theology is contextual, yet for the most part, it is only theologies developed in the Global South that are referred to as contextual theologies in a categorical way.[9] These theologies address the specific challenges that exist where faith is experienced, such as liberation theology in Latin America, and those with a specific context of oppression as their theological locus, for example, feminist theology and postcolonial theology. All these theologies have in common a practical aspect. They aim to give expression to the experience of liberation that oppressed communities undergo as they experience a faith of freedom in Christ Jesus who "set us free, so that we should remain free,"[10] as Paul said in his Letter to the Galatians (5:1).

Grounded in a contemplation of the transcendent, theological methods also advance to contemplate the "other" who shares the same historical reality as the theologian. Within a context of injustice, these "others" are the poor and the oppressed.[11] When contemplating them, we also are contemplating the crucified Jesus. The Latin American Bishops express this conviction by saying, "As disciples and missionaries, Christians are called to contemplate in the suffering faces of our brothers, the face of Christ who calls us to serve them: 'the suffering faces of the poor are the suffering face of Christ.'"[12] Considering the challenge of oppressed communities in Amazonia, Pope Francis describes this spirituality by saying, "A holiness born of encounter and engagement, contemplation and services, receptive solitude and life in community, cheerful sobriety and the struggle for justice" (*Querida Amazonia* 77). The historical reality and its contextual challenges are where the contemplation within faith happens to foster the theological reflection. This is a dialogue between the human and the transcendent that is mediated by history.

Theological methods also include dialogue. It is a dialogue with God, with history, and with the others, particularly the poor and marginalized. Furthermore, dialogue presents opportunities for partners to help us in our efforts to understand the historical challenges faced by faith communities. These partners offer tools—that theology does not have—to examine the socioeconomic aspects of reality, tools coming from social and natural sciences.[13]

Dialogue

Theology is a dialogue: with God, with others, and with the world. It is challenged by an encounter with Jesus. An inclusive dialogue opens us to welcoming everyone. The need and desire for freedom is part of our human nature, a part that enables us to organize societies of justice and harmony. Considering that the message of the gospel is good news for privileged recipients, namely, the poor (Luke 4:16–18), this dialogue creates a space for the voices and visions of the poor and the oppressed to be heard and seen.

Pope Francis has emphasized the Catholic Church's nature as a dialogical reality. In fact, he is recovering a perspective that guided the Second Vatican Council, expressed in the inaugural encyclical of Pope Paul VI *Ecclesiam Suam*. In 1964, Paul VI presented dialogue as a method for the Christian apostolate, rooted in four characteristics: *clarity*, *meekness*, *confidence*, and *prudence*. Dialogue engages people in a way that is charitable and guides them to achieve the truth through collective construction. Paul VI said, "In a dialogue conducted with this kind of foresight, truth is wedded to charity and understanding to love" (*Ecclesiam Suam* 82).

Gaudium et Spes well expresses the importance of dialogue in the relationship with God and the world. The dialogue with God reveals to the Church the human being's dignity and the need to be attentive to the "signs of the times" (*Gaudium et Spes* 4). Grounded in this conviction, the Catholic Church moved from a defensive posture to a dialogical posture of engagement with the secular world: "Everything we have said about the dignity of the human person, and about the human community and the profound meaning of human activity, lays the foundation for the relationship between the Church and the world, and provides the basis for dialogue between them" (*Gaudium et Spes* 40).

This dialogical posture was a new orientation that had a profound impact on the Church's way of engaging historical challenges, which now has resulted in dialogue becoming a key methodological aspect of ecclesial engagement. Marciano Vidal interprets *Gaudium et Spes* as the document that best expresses the spirt of the Council:

> The Second Vatican Council, especially *Gaudium et spes*, determined a new orientation. This orientation can be expressed by a term of great semantic and symbolic meaning, especially in the historical phase of this conciliar event: *dialogue*. This word acquired Catholic citizenship during the pontificate of John XXIII. Then dialogue was embraced and enriched by Paul VI. Sometimes, one does not have in mind how important the first encyclical of Papa Montini, *Ecclesiam suam* (06 August 1964), was a text about dialogue, oriented to support the shift of perspective from the Church towards the world.[14]

This shift impacted not only the Church's relationship with secular realities, but also the Church's way of doing theology. According to Vidal, *Gaudium et Spes* was the most cited document in the postconciliar period.[15]

To bring the innovations of Vatican II to the Latin American context, the Conference of Latin American Bishops (CELAM) embraced this dialogical perspective during the Conference of Medellín (1968) and then expanded its use at Puebla (1979). CELAM's meetings opted for following this spirit of dialogue, by encouraging a liberating education based on critical dialogue because this is what "Latin America needs to redeem itself from unjust servitude and, above all, from its own egoism."[16] Puebla affirmed that the Catholic community must be a "bridge of contact and dialogue."[17] Then it added, "In an attitude of sincere listening and welcoming, in this contact and dialogue we must address issues that are raised from their own temporal environment."[18] The last meeting of CELAM, in Aparecida, Brazil (2007), also embraced dialogue as a way of announcing the good news and denouncing social sin, "a dialogue from different cultural worldviews: celebration, inter-relationship, and revival of hope."[19]

Cardinal Archbishop Jorge Mario Bergoglio, who was at Aparecida and served as chair of the writing commission responsible for drafting the Final Document, exercised his ministry in the streets and slums of Buenos Aires using this dialogical posture. Later, as Pope Francis, he brought it to his pontificate, returning to the spirit of dialogue and collegiality of Vatican II.[20] He usually begins texts and documents by affirming that he is offering a reflection so as to "enter into dialogue with all people" (*Laudato Si'* 3). In the apostolic exhortation *Evangelii Gaudium*, Francis argues that social dialogue is important to construct peace (nos. 238–58). He states, "Evangelization also involves the path of dialogue. For the Church today, three areas of dialogue stand out where it needs to be present in order to promote full human development and to pursue the common good: dialogue with states, dialogue with society—including dialogue with cultures and the sciences—and dialogue with other believers who are not part of the Catholic Church" (*Evangelii Gaudium* 238). In his encyclical *Laudato Si'*, Francis stresses, "Today in view of the common good, there is urgent need for politics and economics to enter into a frank dialogue in the service of life, especially human life" (no. 189). Moreover, in his latest encyclical, *Fratelli Tutti*, Francis shows his identity of a person who speaks from his experience with Jesus to dialogue with everyone: "Although I have written it from the Christian convictions that inspire and sustain me, I have sought to make this reflection an invitation to dialogue among all people of good will" (no. 6). Dialogue became a mark of Francis's ministry as the Bishop of Rome as well as his methodology for doing theology.

The dialogical method proposed by Pope Francis goes beyond having only the secular society and its natural and social sciences as interlocutors. He clearly recognizes that these interlocutors are mediations that are necessary if theology is to contribute to an integral development of the world in which all participate in the common good with shared responsibility. The natural and social sciences are mediations for doing theology as it has been developed for over fifty years by liberation theology. Moreover, Pope Francis brings other interlocutors into this dialogue: the poor and the marginalized, expanding the perspective that became the heart of liberation theology: the preferential option for the poor, an "ethical imperative essential for effectively attain the common good" (*Laudato Si'* 158).

The poor and the marginalized have "much to teach us. Not only do they share in the *sensus fidei*, but in their difficulties they know the suffering Christ. We need to let ourselves be evangelized by them" (*Evangelii Gaudium* 198). Other traditions, such as those from indigenous peoples, also have something to teach us and a contribution to make to the world. In Francis's mission to address the global issue of the ecological crisis, he recognizes: "The wisdom of the original peoples of the Amazon region 'inspires care and respect for creation, with a clear consciousness of its limits, and prohibits its abuse. To abuse nature is to abuse our ancestor, our brothers and sisters, creation and the Creator, and to mortgage the future'" (*Querida Amazonia* 42). Dialoguing with the wisdom of indigenous peoples of Amazonia as well as the wisdom of other religious traditions, Francis articulates a theology that has ethical consequences: "If God call us to listen both to the cry of the poor and that of the earth, then for us, the cry of the Amazon region to the Creator is similar to the cry of God's people in Egypt (Exod 3:7). It is a cry of slavery and abandonment pleading for freedom" (*Querida Amazonia* 52).

Theology is an encounter of contemplation and dialogue in which the transcendent is present in the immanent. The experience of faith occurs within an historical reality. In attentiveness to the historical and contextual issues that impact people's lives, the mystery of the incarnate God is revealed as God's presence is manifested in people's lives and in their journeys toward liberation. This reality is a theological locus, always existing in time and space, and revealed in human faces, most of which are the faces of those who suffer. Although being local and historical-contextual, this reality discloses some universal aspect of God's revelation in the history of salvation that needs to be interpreted, as it gives rise to new historical meanings in different places and times. People in each place and time have their own struggles and experiences, all of which require tools and interlocutors for the development of a theology that unfolds through contemplation and dialogue.

A METHODOLOGICAL FRAMEWORK FOR THEOLOGY

After proposing that theological methods need to be grounded in contemplation and dialogue, I now focus on forgotten people who also possess knowledge that they are positioned to offer as a contribution to the development of academic theology, locally and globally. Of course, in the presentations of Pope Francis, we are witnesses to his recognition of the fact that the traditions and experiences of the poor and marginalized have something to teach us. The "forgotten ones" in theology are those on the bottom rung of society and/or at the margins of the Western theological status quo.

For the latter, I only have to say something very simple because what is stated above shows the contribution from the theology matured outside the Global North and its traditional theological methods. With his own method and theology, Pope Francis presents this contribution better than me. I only add that there are prejudge and ignorance—mostly shaped by a colonizing mentality in the Global North that still sees the rest of the world as servants, which prevents most theologians from the north from engaging with theologies and methods developed in the Global South. Things have improved over the last few years. Francis has contributed to that, but it is still far from an authentic dialogue among peers with significant collaboration. I am a Latin American theologian who reads and values the theological production in the Global North. I even write in English and Italian, dominating languages in the north and in the hierarchy of the Church. This is a common approach of most Global South theologians. They have interest in the theological material created in the Global North and, of course, in the classical texts from the Tradition. But there is no reciprocity from the north. The Catholic Church is universal, a global Church; so, is theology. The development of theology cannot be done without a global dialogue in which people from all over the world can sit around the same table as peers.[21] Theological methods must liberate themselves from a colonizing mentality toward a fruitful dialogue.[22]

However, theologians should not only dialogue among themselves. They need to include the poor and the oppressed who possess a knowledge and wisdom that must be received and included.

In the Gospel of Matthew, Jesus says, "I bless you, Father, Lord of heaven and of earth, for hiding these things from the learned and the clever and revealing them to little children" (11:25). In this narrative written for the Matthean community, Jesus acknowledges with sensitivity that the poor and the little ones have understood God's revelation. Similarly, in Luke's Gospel, Jesus inaugurates his mission with a text from the prophet Isaiah, as he affirms, "The spirit of the Lord is one me, for he has anointed me to bring the good news to the poor...and free the oppressed" (4:18). It is evident that the poor are the privileged hearers of the Word and the first to receive the good news. They are the little children of God who have something to teach us.

Theology cannot dismiss the contributions of the poor and the oppressed and their understandings of their experiences of God, specifically, their encounter with the transcendent that occurs in their historical reality of poverty and suffering.[23] If theological methods are to be truly dialogical, they must include the poor as interlocutors precisely because their experiences and realities matter in our efforts to receive and understand God's revelation. Here, it is very important to understand who the poor are for liberation theology. Maria Clara Bingemer, in one paragraph, is one of the Latin American liberation theologians who best presents the concept of poor:

> In liberation theology, the concept of "poor" corresponds to the "wronged," the "oppressed," "victims" of a world structure that is not fair. Therefore, this structure does not correspond to the justice wished by God. Theologically speaking, the recipients of this Option for the Poor cannot be simply identified with the "economically poor," nor with the "good poor" or with those who are "poor" in any sense, or those who are "poor in spirit"....But rather with the "wronged," whether or not they are economically or metaphorically poor. All human problematic that can become injustice—even when it is not related to "poverty" in literal or economic meanings—is object of the Option for the Poor, because this is an option for justice. Hence, ethnic, gender, and cultural discriminations among others—as forms of injustice that they are, and even when they do not necessarily occur in a context of

> economic poverty—are an object of the Option for the Poor. They are an object, not because they are forms of poverty...but rather because they are forms of injustice.[24]

For the powerful and the privileged, dialogue with the poor (the wronged) is an exercise in humility that demands engaging in the reality of the poor, listening to their voices, and sharing their experience. It begins with a preferential option for the poor that involves a concrete commitment to be a companion of the unfortunate,[25] to celebrate faith with them, and to witness firsthand their oppression. Leonardo Boff and Clodovis Boff, in describing the method of liberation theology, stress that the first step of its method is participation in the faith and liberating praxis of the poor and the oppressed. Theologians join the poor in their suffering and struggle for liberation and justice in an experience of community.[26]

This method, that began with the poor, those who were oppressed socioeconomically, expanded to other oppressed and marginalized groups, resulting in other liberating and contextual perspectives.[27] According to the feminist theologian Vélez Caro, they are "from the historical praxis of liberation, but they focus on particular realities and concrete agents who, from their living experience, make theology to shade lights in their realities from the perspective of faith in order to transform situations incoherent with God's will."[28]

Engaging with the poor and the oppressed, we recognize realities that are incompatible with God's will for abundant life with dignity and justice for all.[29] This requires hermeneutical mediations to understand the structures that prevent societies from realizing God's desire for justice. One mediation is the poor themselves, who reveal the concrete impacts of violence created by injustices against them. Another mediation is the Sacred Scriptures and the Tradition that help us to read the world and the signs of the times in the light of God's revelation. The third mediation is those sciences necessary to examine the mechanisms and phenomena responsible for injustice and oppression. Traditionally, liberation theology has used social sciences[30] as a mediation to understand the existence of institutionalized violence against the poor,[31] but this mediation is not restricted to social sciences. Pope Francis, for example, includes natural sciences in his examination of the reality and the impact of the ecological crisis. By way of a personal example, in my subdiscipline of theological ethics and my main focus, which is health care, I use health sciences and public health studies as meditations in my engagement with the experiences of the poor, and their vulnerability to falling ill and dying prematurely because of lack of health care.[32]

Listening to the poor as a mediation leads us to learn about their suffering and knowledge. This leads to the need for an anthropology of suffering to support justice in health care as a human right from the perspective of the poor.[33] Hence, a liberation ethics[34] is developed from the praxis of the poor, their faith, and the support of the sciences needed to understand the reason for their vulnerability. Liberation ethics is a process of mutual learning, a result of an exercise of the transcendental spirit amid the historical praxis of the poor. It is a dialogical movement of listening to the poor and being open to learn from them. Far from a romantic vision of the poor, liberation ethics is a fruit of a practical engagement in the life, suffering, faith, hopes, and struggles of the poor. Therefore, liberation ethics is grounded in an interdisciplinary method of doing theology with two dimensions that reflect the hermeneutical circle of liberation theology.[35]

The first dimension is the reality of the poor and their historical praxis of faith and liberation. They do not develop an ethics as a systematic reflection on the moral act. They simply act morally, and this act is shaped by their historical experience.[36] The biblical mediation brings the preferential option for the poor as it is "implicit in our Christian faith in a God who became poor for us, so as to enrich us with his poverty" (*Evangelii Gaudium* 198). This option is a theological principle grounded on anthropological and sociological features that see the poor as privileged recipients of the gospel and as suffering as victims of violence against their dignity.

The poor live an experience of being poor as victims of social violence. This experience shapes their worldview and their faith. Consequently, this generates an historical praxis that is a liberation ethic of resistance, struggle, and hope. The experience of the poor provides them an existential protection and a knowledge that those who are outside this reality cannot understand. This occurs in the same way for Black theology in the United States that names *Black experience*. The Protestant theologian James H. Cone develops this concept in the context of racism in the United States, as an experience of suffering within the Black community under white supremacy. He stresses the suffering of Black people, as victims of white supremacy, and their identification with the cross of Jesus. He presents a theology grounded in the *Black experience* and the cross of Jesus, a paradoxical religious symbol that inverts values. According to him, the Black experience is marked by suffering and the presence of Jesus's cross among them that leads them to struggle for justice.[37] Cone argues that whoever does not have this experience or is distant from it cannot understand the suffering of Black people,[38] and their liberating knowledge grounded in the Black experience of faith in the crucified Jesus.[39]

I mention Cone as a matter of illustration of an experience in the U.S. context that has similarities with the Latin American one presented in this book. Returning to Latin America, Argentinian liberation theologian Emilce Cuda, in her account of "Theology of the People," an Argentinian branch of liberation theology, affirms that this theology is situated in a cultural ethos, that is historical with a practice of the people for liberation, but is also transcendent because it seeks salvation. Sharing this cultural ethos, historical and marked by faith and struggle for justice, "the theologian and the poor constitute identify and knowledge at the same time, and in that theological and sapiential moment, the way of salvation takes place."[40] Similar to the *Black experience*, the culture ethos in which the Theology of the People is inserted leads to a "Theological ethics…[that] asks us to build bridges, to seek conversion, to practice compassion, and to do theological ethics incarnating in a culture that is the victim of those unjust relationships that promote accumulation and consumption as the only good, causing some to fall into selfishness and idolatry, and other into need and agony."[41] This is liberation ethic of resistance, struggle, and hope, embodied in the practice of the poor.

The experience of the poor and their knowledge cannot be understood far from them, without breathing their cultural ethos. In a paradoxical relationship between suffering and faith, this experience constitutes a twofold liberation ethics: one is the existential protection that their faith provides by encountering Christ amidst suffering. So, their moral action is in the atmosphere of this existential protection that includes their values, principles, struggles, fragility, and hope. This is their *ethos*, but it is necessary to clarify what this means. *Ethos* is the transliteration of two Classical Greek words *ἦθος* (spelling with eta) and *ἔθος* (with epsilon). Although the meaning of these words is connected, they differ in their origin. *Ethos* (with eta) goes beyond the Latin translation *moris*, from which comes the modern meaning of ethical and moral. *Ethos* (eta) means the house of humankind. It is a place of permanent and habitual protection as a *praxiological framework* shaping a style of life and action. Henrique de Lima Vaz defines this ethos in this way: "The space of ethos, while human space, is not given to man, but it is built by him or unceasingly rebuilt. The house of ethos is never finished and ready....The space of ethos soon becomes comprehension and expression of the being of man as a radical requirement of duty or of good."[42] *Ethos* (with epsilon) is the behavior, as the result of a constant repetition of the same acts. It could be translated by habit. It is the ethos expressed by any individual's acts that translate his/her ethical personality. This expression articulates *ethos* (eta) as character and *ethos* (epsilon) as habit.[43]

The ethos of the poor is their existential house where they live as a suffering people as they journey in faith and hope. It is paradoxical because, even amid their vulnerability and oppression, they know how to survive and where to find their praxiological framework. This leads us to the second aspect of their liberation ethics: historical praxis. This praxis is an action of liberation from their ethos through resistance to the dominant status quo and struggle for justice. Just as Antonio Gramsci notes that the dominant culture is not passively absorbed by the popular culture,[44] there is a process of recreation of the dominant culture through the ethos of the poor, or their hermeneutical lens. This is also the knowledge of the poor, a part of their historical praxis of liberation. This knowledge is sometimes confused and fragmentary. In addition, one who is not among the poor nor in the atmosphere of their ethos, cannot understand this knowledge, neither can he or she recognize they have something to contribute to the process of liberation and justice. Gramsci was aware of this when he proposed the idea of the *organic intellectual* that later was embraced by liberation theology, particularly in the experiences of intentional communities (*comunidades inseridas*) in Latin America.[45] Therefore, among the poor, the dialectic occurs as an ongoing construction of a liberation ethics grounded in the experience of the poor (their ethos) and their historical praxis.

When one transcribes this experience from contemplation and dialogue with these mediations (knowledge of the poor, Scripture and Tradition, and sciences) into a systematic writing, we have a theological product, showing elements of the transcendent present in the history of the poor and oppressed. It is a local understanding of God's revelation and its ethical implications.[46] As such, it cannot be simply imposed as universal or automatically translated into other contexts. The dynamism and challenges of each context requires discernment with contemplation and dialogue. However, a local understanding has elements of the universal that can dialogue within any context and theology in their effort to understand God's mystery in history.

CONCLUSION

Narratives have a power to lead us to discover the beauty and the challenges of believing in an incarnate God while living in a reality full of contradictions. It seems that the more spontaneous a narrative, the more meaningful it is for people and communities. In *Querida Amazonia*, Pope Francis states,

> Popular poets, enamored of its immense beauty, have tried to express the feeling this river evokes and the life that it bestows as it passes amid a dance of dolphins, anacondas, trees, and canoes. Yet they also lament the dangers that menace it. Those poets, contemplatives and prophets, help free us from the technocratic and consumerist paradigm that destroys nature and robs us of a truly dignified existence. (no. 46)

Francis then quotes a Brazilian poet, Vinicius de Morais, known and criticized for his bohemian lifestyle and not one whom a traditional theologian would expect to be quoted by a pope:

> The world is suffering from its feet being turned into rubber, its legs into leather, its body into cloth and its head into steel....The world is suffering from its trees being turned into rifles, its ploughshares into tanks, as the image of

> the sower scattering seed yields to the tank with its flame-thrower, which sows only deserts. Only poetry, with its humble voice, will be able to save this world. (no. 46)

A mystic certainly sees God as a poet with a humble voice. The prophet Elijah had difficulty recognizing God because He did not manifest himself in a hurricane, but rather, in a gentle breeze (1 Kgs 19:11–13). Sometimes, theological endeavors and methods get lost in the technicalities, bureaucracy, and assumptions, thus, forgetting to listen to the humble voices that point to the presence of the transcendent in the immanent reality of the little ones.

A Liberating Method

Liberation theology is a way of doing theology from the perspective of the poor having them as companions in a process of transformation toward justice and life with dignity. The perspective of the poor is a movement of being in solidary with them, sharing the bread, praying and acting with them for social transformation.

A liberating method is oriented from the engagement with oppressed communities and historically marginalized social groups in a process of collective action and construction of systematic knowledge. Liberation is liberating from oppression and creating opportunities for the poor, the oppressed, and the marginalized to flourish with dignity. Considering the reality and the experience of faith of the poor, a liberating method develops an engagement with impoverished and marginalized communities that aims to work with them for their process of liberation from a praxis that reflects a faith incarnated in history. Therefore, the first and foremost movement of liberation theology is to join the poor and the oppressed in their reality and experience of suffering. At the center of this method is a movement of compassion, that is, *suffering with*....In compassion, solidarity, and companionship with the poor, we create liberation theology. Hence, the process of liberation is not an act *from above*, but a movement *from below* in which the poor liberate themselves, with us among them. This occurs in a process of mutual learning based on compassion and mercy.

The Spanish word for mercy is *misericordia*, which means a deep feeling coming from the bottom of the heart toward the other who is suffering. This movement is not easy, but it is a movement that generates an action to care for the other or, at least—when concrete help to address a social problem and suffering is not possible—being in solidarity of the other, walking with him/her in his/her experience of suffering is always possible.

Being with the poor, we are challenged to see and to understand the reality of poverty and injustice from their eyes, cultural identity, and expression of faith. With the poor, a liberating approach engages in all factors responsible for creating poverty and oppression, to understand them in a dialogue that includes specialized knowledge of these factors, teaching from the religious tradition (Bible, Tradition, and Magisterium), and the knowledge originated in the experience of the poor. Actions of social ministry (such as in global public health, in which I am engaged) and "missions" to help to poor are opened to learn from the poor, including their voices and agency in any process of liberation.

Engaging with the poor, their partners, such as theologians, academics, scientists, experts, and anyone who wants to contribute to change realties of poverty and oppression, have something to offer to the process of liberation. But the poor are not mere recipients of external "authoritative" knowledge. They also have something to offer, a contribution of a marginalized people who do not want to be in this position anymore. A liberating method recognizes that effective actions occur when we work together, with the agency of the poor. Below, I suggest a *liberating method for theological ethics research in global health*, structured in three basic steps. (I offer a version adapted for theological bioethics focused on global public health challenges, but it can be use in other areas and social challenges.) The entire framework is sustained by what Leonardo Boff and Clodovis Boff call a "preliminary stage," that is, joining the life of the poor, sharing their experience of faith and struggles for life, as an authentic companion of the poor and the oppressed.[47]

First, it is bibliographic research that is developed while you are already a companion of the poor in their social and ecclesial experience. It consists in academic research on social justice, global health, health inequalities, social determinants of health, and the reality of the poor in impoverished communities and regions. This step aims to raise data about these issues and sociological analysis on population health and the living conditions of vulnerable groups where is the focus of your study and your experience of personal engagement with the poor as their companion. This step also targets selection of theological and anthropological sources able to provide theoretical foundations for the development of the study.

Second, the core of this research is based on the liberation theology method: *see–judge–act*. It deepens the movement of joining the poor in their reality to share lives and to hear their voices. Among the poor, the goal is to hear their voices and to learn from their creativity to survive in very adverse conditions through an experience of companionship. Then this leads to the development activities in which the poor (and us among them) share their suffering, social concerns, struggling to access health-care services, and hope for social justice. Hearing these voices mean to have contact with narratives that express the experience and knowledge of the poor. This will provide concrete material to confront the theoretical first step.

Explaining this method in terms of liberation theology means:

- See: being with the poor, caring about them, and listening to their stories of suffering and hope. This also means to observe the reality and how socioeconomic injustices impact the reality from the eyes of the poor and the oppressed.
- Judge: understanding the reality of the poor, the causes of their suffering and lack of basic needs, and difficulties to access health-care services. This part also addresses the role of faith in the life of the poor and their struggle for justice and liberation. It is an effort to understand the mechanism of structural violence from a theological perspective.
- Act: observing the actions that have already been done by the local community for social justice and to access health-care services. It aims at strengthening these initiatives (if there is any) and developing new actions that can empower the poor in the local community to become aware of the reasons for their social suffering and enable them to struggle for health-care advocacy.

Third, it is the analysis and confrontation of all data from the bibliographic research and experience among the poor. Projects, actions, and texts will come from this experience of liberation and companionship among the poor, which their voices can be amplified, and their agency supported and promoted.

Through this liberating method, community members are truly engaged in the work, helping to inform research, practices, and sharing their experience directly and indirectly related to health and access to health care. Considering global public health, a liberating method must create participation of local communities in which the voices and experiences of the poor engage in the development of strategies of health-care delivery and inform health policies. In addition, we celebrate faith and life with the poor, vigorously participating in their communitarian activities and faith celebrations. Together, this favors a process of collective actions, contributing to the empowerment of people in a process of conscientization and the development of community's action plans for their engagement in the public health care and other social challenges. It is an experience of companionship in which the participants are agents in their own social context. They become agents of a social action in which there is an interaction between research and action with mutual learning. The final role of the theologian is to systematize this and give back to the community and beyond, offering it as contribution to the dialogue in other contexts.

2

"Anointed to Evangelize the Poor"

An Exegetical Study of Luke 4:16–30

After discussing contextual theologies and liberating methods, this chapter begins the development of a Christology, that will extend across three chapters, from a biblical passage (or pericope). This work is a contextual theology grounded on a liberating method of doing theology developed from the experience of faith and social struggle of Latin American communities, particularly in Brazil, and all theological analysis is generated from this experience. That does not make this book an isolated work that presents a particular God, but rather offers the universal God experienced in a particular reality. It follows Pope Francis's perspective that the universal is real in particular realities.[1] In this case, the biblical passage is understood from a historical reality, where concrete experiences of faith take place, in dialogue with academic studies of theological matters. Theology is only the second act of faith, a systematic reflection of a faith experience. Theology serves the community of faith, helping it to comprehend its experience and to discern the challenges of developing the embodiment of faith in any historical period. Even biblical texts are not faith themselves but are built on people's faith. As theology, these texts reflect an experience of the faith of communities. But biblical texts have a unique dynamism, in which faith is revealed through them, and this revelation becomes food for our experience of believers at anytime, anywhere. Therefore, the Scriptures have a privileged place in our communities that any theological reflection is unable to occupy. Biblical texts speak to communities and their historical struggles with a proximity that is impossible for theology to have. There is an identification between Scriptures and the community of faith, something universal for the Christian faith that is visible in the particular of each individual community. In this sense, the theological reflection of this book is realized from a *locus*, that is, a particular historical reality, by having a biblical passage as the starting point of this reflection (or theological systematization), considering the organic relationship between the text and the community of faith.

When I was a student of theology, I had a professor who liked to state repeatedly that good Catholic theology was based on Sacred Scripture, enriched by tradition and the magisterium of the Church seen from a historical experience of faith. The Bible is always the first source, or rather, the Word of God is the primordial source from which theology springs. Sacred Scripture is the main expression of this Word, but it is also revealed, understood, and embodied in the course of the salvific history and the faith experience of communities. God's revelation takes place in the Word, its fullness manifest in Jesus Christ. But comprehension of revelation is not completely understood as a single act after an encounter with the Word. Guided by the freedom of the Spirit, revelation has an ongoing dynamism, manifest also in events and words throughout history (*Dei Verbum* 2) and new interpretations, with the assistance of the same Holy Spirit (for example, *Catechism of the Catholic Church* 94; *Dei Verbum* 12). God is present in history, walking alongside the people. The Dogmatic Constitution on Divine Revelation *Dei Verbum* affirms,

> Sacred theology rests on the written word of God, together with sacred tradition, as its primary and perpetual foundation. By scrutinizing in the light of faith all truth stored up in the mystery of Christ, theology is most powerfully strengthened and constantly rejuvenated by that word. For the Sacred Scriptures contain the word of

> God and since they are inspired, really are the word of God; and so the study of the sacred page is, as it were, the soul of sacred theology. (no. 24)

In the spirit of the Second Vatican Council, which promoted the study of Sacred Scripture (that is, the soul of theology), I suggest an exegetical analysis of a biblical passage as a source to enrich the study of theology, in this case an exercise of Christology, with two goals: first, to enrich the interpretation of a Christian experience from the reality of a faith community; and second, to offer a new recourse for strengthening the encounter with Jesus and the embodiment of this encounter into the social life. In other words, the biblical analysis originates in a particular reality and returns, as systematic and moral theologies, to realities that communities experience in their faith in Jesus.

The biblical text chosen for this exercise of theological service is from the Gospel of Luke. Thus, Luke functions as a model that works with any other biblical text, particularly from the New Testament, when the main goal includes something related to Christology. The first step is an exegetical study to better understand the text and its context, as well as the writer's intentions and theology. This passage from Luke is chosen for its literary and theological richness. In addition, some limitations in Latin American studies are outlined in chapter 4 to link their academic analysis to the way communities read this text as part of *leitura popular da Bíblia* (a communitarian way to read the Bible in impoverished realities)[2] and the identification with this text. Luke 4:16–30 marks the beginning of Jesus's public ministry. Moreover, Luke 4 has a key role in the Gospel of Luke that helps us to understand his entire work, including the Acts of the Apostles. Therefore, before I move forward with a specific examination of this passage, it is worth beginning with an overview of the Lukan writings.

Luke wrote a single work divided into two volumes: the Gospel according to Luke and the Acts of the Apostles. One text continues the other, but in the Bible, they were set apart. The unity between Luke's Gospel and the Acts of the Apostles as well as their theological continuity within the author's objective are clear when one reads the Gospel as a continuation of Acts, as if they were a single book. As a comprehensive single work, it is possible to see how the proclamation of the good news begins in a small Galilean village with Jesus of Nazareth, who is the gospel, and then expands beyond the borders of Palestine through the mission and preaching of his followers. All of this occurred under the guidance of the Holy Spirit, who spurred Jesus in his ministry (see Luke 4:14) and urged the apostles to continue the proclamation of the good news (see Acts 2:1ff.). Crossan and Reed highlight that "Luke's two-volume gospel tells how the Holy Spirit took Jesus from Galilee to Jerusalem in the first volume [the Gospel of Luke] and the Church from Jerusalem to Rome in the second one [the Acts of the Apostles]."[3] At the center of this great work is the passion, death, resurrection, and ascension of Jesus.[4]

Luke's work has a historiographical character, which can be seen in its prologue (Luke 1:1–4). He speaks of having heard eyewitnesses and having carried out an accurate investigation, but Luke's goal was not to offer a historical biography of Jesus and his first disciples. He wrote a text with a historiographical mark, in addition to missionary and apologetic goals. François Bovon argues:

> [Luke] wants to demonstrate the respectability of the "way," that is, the Christian message and the Church; to illustrate the strength of the mission, highlighting its successes; to manifest the support that God gave to Jesus and then to the witnesses [Jesus's disciples]; and, even more, to proclaim that Jesus' life fulfills the promises of Scripture, reveals God's affection for the people and nations, and offers an opportunity to return to the living God.[5]

The work of Luke has an addressee, that is, a person to whom he writes, Theophilus. Nothing is known about him, as his name appears only at the beginning of the Gospel (see 1:3). There is a hypothesis that Theophilus was a wealthy Christian responsible for funding Luke's historical research, but nothing has been proven.[6] Another hypothesis is that Theophilus is a fictional character, a symbolic name because it means *son of God*. Hence, Luke's recipients were all who believe in Jesus as the Son of God, becoming the children of God. Regardless of Theophilus being a symbolic name or a real person, Luke is clear that his work has also non-Jews as recipients. When he explains Jewish institutions (see Luke 22:1–7), he omits tough questions for those considered pagans or Gentiles, as they appear in Matthew 10:5, which says to the apostles, "Do not make your way to gentile territory."[7]

Luke wrote in *Koiné* Greek, with popular and common characteristics as this language was spoken in the region. But we find elements in Luke's *Koiné* text with a more sophisticated writing style, so much so that some sentences are very close to classical Greek. For example, the prologue (Luke 1:1–4) and Paul's speech in Athens (Acts 17:22–31) seem to suggest that the author was very carefully choosing the terms and organizing these texts. The speech on the Areopagus is well written, which shows the ability that the nascent Christian community had to dialogue with Greek culture.[8] Luke also avoided strong terms that could be misunderstood by a non-Jewish audience, like those found in Mark. Thus, he changed some terms from one of his sources and corrected the Semitism found in Mark's Gospel. For example, the author of Mark heavily used the Greek linking particle *kai* (and) to link one idea or text to another; Luke developed a more sophisticated linguistic way to articulate his text. This points out the author's erudition. However, the fact that he also used a Greek very close to people's common way to speak on the streets and in the markets of the local region of Galilee and Palestine reveals his social concern. Therefore, Luke followed Mark's framework, one of his sources, but left spaces to make insertions with which he imprinted his style and theology on the text, adding information and/or adapting material from sources according to his theological and missionary objectives. In addition to Mark, Luke had as sources the *Q Source* (a common source for both him and Matthew) and a source of his own, which produced unique texts not found in the other three Gospel narratives.

The tradition established the author of this great work as being Luke. This name was also that of a physician whom Paul referred to as the "beloved doctor" in Colossians 4:14 and who accompanied him on some missions (see Phlm 24:2; 2 Tim 4:11). However, there is much controversy over the identity of the author of the Gospel of Luke and Acts. Some argue that the author of this double work was not Luke, to whom Paul referred. The Lukan author would not be a companion of Paul, due to some differences found between accounts of the same facts told by Paul and by Luke, such as the Council of Jerusalem (cf. Acts 15:1–21; Gal 2:1–14). Those who support this argument explain that the first-person plural used by Luke in Acts (see Acts 16:10) suggests that the author's presence alongside Paul during his missions is merely a literary stylistic element.[9] However, the author of Luke–Acts was part of a Pauline community. The place and date of the writing of the Lukan work are uncertain. It seems certain that it was written outside Palestine (where, exactly, is unknown) after the destruction of the temple of Jerusalem, between the year AD 70 and 90.[10]

The Lukan literary genre is usually classified as historical or biographical, due to the difficulties of specifying if it meets the criteria of one or the other. In certain aspects, the Gospel looks like biographical text, but the author suggests the entire history of the people of Israel is somehow involved in the life of the main character.[11] Telling the story of Jesus, Luke offered key facts of the story of the people of Israel, because, in Jesus, the promises of God in the covenant were fulfilled.

Let us consider the overall structure of the Lukan work to get a general context as we move into a more in-depth study of the pericope Luke 4:16–30. According to the Chilean biblical scholar Pablo Richard, Luke's work is structured as follows:

Historical prologue of the entire work Luke–Acts – Luke 1:1–4
Theological prologue of the entire work Luke–Acts – Luke 1:5—4:13
- A – Ministry of Jesus in Galilee – Luke 4:14—9:50
- B – The Journey of Jesus from Galilee to Jerusalem – Luke 9:51—19:44
- C – Ministry of Jesus in the temple of Jerusalem – Luke 19:45—21:38

Center:
- Passion and death of Jesus – Luke 22—23
- Resurrection of Jesus – Luke 24:1–49
- Testament of Jesus – Luke 24:44–49; Acts 1:6–8
- Exaltation of Jesus: ascension – Acts 1:9–11

A – The movement of Jesus in Jerusalem – Acts 1:12—5:42
B – The movement of Jesus from Jerusalem to Antioch – Acts 6:1—15:35

C – The movement from Antioch to Rome – Acts 15:36—28:31.[12]

Luke did not write a theological treatise or essay as we understand it today.[13] However, there is an underlying theology driving his book, with the aim of carrying out a theological project[14] in which he seeks to present the history of salvation that began in ancient Israel, had its high point in Jesus Christ (fulfillment of God's promise), and then continues in the life of the ecclesial community. Luke concretized this project by presenting an access to revelation through contacting the past, specifically the story of Jesus (to whom the author, Luke himself, did not have firsthand direct access. He was not an eyewitness, but part of the second or third generation of Christians). However, learning about this history is not enough to understand its meaning. The Word (Jesus, the Word of God) gives meaning to events, so that they can be understood. This explains, for example, why the verb *evangelize* is so important in Luke's work.

The continuity between the time of Jesus and the time of the Church must be guaranteed. Historical memory has this function in Luke, but memory alone does not guarantee continuity. The action of the Holy Spirit is responsible for the continuity. Luke makes this clear, showing in key moments the Spirit's intervention in this process.[15]

Within this theological project, we perceive the theological characteristics of Luke, marked by a universal perspective of salvation and an increasing openness to non-Jewish people, that is, pagans or Gentiles.[16] The aspect of mercy is strongly present in Luke (the parable of the *merciful father*, inaccurately known as the prodigal son, for example, appears only in Luke 15:1–32). His text radiates joy in a fervent proclamation of the gospel and that the saving mission of Christ was prepared by the Scriptures because Jesus fulfilled the prophecies.[17] Finally, Luke has a strong concern for the poor and the most marginalized. His Gospel is often called the "gospel of the poor." It seeks to show how important it is for the community to live out an ideal of poverty in a fraternity of people who share everything. Luke even exalts poverty and criticizes wealth (see Luke 6:20; 18:18–27; 19:1–10; Acts 11:27–30).[18]

Now that we have learned a little about the Lukan work, we have a foundation on which to develop a more specific study of a biblical passage of the Gospel. This introduction to Luke's work was important because we will find these many general elements exposed here in Luke 4:16–30. In addition, this introduction helps us to know the context of the work in which this pericope is inserted as a significant piece of a larger project.

LITERARY ANALYSES

In the following literary analysis of the text, we will avoid, as far as possible, presenting historical and theological elements that will be discussed later.

As with any text that we begin to read, the first contact is with its writing—the way it presents itself to us as a literary text, its literary beauty. After entering the text, reading the book through the way its author articulated words and phrases, we begin an exercise of understanding it and, if the text manages to attract our attention, we want to deepen our understanding even more by increasingly paying attention to details, asking questions, and confronting ideals with other material related to the topic. When we begin to read a text from the Bible, letting ourselves be gripped by the literary beauty of its verses is the first step for a community reading in a biblical circle. Such a step might lead us toward an exegetical study to seek answers to our questions and to better understand the text and its relevance for our lives and for the community of faith. This exercise of reading and literary enchantment is the invitation that I now extend to everyone regarding Luke 4:16–30 for your individual or community reading. A literary activity, the pleasure of reading a good text, is a spiritual contemplation—because we read a passage of the Scripture—and a study (or an academic exercise with the help of those who examined this text before us) of understanding and learning from a primary source for our Christian ethical life.

Luke 4:16–30[19]

I offer a translation of this pericope made by myself, with all the limitations that this might have. The reason for that is I want to respect the most literal aspect of the text, leaving aside certain arrangements that English language (or any modern European language) would require. This literary translation aims to help us to understand the construction of the Lukan text better, showing as much as possible the author's style of playing with words and expressions, as is clear in original language:

> 16 And he come to Nazara, where he was raised, and entered, accord with his custom on Saturdays, into the synagogue and stood up to read,
>
> 17 and was given to him a scroll of the prophet Isaiah. He unrolled the scroll and found where it was written:
>
> 18 *The spirit of the Lord is on me,*
> *for he has anointed me.*
> *To bring the good news to the poor,*
> *to set the captives free*
> *and to sight to the blind,*
> *to set the oppressed free*
> 19 *and to proclaim the year acceptable of the Lord.*
>
> 20 Then having rolled up the scroll, gave it back to the servant and sat down; and the year eyes of all in the synagogue were fixed on him.
>
> 21 He began to speak to them: "Today was fulfilled this Scriptures to your ears."
>
> 22 And all give testimony of him and was amazed at the words of grace coming out of this mouth and say: "Is he not the son of Joseph?"
>
> 23 And he replied: "Surely, you quote me the saying: 'doctor, heal yourself.' 'The things we have heard that occurred in Capernaum, do the same here in your own country.'"
>
> 24 And he continued: "Amen: I tell you that no prophet is welcomed in his homeland.
>
> 25 For that, in truth I tell you: there were many widows during the days of Elijah in Israel when the heaven was shut for three years and six months, when great famine raged throughout the land;
>
> 26 But Elijah was not sent to none of them, rather to a widow woman at Zarephath of Sidonia.
>
> 27 And there were many lepers in Israel during Elisha's time, the prophet; and none of them were purified, only Naaman, the Syrian."

28 All were full of fury when they heard these things at the synagogue,
29 And, standing to their feet, hustled him out of the town, taking him to the brow of the hill upon which their town was built, intending to throw him off the cliff,
30 he, however, passed straight through them, walking away.

After the first contact with the text, by reading it several times, I offer an examination to understand it deeply. The first question is to see what is before and after the passage, to check if, in fact, these verses in chapter 4 are what biblical scholars call a pericope, that is, a biblical passage with an internal coherence by itself within a literary unit.

Within Luke's work, we find several chapters about Jesus's activity in Galilee before going to Jerusalem. These chapters correspond to Luke 4:14—9:50 and form a literary block. In 9:51, the reader clearly realizes the author's transposition to another context (particularly in a different geographical region), since Luke affirms that Jesus took the way to Jerusalem. Our pericope is within this literary block from chapters 4 to 9. Therefore, it seems plausible to limit Luke 4:16–30 as a pericope due to the literary transpositions coming before (4:14–15) and after (4:31–33) the selected passage for this study.

Verses 14–15[20] function as an introduction to the literary block about Jesus's ministry in Galilee. They also serve as a transition[21] from one scene to another in which there is a rupture of stories. Jesus was in the desert being tempted by Satan (4:1–13) and is now in Galilee to begin his public life. Verses 14–15 constitute a *summary* (technical term for verses that aim to close a story and/or open a new one) and present Jesus as the one who is guided by the power of the Spirit. They report the anticipated success during the ministry in Nazareth and prepare for a dramatic scene in the synagogue.

Verses 30–31[22] are also a *summary*, having the function of switching from one scene to another. They mark a change of narrative and context. Both summaries frame Luke 4:16–30. They are linked by the terms *edídasken* ("taught"; see v. 15) and *en dídaskon* ("was teaching"; see v. 31). Several times, Luke highlights Jesus as the one who teaches during his ministry in Galilee.

Luke 4:16–30 is objectively organized around the speech of

Jesus and the reaction of his listeners. Luke used Mark 6:1–6 as a source for his narrative, but altered the material he had at hand, adding and modifying it for his purposes. Luke 4:16–24 originated in Mark, and verses 25–30 were Luke's own addition, certainly from a source to which the other evangelists had no access.[23] This text has a programmatic character, functioning as a platform.[24] Luke presents Jesus's program in Galilee. Jesus is the anointed one of the Lord who announces his program of evangelization of the poor and will suffer because this project will be rejected. "Jesus had been anointed with the Spirit to announce the good news to the poor, but the poor, the blind, and the captives are, above all, outside Israel."[25]

This pericope is divided into two great scenes: verses 16–21 and 22–30. The first scene revolves around Jesus's reading of a text from the Prophet Isaiah and his talk about the fulfillment of the Scriptures; the second revolves around Jesus's speech about the nonacceptance of the Prophet in his own homeland and the violent reaction of the listeners:

vv. 16–21: the account on Jesus's teaching in the synagogue and the admiration of the listeners.
v. 21: Jesus utters a strong phrase.
v. 22a: listeners are amazed at Jesus's wisdom (positive reaction).
v. 22b: a question about the origin of Jesus.
vv. 23–27: Jesus reacts to questioning and challenges his listeners.
vv. 28–29: listeners are enraged at Jesus's words and want to kill him.
v. 30: Jesus walks his way.

In the narrative, there is a movement of *ascending* and *descending* in relation to Jesus himself. He *stands up* to read and *sits down* to teach. The author structures the first part of his text (verses 16–21) within this movement with a solemnity in the middle. This structure forms a *concentric circle*, as exegetes refer to it:

A – stood up (*anéste*)
B – was given (*epedóthe*)
C – unrolled[26] (*anaptúxas*)

Solemnity: Jesus reads a text of Isaiah 61:1–2; 58:6:

C – rolled up (*ptúxas*)
B – gave it back (*apodoús*)
A – sat down (*káthisen*)

Arguing in favor of this literary structural understand, Brendan Byrne affirms,

> The ascending-descending patters lends maximum solemnity to the text read by Jesus. The drama continues in the subsequent note (v. 20b), that "the eyes of all in the synagogue were fixed on him" followed by the solemn pronouncement of the great "Today."[27]

Before continuing with this drama in the narrative, it is necessary to take a closer look at the text in which Luke quotes Jesus as reading in the synagogue. Luke uses a Septuagint text (a Greek translation) and not the original Hebrew writing.[28] The text of the Prophet read by Jesus is assembled by Luke from three verses of Isaiah 61:1–2 and 58:6. The author of the text makes this montage according to his purposes. In parallel Gospel texts to Luke—Mark 6:1–6 (one of the sources) and Matthew 13:53–58—the scene in the synagogue is reported very succinctly, without the Lukan drama and with no reading of the Prophet Isaiah.

Luke 4:18–19	**Isaiah 61:1–2**
v.18 *pneûma kyríou en' emè,* The spirit of the Lord is upon me,	*pneûma kyríou en' emè,*
oû eíneken échpisén me for he has anointed me	*oû eíneken échpisén me*
Eùaggelísasthai ptochoîs. To proclaim the good news to the poor.	*Eùaggelísasthai ptochoîs.*
Apéstalkén me Sent me	*Apéstalkén me*
[...]	*lásasthai toùs suntetrimménous tê kardía*|, to heal the broken-hearted,

Kerúxai aìchmalótois áphesin, to set the captives free,	*Kerúxai aìchmalótois áphesin,*
Kaì tuphloîs anàblepsin. and to give sight to the blind.	*Kaì tuphloîs anàblepsin.*
Isaiah 58:6	
Aposteîlai tethrausménous en aphései, to set the oppressed free,	*[Aposteîlai tethrausménous en aphései]*
v.19 *knrúxai eniautòn kyríou dektón.* to proclaim the year acceptable to the Lord.	*Kalésai eniautòn kyríou dektón.*
	Kaí enéran antapodóseos parakalésai pántas toùs penthoûntas. And the day of vengeance for our God to comfort the bereaved.

In this comparative picture, we realize that Luke's quotation of Isaiah is, in fact, a montage. Luke manipulated the Prophet's text by omitting two pieces from Isaiah 61:1–2 and adding one from Isaiah 58:6. Perhaps Luke excluded the harsh phrases, "healing the broken-hearted" and "the day of vengeance of our God," because they would not suit his theological project in which one of the objectives was to show a God concerned with the poor at the social level and not just spiritual poverty as the expression "broken-hearted" could be interpreted. I suggest this in consideration of the Beatitudes in Luke 6:20–23 and the author's concern with social poverty.[29] Luke also presents God as a merciful Father (Luke 15:11–31), who goes after the lost sheep (Luke 15:4–7) and demands that the followers of his Son are "moved by compassion" to act (Luke 10:29–37). Presenting God as this very merciful Father seems incompatible to an emphasis related to "the day of God's vengeance."

The addition of "to send the captives free" points out a parallel with what was presented in the previous sentences. The term *aphései* ("freedom") in the text of Isaiah 58:6 corresponds to one of the actions of the Messiah, as he comes to free the oppressed and those who are in captivity, actions that happen in the Sabbath year, a tradition certainly present in Luke's mind, since Jesus comes to fulfill

God's promises. We will return to this issue when dealing with the context where this text was developed. The terms *aphésai* and *dektón* (*acceptable*, referring to the Jubilee year) are central to understanding Luke's purposes in putting together this quote because these terms reflect the Jewish tradition of the *seventh year* (Sabbath year) and the *Jubilee year*.

The significance of reading the text of Isaiah is understood from the lens of verse 21 in which Jesus says, "Today was fulfilled this Scripture to your ears." The use of "today" shows that Jesus is the true Messiah. He is under the anointing of the Spirit, revealed in the baptism in the Jordan (see Luke 3:22). Once again, the text presents the action of the Spirit on Jesus, who will now carry out his ministry from the script composed by the Prophet Isaiah centuries before. "The year acceptable of the Lord" begins; this is the inauguration of the age of the Messiah announced by the prophets.[30]

In the second part of the text (vv. 22–30), Luke presents the reaction of the listeners, which, at first, is positive, as they are amazed at Jesus's words, but then they begin to question themselves and no longer accept him. The text makes clear that the reason for the rejection of Jesus is not because of the teaching given, but because he was a Nazarene and the son of Joseph, a poor person known by all. "Is he not the son of Joseph?"[31] Faced with this questioning, Jesus makes a provocative and ironic speech, stating that the Prophet is not accepted in his own homeland, based on the stories of two well-known prophets, Elijah and Elisha, who were sent by God to heal foreigners (Jesus refers to the passages of 1 Kgs 17:8–24 and 2 Kgs 5:8–14). The writer uses well-known images of the people present in the synagogue and a proverb that is widespread in the region, probably to be clear about what he wants to convey in this text. Hence, he offers the reader the reason for the fury of those present in the scene, even to the point of desiring to kill Jesus.

Referring to Jesus as a prophet and showing the rejection of him link this text to Jesus's infancy narrative earlier in the Gospel and that of his resurrection at the end of the Gospel. Among the several titles Luke employs for Jesus, the most used is *Kyrios* ("Lord"; see Luke 7:3, 19; 10:1, 39, 41; 9:54; 10:17; 10:40; 11:1, 39; 12:41; 18:41; 19:8). Jesus is also a great prophet (Luke 7:16).[32] It is the death of this powerful prophet that the disciples of Emmaus mourn:

"The things about Jesus of Nazareth, who was a prophet mighty in deed and word before God and all the people" (Luke 24:19).

Luke 2:34–35 provides the second oracle of Simeon: "This child is destined for the falling and the rising of many in Israel, and to be a sign that will be opposed so that the inner thoughts of many will be revealed—and a sword will pierce your own soul." This is precisely what happens in Luke 4:22–30. Jesus is a sign of contradiction: first they accept him; then they reject him. The text shows that the positive reaction at first was superficial and Jesus, capable of revealing what is in the depths of the heart, demands a deep and authentic conversion. The initial approval of Jesus by the Nazarenes was a superficial attitude and not a real conversion.[33]

The total rejection in the synagogue of Nazareth serves to prepare the reader of Luke's book for the rejection that Jesus will suffer in Jerusalem before the Sanhedrin.[34] So, when the reader gets there, he/she will understand why Jesus was rejected and killed by the authorities of the nation and only accepted by the little ones.

THE CONTEXT

According to John Dominic Crossan and Jonathan L. Reed, the job of an exegete (an expert in textual analysis, particularly of old texts, such as the Sacred Scriptures) is like the work of an archaeologist.[35] Both have to carry out excavations. When a site is found, the archaeologist needs to excavate the ruins and seek answers to the artifacts found and relate them to what he/she has known in history. The exegete must engage in the same process with texts, excavating the layers between facts, oral transmission, and writing, to seek answers to their questions and hypotheses. This must be done considering historical knowledge and archaeological discoveries to make proper connections. Therefore, concerning literary study, it is not enough simply to understand a biblical text better; it also requires a historical-critical work to excavate the texts. In this perspective, I now approach Luke 4:16–30 to complement the literary analysis outlined above.

Luke presents the synagogue as a specific building where the Jews gathered to hear the Scriptures and to pray. It is plausible to presuppose a place because the writer says *kaí eìsêlthen* ("and entered").

He uses the third person singular aorist of the verb *eìserchomai* ("to enter"). Archaeological excavations have not found the existence of a synagogue in Nazareth during Jesus's time.[36] Nazareth was a very humble and poor village in Galilee.[37] A meeting to read and meditate on the Scriptures probably took place outdoors, perhaps under a tree near a lake or a river.

The excavations carried out under the later Christian structures found no synagogue, no fortifications or palaces, no basilica or bathhouses, and not even paved streets. Absolutely nothing. Instead, it found presses to produce olive oil and wine. Cisterns, silos, and millstones were scattered around, and pits speak of a rural population that lived in very simple hovels.[38]

Excavations indicate that Nazareth was a poor area, made up of Jews who migrated there because of the expansionist policies of the Hasmonean period.[39] Its population was around two to four hundred inhabitants. Nazareth was an insignificant village of Galilee, overshadowed by the magnitude of the cities of Sepphoris and Tiberias that had significant growth under the rule of Herod Antipas, the tetrarch of Galilee and Persia between 4 BC and AD 39.

Like the entire population of the Galilee region, the people of Nazareth suffered from high taxation. There was probably a triple taxation: taxes collected for the Roman Empire; taxes for the maintenance of the temple, that is, the religious tribute; and certainly, Herod the Great created his own taxes to finance his enormous constructions. His successor, Herod Antipas, continued the constructions to restore Sepphoris and to build Tiberias. All this made the peasant population increasingly impoverished and generated great social inequality, with very many poor and a few rich. High taxation caused small landowners to become indebted, who were forced to pledge their land and even lost it. There was a rural exodus, a generalized decline in the socioeconomic structure. To maintain the two developing metropolises, the peasant people of Galilee paid high taxes. As a result, poverty increased, leading to the appearance of thieves and many beggars.[40]

The situation in Nazareth during Jesus's time was indeed very sad, with massive socioeconomic issues. When Luke wrote, however, he was recalling the stories and words of Jesus in another context, certainly with similarity to Nazareth and its particularities. As Luke wrote right after the events of Jesus about which people still had a fresh memory, his concern was not simply to tell a biography but rather carry out a theological project and answer questions specific to his time, a few years after Jesus's death. Thus, Luke contextualized and adapted the material at hand according to the reality of his community; a process that virtually occurred with all New Testament texts. The evangelists applied what they learned and remembered about Jesus to the present needs and challenges of their communities.[41] The most important thing was the certainty of the real presence of the living and risen Christ in the local community experience. The Gospel's narratives were developing considering this dynamic contextual encounter of faith, and not simply repeating a historical biography. This explains why Luke made changes in the text from one of his sources (Mark 6:1–6), added that Jesus read Isaiah (also presented with edits from the evangelist), and presented new elements (vv. 22–30) coming from a source possibly only known by Luke or his own creation.

In all cases, Luke demonstrates a good knowledge of Jewish traditions and presents Jesus's going to a synagogue according to custom. The expression *katà tò eiothòs* ("*according to the custom*") is very strong. It indicates the power of prayer in the synagogue and in Jesus's own life (Luke always presents Jesus as the one who takes time to pray by himself). This custom of going to the synagogue for reading the Scriptures and praying linked the present to the past (the Traditions of Israel) and was a way to express communion.[42]

The Sabbath ritual in the synagogue consisted of two main parts: the *parashah*, a reading of a text from the Torah, and the *haphtarah*, a reading of a text from the prophets.[43] The text of the prophets could be read by any adult male, who had the freedom to choose the quotation. After the reading, there was the moment of explanation, usually carried out by someone with knowledge of the Scriptures and the Traditions. Luke portrays the second moment of the rite and presents it according to the local custom: someone *stands up* to read and then *sits down* to teach, just as Jesus does. Luke presents an educated and wise Jesus, knowledgeable of the Traditions because he also read, in addition to teaching (other Synoptic Gospels only highlight the teaching aspect and do not say that Jesus reads). Knowing how to read and write was a privilege for few in the Galilean region, especially in Nazareth, an impoverished agricultural village. This raises the question of how Jesus learned to read;

a carpenter's son would certainly not learn anything other than his father's profession. This does not mean that Jesus did not have a great knowledge of the Scriptures, because oral transmission was very strong, and it does not exclude that he knew how to read, as Luke shows Jesus with this skill.[44]

Luke wrote from a context in which the Christian faith was expanding, and communities were being formed. Although this was a time of great excitement for these communities, they also suffered from persecution and internal conflicts. For a Christian community, Jesus was the true Messiah. Luke demonstrated this truth by putting it in Jesus's mouth: "Today was fulfilled this Scripture to your ears" (v. 21b). Jesus was the fulfillment of God's promise in the Old Covenant. Luke expanded the scope of this promise. Its fulfillment was first to the Jews, but they rejected it, and then it had turned to the non-Jews, the Gentiles, as well. The text is not limited to show a simple announcement of "Today was fulfilled this Scripture," but the author developed the path that Jesus was going to take to bring salvation to all—that is certainly among the reasons Luke presented for why God sent two prophets to help foreigners (non-Jews)—and to understand salvation as good news proclaimed to the poor.[45]

There is a time gap between the historical Jesus (his life until his crucifixion and death) and the writing of Luke's text. This creates a challenge to learn from the Gospel precise, original elements of Jesus's historical life and to distinguish it from what was created and montaged by Luke, based on the paschal experience and its relevance for the historical time of the community, years after Jesus's death. The paschal experience, that is, the faith encounter with the risen Christ, guarantees that Jesus is alive and concerns itself with the problems in the reality of these communities. This complexity of two different contexts and the time distance between them do not dimmish the dynamic vigor and message of a biblical text, as it was written under the inspiration of the Holy Spirit, which makes this text a living document.[46] Luke's community was certainly made up of many Christians of pagan origin (non-Jews, most from Hellenistic culture), especially if we accept the tradition that suggests Luke as Paul's companion in his mission to the non-Jews. Knowing this makes it understandable when Jesus says, "I tell you that no prophet is welcomed in his homeland" (v. 24), supporting the statement referring to 1 Kings 17:8–24 and 2 Kings 5:8–14. Two prophets highly respected in Israel, Elijah and Elisha, who, as noted earlier, were sent by God not to help their fellow Israelites, but foreigners. Here, Luke portrays the Jewish people's rejection of Jesus. Most Jews rejected the fulfillment of God's promise, which caused Him to turn to pagans, who accepted Jesus and believed in the words of Scripture about the Messiah. With this, Luke also sustains the faith of his community or the Christian group from/for which he wrote.

Luke 4:16–30 also has an allegorical character, as it portrays what will happen to Jesus throughout his life: rejection, condemnation, and death in Jerusalem, which also happened to Paul. There is a relationship between what happened with Jesus in the synagogue and Paul's fate, as described in Acts, during his mission.[47]

According to Crossan and Reed, Luke 4:16–30 is structured in five steps: (1) synagogue situation; (2) scriptural fulfillment; (3) initial acceptance; (4) eventual rejection; and (5) lethal attack.[48] Luke's pericope shows Jesus first addressing the Jews, who did not accept him. Then he quotes two prophets referring to the fact that they were sent to non-Jews. This has an interesting similarity with Paul's missions and preaching in the Acts of the Apostles. When he arrives at a new city, Paul first goes to a synagogue to speak about Jesus to the Jews and, if there are no results, he turns to the pagans (Acts 13:13–52; 14:1–7). The most interesting thing is that these five steps seem to be carried out on Paul's path.[49] Let's look at the parallel:

Steps	**Jesus in Luke 4:16-30**	**Paul in Acts 13:14-52**	**Paul in Acts 17:1-9**
Situation of the synagogue	4:16-17	13:14-16a	17:1-2
Fulfillment of the Scriptures	4:18-21	13:16b-41	17:2b-3
Acceptance	4:22	13:42-43	17:4
Rejection	4:23-28	13:44-49	17:5
Attack	4:29-30	13:50-52	17:5b-9[50]

It remains now to say something about the socioeconomic context, which Luke had in mind when writing this text, especially regarding the poor as recipients of the proclamation of the good news and the liberation of the oppressed.

LIBERATION AND POVERTY

To understand what is behind Luke's text, regarding the liberation from oppression and poverty, it is necessary to bear in mind two words highlighted in the literary analysis: *aphései* ("free," which could also be translated as liberation) and *dektón* ("acceptable").

The term *aphései* appears twice in the Lukan quote from Isaiah. The first time, it says, "to set the captives free" (Isa 61:1), and the second time it says, "to set the oppressed free" (Isa 58:6). *To set free* has high meaning for Luke. It is linked to a context of liberation from the exploitation of the rich over the poorest, an integral liberation of the human being that includes the socioeconomic dimension.

I argue that Luke's liberation means liberating from the shackles of social exploitation. Everything seen until here leads to this interpretation: the reality of the community of faith where the texts originated, the context that surrounds Isaiah's text, and Luke's emphasis on poverty in contrast to wealth, which is responsible for exploitation and oppression. All these aspects and challenges faced by Luke are similar to the context of many Catholic communities today, particularly in the Global South, where members of these communities have a great identification with the message of liberation in Luke 4 amid poverty and oppression.

Luke wrote within a community made up of people converted from Hellenistic beliefs with their plurality of deities, possibly possessing material goods, that is, wealth. Therefore, he knew the risks of wealth, and valued poverty and humility within a simple life sustained by fraternity, in which the community must seek to help the poor and needy. In this sense, when referring to the phrase "to give sight to the blind," the author also shows that Jesus removes believers from the darkness to place them in the true way of life and salvation, a path that necessarily includes the evangelization of the poor and the embodiment of a humble life. Later in the Gospel, Luke describes Jesus realizing this ideal service and commitment to humility in his ministry (Luke 7:21; 18:35).

"To send the captives free" refers to Israel's tradition of the *seventh year*, that is, the *sabbatical year*, known as the "year of remission," a prescription of the Torah, from Deuteronomy 15:1–8. It is a beautiful text that categorically says which specific attitudes must be carried out in the year of remission, such as forgiving debts, not exploiting others, and fighting for justice so that the poor will no longer be lost amid Yahweh's nation, for he will bless the people. "In the sabbatical year, every seventh year, remission of debts and freedom of enslaved debtor were commanded."[51]

The second time that Luke uses *aphései* refers to the liberation of the oppressed, making an addition to the quoted text of Isaiah 61:1–2. Luke borrowed the phrase "to set the oppressed free" from a very interesting context in Trito-Isaiah,[52] in which the prophet complains that Israel is neglecting its duty of hospitality and social justice. Isaiah 58:5–7 asks why Israel is not living the duty of breaking bread with the hungry and welcoming the homeless into their home. This reveals that the ministry of Jesus implies fulfilling the program of social justice and hospitality according to Isaiah 58:

> Whether Luke's use of *aphesis* reflects a similarly deliberate allusion to them is not so certain. However, there are good grounds for finding this sense of "release" included in the program of liberation that Luke has Jesus inaugurate here. The heart of that liberation is freedom from the bond of sin. But spiritual "release" is, in Luke's perspective, a beachhead and pledge of a liberation that will encompass the totality of human life, including the socioeconomic structures of society.[53]

Related to this context of liberation and present in the traditions of Israel is also the second term highlighted: *dektón* ("acceptable"). The Lord's anointed one came to "proclaim the acceptable year of the Lord" (v. 19), a phrase from Isaiah 61:2, but which also appears in the text of Isaiah 58 at the end of verse 5. The tradition, here, comes from Leviticus 25, the Jubilee year, celebrated every fifty years. In that year, peasants were given the opportunity to return to their lands and rural homes that had been lost due to debt or any other type of exploitation. The Jubilee year was a new opportunity to renew life with a fresh beginning, after a time far from the dignity deserved. For one reason or another, peasants (actually *campesinos*, a Spanish word with a close meaning to a group of rural workers of the old Israel) had become indebted to the point of losing their property and even their freedom, and, as a result, their family would be exploited by landlords. The Jubilee year was the year of truce or suspension of hostilities and exploitation, a year that enabled one to recover lost rights and start again.[54]

Luke omitted from his quotation of Isaiah 61:1–2 the reference to "the day of vengeance for our God." He certainly did it intentionally. It seems that Luke did not want to anticipate the idea of a judgment of the Lord. He postponed this conception to later in the book, within the narrative of Jesus's long journey to Jerusalem (see Luke 9:56—19:44). The ministry that begins now is not the one of vengeance, but the one of God's grace, the pleasant or acceptable year (*dektón*) of the Lord, which will be extended and promoted through the actions of the Church. Between the present time and the judgment, there is a space for conversion, in which the history of salvation takes place. Following Isaiah's perspective, Luke draws attention to the recognition of "the acceptable year of the Lord," a central idea for understanding Jesus's ministry. According to Brendan Byrne, the Gospel of Luke has a great underlying question running through the entire text: "Who will accept what is *acceptable* of the Lord and who will not?" Conversion of heart is required for an affirmative answer to this question.[55] Some convert and accept; others do not. This is the drama of this pericope. The text shows that Jesus's listeners in the synagogue first accepted the message, but then they rejected it, because it was not an acceptance coming from the heart with real conversion. Whether one accepts God's project carried out in Jesus Christ or not is the greatest challenge posted by Luke's Gospel. This project is not only a spiritual work, but also a commitment to liberation and social justice for the poor.

THE POOR AS THE PRIVILEGED RECIPIENTS OF THE GOSPEL

As a core part of Jesus's project presented in Luke 4:16–30, the announcement of the good news focuses on the poor, as its privileged recipients. Jesus is the anointed one of the Lord, the true Messiah, who announces liberation and the acceptable year of the Lord to the poor in a special way. The primacy of the poor in Luke's text is very clear, but there are some who cast doubt about who these poor are, and to which poverty the evangelist is referring. The reader who is following this chapter from the beginning certainly will have identified to what poverty Luke refers, but let us take a closer look at this essential aspect of the mission of the anointed one.

Luke presents the mission of Jesus as an announcement of the good news to the poor, continuing the tradition of Mark and Matthew. The Synoptic Gospels highlight this fundamental aspect of Jesus's ministry, that is, Jesus's service to the poor and outcast. The good news is the announcement of the coming of the kingdom of God,[56] which is not just something for a distant future or for another world in the eschatological time. Instead, the kingdom occurs in the presence of Jesus,[57] who creates a historical movement of moving forward toward justice for the poor and the oppressed. The Lord's anointed one not only announces the kingdom of God, but also anticipates it with his action of favor to the poor. Following this action is the historical forward movement.

When Luke refers to the poor or to poverty, it is very difficult to say that he is only talking about spiritual poverty.[58] Luke's Gospel has a strong social imprint. Hence, it is not an exaggeration to suggest that Luke is the Gospel with the greatest social concern.[59] This does not diminish the importance of spiritual poverty, but rather complements it. Two well-known passages in the Gospel clearly support the statement of Luke's social concern: the Magnificat (Luke 1:46–55) and the Beatitudes in the Sermon on the Plain (Luke 6:20–30). In these texts, the evangelist was not afraid to affirm God's preference for the poor and the little ones, and his aversion for the rich. Mary's song says clearly, "He has brought down powerful from their thrones, and lifted up the lowly; he has filled the hungry with good things, sent the rich away empty" (Luke 1:52–53). In the Beatitudes, the high point of Jesus's preaching during the ministry in Galilee, he declares that blessed are the poor, the hungry, those who mourn and those who are persecuted because of Jesus, because theirs will be the kingdom of God. They will be satisfied, will be able to laugh and have great reward. It will happen differently with the rich, as these harsh words communicate: "Alas for you who are rich: you are having your consolation!" Four harsh *alas* are used against the rich and powerful in contrast to the four *blessed* (or happy) in favor of the poor, the hungry, and the oppressed (see Luke 6:20–26). Luke has a great aversion to the rich and offers an ideal of poverty to a community of christological faith. "We see how the community seeks to live an ideal of poverty, sharing goods and meeting the needs of the poorest."[60] In Acts, one finds the community of Antioch in solidarity with the community of Jerusalem (see Acts 11:27–30), an example of social fraternity among different groups.

Wealth is heavily criticized by Luke, but God always wants to save his children. He is a merciful God who finds a way to rescue the rich. Thus, Luke demonstrates an opportunity given to the rich, so they can also be saved. Although "it is easier for a camel to pass through the eye of a needle than for someone rich to enter the kingdom of God," nothing is impossible for the merciful God (see Luke 18:24–27). However, a call to conversion to accept the *acceptable* of the Lord, his year of grace is always present, as an opportunity for all to change their life. Luke stresses that the conversion of the rich and the oppressors is possible, as happened with the senior tax collector Zacchaeus, who said to Jesus, "Look, half of my possessions, Lord, I will give to the poor, and if I have defrauded anyone, I will pay back four times as much." Jesus confirms God's love to save everyone: "Today salvation has come to this house" (Luke 19:1–10).

When Luke quotes Isaiah 61:1–2, considering the entire Lukan work, knowing the context of Galilee at Jesus's time, and the reality for which Luke wrote and was interested, it is very difficult to deny the socioeconomic dimension of the Gospel in order to sustain a thesis that Luke only refers to the spiritual poor when affirming the poor as recipients of the good news. Luke speaks of the human being in all its dimensions of life, and of the privilege of the hungry, exploited, oppressed, and miserable poor as the primary recipients of the proclamation of the Gospel, the good news. It is not possible to understand the proclamation of salvation unless the good news is proclaimed to the poor.[61] It is not possible to understand the ministry of Jesus and the historical concreteness of the kingdom of God manifest in his presence in the world without going through the proclamation of the Gospel to the poor:

> The addressees of the proclamation of the gospel are the poor, impoverished and weakened by the ambition of those who govern them. The extreme limit of this condition is marginalization: the people (*povo*) lost their freedom and any ability to critically see reality; they live

> continually under pressure from inside and outside, and increasingly lose their lives without minimal condition to flourish as a result from the lack access to the goods needed to sustain life. Jesus' mission, therefore, is to bring a word of hope to these exploited and oppressed people and, at the same time, to carry out the action that concretely frees them from the situation of marginalization.[62]

Jesus's contemporaries' perspective of hope was related to four levels: sociopolitical, religious, existential, and apocalyptic.[63] Faced with the hope of the people, Jesus announces the kingdom of God, which encompasses these levels (realized in the present and in the future). But the main characteristic of this kingdom points to something beyond these levels of hope because the kingdom of God itself is anticipated within the historical presence and action of Jesus. "The distinctive feature of Jesus is that he does not limit himself to announcing the arrival of a kingdom. He anticipates it with his action, explains it with his word, and makes it visible with his person."[64]

The poor are the privileged recipients of the proclamation of the good news. Thus, Luke 4:16–30 offers us the program of Jesus's ministry in Galilee. It is a program that Jesus will carry out. At the same time, the presentation of this program is a call for the Christian community to carry it out from a deep conversion in the encounter with the carpenter's son, the prophet of Nazareth. Unlike other leaders who call followers for themselves, Jesus invites people to do what he does, to carry out the same program of the kingdom of God and to continue the proclamation of the good news to the poor, within a community life that, in turn, is characterized by the poverty and simplicity of its members. The call of Jesus is an invitation to the others, particularly the impoverished. In Luke's Gospel, therefore, poverty and the poor are referred to in two aspects linked to both words themselves: first, poverty has a subjective-existential aspect, the community of disciples of Jesus Christ who embodied a poor life; and second, the poor have an objective-practical aspect, the disciples who continue the master's mission in the proclamation of the good news to the poor, as privileged recipients of the gospel.

Having developed an exegetical and hermeneutic exercise of a biblical passage, the next step is to develop a systematic theology, beginning from the theology of the text and moving on to dialogue with the Catholic tradition seeking to offer a contribution to our context, that is, the historical reality of our communities of faith today. Although this chapter introduced some theological elements of Luke 4:16–30, the challenge now is to explore a theological reflection inspired by this pericope within a dialogical approach with ethical implications.

3

The Joint Action of the Word and the Spirit in Communion with the Father

Based on our exegetical study of Luke 4:16–30, this chapter presents a systematic theological reflection inspired by this biblical passage. This theological account is fundamentally on the mystery of Jesus, as son of God and the second person of the Trinity, developed from a concrete experience of a community of faith. Therefore, I offer a christological perspective from a reality strongly marked by poverty and the plurality of the people (*povos* or *pueblos*) where I come from and learned how to believe in Christ. This reality is a Latin American context, particularly small communities in Brazil.

The word *people* used in this chapter has an important meaning for this Christology. I use "people" as a translation of *povo* (in Portuguese) or *pueblo* (in Spanish), a singular noun that does not simply represent more than one individual (*pessoa/pessoas*), as with the plural of *person* conveyed by the sematic meaning of the English word *people*. Rather, *povo* is a collective noun that represents a group of individuals who share an identity, a history, and an experience. This meaning is found in the Vatican II document *Lumen Gentium* when it defines the Catholic Church as *people of God—Populus Dei* in the original Latin with the same meaning of *povo/pueblo*. *Povo* can be plural, *povos* (*pueblos*, *populi*) to represent more the one *povo* with their identity, so we say *povos indígenas* (indigenous peoples). This does not mean several indigenous individuals, but more than one ethnic group of these original *povos*.

The life and identity of a *povo/pueblo* is very important for the experience of Christian faith and doing theology. One of the Latin American liberation theologies is known as *teologia del pueblo*[1] (theology of people) and has a huge influence in Pope Francis's way of doing theology.[2] On the concept of *pueblo/povo*, Francis says, "The word 'people' [*pueblo*] has a deeper meaning that cannot be set forth in purely logical terms. To be part of a people is to be part of a shared identity arising from social and cultural bonds. And this is not something automatic, but rather a slow, difficult process of advancing toward a common project" (*Fratelli Tutti* 159).

Francis's dream of a "church that is poor and for the poor"[3] certainly reflects his own experience of Catholic communities marked by poverty in Argentina. In a context of poverty and oppression, the Church in Latin America shows that "the Church is people of oppression who find in Jesus Christ hope for its own liberation... and receive from the Holy Spirit strength and courage to struggle for this liberation."[4] As a theological concept and a historical manifestation of those who follow Jesus, the people of God acquires a historical manifestation in small communities that see themselves as a people who experience Jesus Christ within the reality of poverty and suffering. This experience of faith is the locus of the Christology offered in this chapter, deriving from its dialogue with Luke 4 and the significance this text has in inspiring the people of christological faith.

Thus, the Lukan pericope inspires elements for theological reflection on the mystery of Jesus Christ, having the poor and diverse reality of Latin America as the place where faith in Christ is embodied. In light of the reality of the poor, I approach the mystery of Christ—a mystery with historical presence in the world of the poor—in order to show a christological faith[5] that, incarnated in the history of a portion of the people of God existing in Latin America, becomes a liberating faith.

New Testament texts were written after the paschal experience of Jesus's resurrection. This experience made the disciples look back, that is, reflect on the time when they were with the historical Jesus, and interpret everything he said and did in light of his resurrection. Hence, the disciples came to a full faith in Jesus as the Messiah and the Son of God. The memory of the historical Jesus plays a decisive role in the unfolding of the christological faith, as it allows the connection between Jesus of Nazareth and the faith-interpretation of Jesus Christ after the resurrection. Thus, the Church, as a community of believers, legitimates its interpretation of faith in who Jesus is.[6] Every biblical text, no matter how much it brings biographical elements of Jesus of Nazareth, was written in light of and impacted by the paschal experience. It is written in the context of faith in Jesus who died on the cross, rose again, and is alive in the historical struggle of the community of his followers. Presenting anything about Jesus's life is not just speaking about the story of a wonderful man, but it is to talk about the faith in the Son of God. The apostolic Church made explicit the Christology that was in the historical Jesus of Nazareth, a Christology implicit in everything he did and said.[7] This was the maturing process of a community (actually, communities that many times did not have direct communication among themselves) that heard Jesus preaching the kingdom of God and now identifies him with the kingdom itself. The community preaches the risen and living Christ as the object of *kerygma*, the first proclamation of Jesus, as Son of God and redeemer, to those who did not know him.

The first Christian communities had the paschal experience within specific contexts, with their own difficulties and challenges. The encounter with the living Christ took place in the reality in which a community was inserted. Thus, remembering Jesus and his life was from the lens of the specific context of each Christian community. The New Testament shows Jesus from those lenses. Some narratives present Jesus in one way, highlighting specific aspects understood from the experience of a community where the text originated, others present Jesus in a different way that is more relevant for their experience of faith and historical challenges. From this diversity of experiences of the living Christ springs a plurality of New Testament Christologies,[8] that are not in opposition to one another, but rather complementary.

In the development of theological reflections of faith in Christ throughout the tradition of the Church, the complementary aspects of the plurality of christological perspectives made possible the systematization of what is known today as Christology, a theological discipline that is not monolithic and inflexible, but plural and dynamic. The existence of four Gospel narratives allows us to see this plurality of faith experiences and interpretations of the memory of Jesus of Nazareth. As a community is challenged, it looks at the life of Jesus in a way that helps clarify and even address concrete problems because Christ is alive and present in the history of a community through his Spirit, that is, the Holy Spirit. The four evangelists, whether one author or several for each Gospel, wrote their narratives according to the concrete experience of the community in which they were inserted as a member, a fellow faithful. Even similar texts—such as Luke 4:16–30; Mark 6:1–6; and Matthew 13:53–58—were elaborated from a concrete historical experience, reflecting differing points of view concerning issues regarding a given context. This, for example, allowed Luke to add specific details to his version while he was recounting the same fact presented by Mark and Matthew. Another example is the text about Jesus driving the dealers out of the temple. In the Synoptic Gospels (Mark 11:15–19; Matt 21:12–17; and Luke 19:45–46), this fact is narrated shortly before the arrest of Jesus, closely related as one of the reasons for his arrest. The Gospel of John narrates this scene at the beginning of the Gospel (see 2:13–22), with no direct connection with the arrest of Jesus. John wants to show the Johannine community's break with the synagogue, as Jesus's followers were expelled from this Jewish institution. John presents a conflict between Christians and synagogue leaders.[9] This difference in the chronology of the fact is possible because the goal of writing a Gospel was not simply to offer a biographical text of a great man from Nazareth, but rather to offer a text with historical elements marked by theological truth able to impact the existence of the community of faith.[10] New Testament writers offer the historical memory of Jesus to show that he is alive, present within his disciples. This is a dynamic presence that sustains the community in its real and existential dilemmas.[11] However, among these christological differences in the New Testament, there is a fundamental point that unites all different interpretations: "They are based on and witness to the experience that Jesus is the bearer of God and of God's salvation. Jesus the 'mediator of salvation from God' is as it were a common denominator of all New Testament Christologies."[12]

Considering today's challenges of communities struggling in contexts of oppression and marginalization, I present a Christology that follows a similar path to New Testament communities in terms of understanding the encounter with Jesus from the lens of historical circumstance. While New Testament communities learned about Jesus's story from oral transmission offered by eyewitnesses and then felt the need to write about it, today's communities have the witness of the first communities offered by texts. Responsible for showing us christological themes and illuminating our reflection, the biblical text has the memory of Jesus of Nazareth, transmitted through the mediation of apostolic communities from their reading of Jesus's deeds and words. Many members of these communities had direct contact with Jesus and transmitted this experience to others. There were those disciples who lived with the historical Jesus and became founders and leaders of the first Christian communities.[13] For those communities, the relation between the Jesus of history, a man from Nazareth who was crucified and died, and the Christ of faith, the Son of God who was resurrected and sent his Spirit, was clear and at the center of their faith. Although we are far from the earthly days of this man from Nazareth, his Spirt makes him to be present in our history where we encounter the Christ of faith after learning from the Jesus of history. This occurs in the local reality of Christian communities, where the universality of faith is embodied. Based on the experience of faith of Christians in Latin America, I offer a christological essay from the theological harmony between the Jesus of history and the Christ of faith. With this, I move forward to present a living Christ incarnated in the concrete reality of our culturally diverse peoples who are injured by the wounds of poverty and oppression.

The practice of Jesus—under the guidance of the Spirit who anointed him to evangelize the poor (Luke 4:18)—and his teaching on setting captives free and proclaiming the acceptable year of the Lord (Luke 4:19) become present today in the life of communities of disciples and missionaries of Jesus Christ, who encounter him in a historical reality through an experience of faith. By the power of the Holy Spirit, Christ makes himself present in the reality of the poor, people who carry the cross of oppression and poverty. They are a "crucified people,"[14] who become the Church, an integral part of the people of God who manifest the Body of Christ in history, a body bearing the marks of suffering due to socioeconomic oppression. At the same time, Christ is among this people, offering hope and strengthening a liberating praxis. Amid people's suffering, Jesus Christ is present as crucified and risen,[15] capable of offering meaning for the poor and sustaining them in the Easter of existence, which is reflected in a social practice flowing from a liberating ethic.[16]

Although some would disagree saying that it is possible to develop a Christology without the influence from where this theology is developed and the local episteme (perspective questioned in the first chapter), any study of the mystery of faith in Christ is done from the social and ecclesial place in which we are inserted, with the cultural and epistemological implications that this locus represents. As much as one tries to elaborate a theology that is detached from a specific context to guide all other theological elaborations, which characterizes some Eurocentric theological approaches, a totally neutral theology is not possible. My christological reflection originates in the experience of an encounter of the poor with Jesus Christ. He makes himself present in the concrete reality of impoverished communities. In this local encounter, Jesus provides a sense and a practice of liberation through the action of his Spirit. From this *chão cristológico* (christological ground), in consideration of the biblical text, and in dialogue with tradition, the christological dogmas are interpreted and acquire meaning in the existence of the poor of our continent, Latin America, but also in the existence of any oppressed group anywhere that encounters Jesus in the middle of their struggle once the christological tradition is read from their local experience. Therefore, I am speaking of a Christology in the encounter with the poor and the plural reality of Latin America as a theological-existential relationship.

In the first chapter, I presented a methodological account of doing theology from local contexts. Many often refer to this as *contextual theology*, sometimes with a pejorative understanding when seen from a Eurocentric paradigm. Moreover, I want to specify my methodological path, considering the current christological endeavor stated in the previous chapter and continued here. Some name this method *Christology from below*[17] because the starting point is the reality of peoples in a local historical context. I see this perspective as legitimate and helpful to aid communities of faith in understanding the meaning of Jesus's presence in their lives. In Latin America,

Jon Sobrino[18] and Leonardo Boff[19] are among those who best offer a Christology from below, beginning from the historical Jesus and the experience of impoverished Christian communities. I do not think that my proposal perfectly fits into this method, although I clearly use it. I take the liberty to use an adapted version of the method of Christology from below, adding two significant aspects: first, the exegetical reflection of a particular Gospel's text, namely, Luke 4:16–30 (offered in the previous chapter). This passage becomes a foundation for my theological exercises, preventing me from navigating in very generic statements. At the same time, Luke 4 is the source for christological themes that will be addressed. Second, the systematic reflection and following ethical implications are from christological themes raised by the biblical pericope and its interaction with the reality of communities who read this text and encounter Jesus within their challenges. These two aspects are in intimate relationship (akin to a nuptial experience, as offered by mystical writers) with the faith experience of the poor in Latin America. In this experience one can see God's presence in history, a Christ with a human face in the face of the crucified people, and a Church led by the Spirit in the proclamation of good news to the poor, that is, to privileged recipients of the gospel announced by Jesus.

The next section addresses two major reflections: the first offers an analysis about the poor in the tradition of the Catholic Church and then in the Church's journey in Latin America; the second is a systematic theological study of christological themes raised from Luke 4:16–30.

THE POOR IN THE LUKAN TEXT AND IN THE TRADITION

In the previous chapter, the exegetical study of Luke 4:16–30 presented the centrality of the poor as privileged recipients of the proclamation of the good news, that is, the gospel. Along with this announcing of the good news is the liberation of the captives and the oppressed, as well as the proclamation of the acceptable year of the Lord, all of which are references to Israel's traditions of the sabbatical year and the Jubilee year, which have profound social implications. The study of this passage of Luke's Gospel led us to understand that when the author writes about the poor and poverty, he primarily refers to the socioeconomically impoverished people, those dispossessed of basic goods, marginalized, and oppressed.

In the synagogue of Nazareth, Jesus affirmed that the proclamation of the good news had the poor as its first recipients. When asked by the disciples of John the Baptist if he was the Messiah, Jesus did not answer yes or no. Instead, he said, "Go and tell John what you have seen and heard: the blind receive their sight, the lame walk, the lepers are cleansed, the deaf hear, the dead are raised, and the poor have the good news brought to them" (Luke 7:22). In the Beatitudes of Luke (6:20–23), unlike Matthew (5:1–12), one does not find an adjective qualifying and restricting the meaning of the term poor. Matthew's expression, *poor in spirit*, leaves room for interpreting poverty as something strictly spiritual. Luke simply wrote, "Blessed are you who are poor: for yours is the kingdom of God" (Luke 6:20). Then, in the other Beatitudes, Luke presents the hungry, those who mourn and those persecuted because of Jesus as blessed people. These conditions indicate exclusion, struggles, and concrete needs, a historical reality belonging the social sphere.

In the Synoptic Gospels, the poor are characterized in two aspects: the first refers to those who suffer and groan because of the lack of basic necessities; hungry, thirsty, naked, foreigners, sick, prisoners; those who cry, that is, all those who live bent over by some concrete weight oppressing them. They are the *anawim*. The second aspect suggests that the poor are those excluded and marginalized by society because they are considered sinners, publicans, and prostitutes.[20] According to Albert Nolan, in the Gospels,

> The poor were in the very first place the beggars. These were the sick and disabled who had resorted to begging because they were unemployable and without relatives who could afford to or were willing to support them. There were of course no hospitals, welfare institutions or disability grants. They were expected to beg for their bread. Thus, the blind, the deaf and dumb, the lame, the cripples and the lepers were generally beggars.[21]

After the beggars, Nolan adds, the category "poor" also included widows and orphans who, having no one to support them, depended on alms; it also encompasses unskilled day workers, often unemployed, peasants, rural workers, and slaves. All of these suffered deprivation and even went hungry and thirsty, but the main suffering was the shame and the contempt felt for the oppression and for being excluded from society. In a broader concept of the poor, the excluded—due to social practices not suited to local customs—were also treated as inferior beings.[22] In current time, everyone who lives a life without minimal dignity—oppressed by their social condition, gender identity, color, ethnicity, and any other form of marginalization—would be the poor in the Gospels. People's dignity was injured by living within exclusive conditions that had social and religious aspects, because both social and religious matters, in Palestine during Jesus's time, were connected. Maria Clara Bingemer explains that the poor were religious people who were marginalized not because of their religion, but rather, due to a social point of view that often was connected to religious condemnation.[23] Perhaps it is not possible to make this distinction between the religiously marginalized and socially marginalized in a radical way, as these two aspects were intertwined most of the time, within a vicious circle. There were no qualms about excluding someone because this person was poor; if one got sick, it was due to the misery in which he lived. In addition, sickness was a result of having committed a sin, all reasons for socioeconomic and religious exclusions.[24]

In Luke's Gospel, one finds the use of the term *poor* corresponding to the meanings presented above, that is, as a category of people who are miserable, oppressed, and excluded socially and religiously. In Luke 4:18, the meaning of poor, privileged recipients of the gospel, is related to the *anawim*, that is, being bent over due to the weight created by the lack of fundamental goods for flourishing with dignity: the weight of oppression, marginalization, and poverty. The poor are real people and Jesus's relationship with them profoundly reveals his personality and mission.[25] In the synagogue of Nazareth, Jesus presents the messianic kingdom that brings the concrete liberation of the poor and the oppressed. "It is the poor, the suffering, the hungry, and the persecuted who are blest, not because their condition itself has value but because their unjust situation is a challenge to the justice of the messianic king. Through Jesus, God has sided with them."[26]

Liberation from sin also involves liberation from oppression in history, of which the poor are victims. Encountering the poor to serve and to proclaim the good news is a way of salvation, one in which we encounter Jesus Christ's face in the suffering face of the poor, the living God revealed by him.

Caring for the poor and embracing their reality, Jesus shows us his partiality for the outcast. Jesus's proclamation of the gospel and relationship with poor reveal the partiality of God[27] because the option of Jesus is the option of God, a merciful Father. "Christ's whole earthly life—his words and deeds, his silences and sufferings, indeed his manner of being and speaking—is Revelation of the Father."[28] The partiality of Jesus for the poor gained a particular manifestation in the Church in Latin America with a theological, ecclesial, and pastoral orientation known as the "preferential option for the poor." Clearly embraced by the bishops of CELAM (Episcopal Conference of Latin American and Caribbean Bishops) in all its conferences since the second one in Medellín (1968), the preferential option for the poor has become the heart of a new way of doing theology, known as liberation theology, and was incorporated by the magisterial teaching for the first time by Pope John Paul II in his encyclical *Sollicitudo Rei Socialis* (no. 39).

In the CELAM meeting in Aparecida, Brazil (2007), the preferential option for the poor objectively states its christological foundation, something clear in Latin America and many theological books and articles, but not visible enough to prevent some people from criticizing liberation theology. For those unformed critics, this option for the poor was a sociological concept responsible for making theology in Latin America move away from Jesus to assume a revolutionary aspect in which the poor were used to sustain any effort of social transformation. In the opening address of the Conference of Aparecida, Pope Benedict XVI addressed this criticism by saying that the preferential option for the poor was an option for the christological faith. This became part of the final Document of Aparecida (no. 392) and was quoted, supported, and promoted by Pope Francis:

> The Church has made an option for the poor which is understood as a "special form of primacy in the exercise of Christian charity, to which the whole tradition of the

> Church bears witness." This option—as Benedict XVI has taught—"is implicit in our Christian faith in a God who became poor for us, so as to enrich us with his poverty." This is why I want a Church which is poor and for the poor. (*Evangelii Gaudium* 198)

In the Gospel of Luke, the evangelist does not leave room for an interpretation of the poor that places them outside the socioeconomic issue of poverty. This clarity points out that Jesus's relationship with the poor reveals an aspect of God's mystery and his option for the poor as privileged recipients of the gospel. In the synagogue of Nazareth, Jesus was anointed by the Lord to announce the good news to the poor. Now that we know who the poor are, we need to understand the good news announced to them. What is the good news to the poor offered by Jesus and embraced by his followers as those who continue his mission in history?

In his ministerial activity, Jesus announced the kingdom of God: "Soon afterwards he went on through cities and villages, proclaiming and bringing the good news of the kingdom, of God" (Luke 8:1). Matthew says that Jesus taught and preached the gospel of the kingdom (Matt 4:23; 9:35), and Mark says that Jesus announced the approach of the kingdom of God: "The time is fulfilled, and the kingdom of God is close at hand. Repent, and believe the gospel" (Mark 1:15). The kingdom of God was at the center of Jesus's preaching. In the Synoptic Gospels, he did not preach about himself, but about the kingdom of God. The post-Easter community, however, identified Jesus as the kingdom itself, moving the kingdom from outside of Jesus to be within him, as presented in the last chapter, with the risen Jesus being the center of the apostolic preaching. The kingdom of God is the good news preached to the poor, a kingdom not only for an eschatological future, but a present reality in Jesus himself, through his life in favor of the poor. According to Jacques Dupuis, "The kingdom of God that is coming about through Jesus's life and action is predominantly addressed to the poor, the *anawim* of God, that is, all the despised categories of people, the oppressed and the downtrodden. For all these, Jesus manifests a preferential option that amounts to a declaration of God's own mind in their favor."[29] The kingdom of God is destined for all people who are victims of unjust structures and oppressed; it is for all who live in inhumane situations. As a broad concept in this kingdom, the poor includes all those who are oppressed and marginalized. The content of the gospel announced to the poor is the kingdom of God.

In the synagogue of Nazareth, the eyes of the listeners saw the realization of the kingdom of God present and active in the person of Jesus, in everything he says and does, as the messengers from John the Baptist witnessed (Luke 7:22).[30] A kingdom destined for the poor[31] can change their lives, free captives, and make the lame walk and the blind see. This kingdom is no longer in a far future, but present and active in Jesus, the Messiah and Prophet,[32] because the Scripture "is being fulfilled today" (Luke 4:21). Jesus is the prophet who announces wonders for the historical present, and with this, he reveals God and the future waiting for us. "With Christ the kingdom has already begun to act in the world."[33]

Jesus placed the poor as recipients of the gospel, whose central content is the kingdom of God. He does not only proclaim something to the poor, but he also joins them as a companion in their existential journey, full of socioeconomic insecurities. Jesus made the life of the poor his own life, by living with them and identifying with their reality, from his birth in a Bethlehem manger until his death on a cross in Jerusalem.[34] In his public life, Jesus had nowhere to lay his head (see Luke 9:57–58). To follow him, it was necessary to sell everything and give to the poor (Luke 18:22). Jesus embodied a total identification with the poor and their poverty, calling his disciples to do the same, a powerful ethical commitment with transcendental roots and immanent realization. The first Christian communities understood this very well. Luke's work is an example of this. As presented in the previous chapter, Luke was very concerned about serving the poor and showing the life of a community strongly marked by poverty and humility. After the paschal experience, the apostolic community turned to Jesus's life and saw how central this poor/poverty aspect was, and how it revealed the face of God. They perceived that the meaning of Jesus's work with the poor and his identification with them not only had a sociological meaning marked by the need for solidarity, but also a theological meaning, because Jesus's identification with the poor revealed God and his preference for the neediest.[35] Although historical in the context of this early community, this revelation is ahistorical, transcendental and, being so, it manifests God's mystery in any local reality and its historical challenges, especially those related to the poor and the oppressed.

The development of the Christian community in the period known as early Church was marked by a life devoted to serving the poorest and by a poor Church. Many who had converted to faith in Christ were not afraid to renounce their possessions and give them to the poor. Poor/poverty was understood as Jesus did, that is, a historical socioeconomic reality. But this social understanding of poverty was not in opposition to the spiritual perspective also part of Jesus's life. Therefore, poverty acquired two closely linked meanings, and one without the other seemed to be meaningless. This complementarity is relevant. The spiritually poor seem to have no meaning without a poor, humble life of service to those who lack access to basic goods to flourish. To be poor and a disciple of Christ, a humble, merciful attitude is necessary, in which one recognizes one's poverty before the immense wealth of God. The *rich poor*, people who are rich, but self-identify as spiritually poor—because they are not God-fearing or Christ-faithful, or because they do not have a mature spirituality—seems to be a later conception in the development of Christianity. In his encounter with Jesus, the rich man was called to leave everything behind and to "sell all that you own and distribute the money to the poor," as a condition to follow Jesus by proclaiming the gospel to the poor (Luke 18:18–30).

In the tradition of the Church throughout the centuries, the terms poor/poverty had acquired many meanings, and at times, they were distant from the first meaning offered by New Testament texts. However, as much as the institutional Church at times in history had distanced itself from the poor, the Church—as the people of God guided by the Holy Spirit—has never abandoned them. The Spirit has always raised up great known and unknown prophets and saints to show the institution to whom the gospel should be preferentially proclaimed and how the gospel teaching should be embodied in the ethical practice of Jesus's followers. Although the institutional Church did not always embody this practice, its teaching never denies this evangelical truth, as one can see in the *Catechism of the Catholic Church*: "The Church's love for the poor…is a part of her constant tradition. This love is inspired by the Gospel of the Beatitudes, of the poverty of Jesus, and of his concern for the poor. Love for the poor is even one of the motives for the duty of working so as to be able to give to those in need. It extends not only to material poverty but also to the many forms of cultural and religious poverty."[36]

The tradition of the Church teaches us that focusing on the poor is fundamental for the Church's mission. The Church fathers, the early Catholic bishops and priests who led Christian communities and offered writings and teachings that provide the first theological foundation of the Christian faith and doctrine, lived out a life of defense of and service to the poor. In doing so, they were true prophets in their time and faithful disciples of Jesus Christ, responding to the challenges of their concrete realities. It is not possible to offer an analysis of the Church fathers' teaching regarding the service to the poor because of the extensive number of texts involved. As a result of this limitation, I illustrate their teaching by highlighting only two Church fathers, and a few elements of their preaching, to help us to understand the centrality of announcing the good news to the poor in the life of the Church and who the poor they talk about are.

First, there is John Chrysostom (347–407): preacher, bishop of Constantinople, persecuted and exiled several times. His last exile being decreed by the emperor of the Byzantine Empire in 407, during which he died. John, the "golden-mouthed" (meaning of Chrysostom in Greek, a nickname he received for his gift of oratory), lived in a context in which the Church, no longer officially persecuted by the Roman Empire, began to have members involved in the seduction of wealth. The Church experienced a paradox: while people with great wealth, when converting to faith in Jesus Christ, deeply identified themselves with him and renounced their possessions in favor of the poor (as was the case of John himself), many became Christians to maintain the same status quo, considering that Christianity was being embraced by the empire as its official religion. Amid this context, John Chrysostom's writings—many of them homilies preached to his community—"frequently refer to evangelical texts on poverty and [he] applies these texts to the societal challenges of his time, with vigor and a lot of conviction."[37] He was not afraid to denounce hypocrisy and to stress that the true disciple was the one who lived by charity.[38]

John Chrysostom was not afraid to criticize the elite, the rich, and those who exploited the poor and the workers. He even criticized the clergy who should have turned to the poor and served them intensely.[39] John's concern with the poor was based on a concern for social justice so that everyone could have the minimum for living with dignity.

> Not to enable the poor to share in our goods is to steal from them and deprive them of life. The goods we possess are not ours, but theirs. The demands of justice must be satisfied first of all; that which is already due in justice is not to be offered as a gift of charity.[40]

The poor of whom John Chrysostom spoke were the same poor to whom Jesus announced the gospel of the kingdom of God. This is a clear source of the Church's tradition that continues the ministry of Jesus Christ in history under the guidance of the Holy Spirit. In addition to commitment to justice for the poor, John brought to maturity theological reflection related to the poor. He suggested that Lazarus's weakness and pain of being a poor man (see Luke 16:19–31) made him available to participate in the heavenly reward and the one who passed by him and did nothing suffered great punishment. "If the rich man who passes by the side of the poor man, Lazarus, suffered such a punishment, and found no relief, what will those who persecuted and scandalized so many have to endure?"[41] John Chrysostom offers a strong theological ethics interpretation of the Gospel through his teaching to his community that connects poverty/suffering to salvation and wealth/exploitation to condemnation. These are harsh words that reveal the love for the poor as central for Christian morality and God's preference for them. Hence, in this practice in favor of the poor, the transcendent is real and immanent within a community.

The second Church father is Basil of Caesarea (330–379), considered the father of monasticism in the Eastern Church. He was also the bishop of Caesarea, where he exercised his apostolic ministry with deep fidelity to Christ and to loving the poor. Basil brought his experience as a monk to his pastoral ministry as an ecclesial leader. During his time as a monk, he learned the real meaning of evangelical poverty, fundamental to being a disciple of Christ, and was not afraid to denounce the avarice of the rich, being a brave servant of the poor. Basil was born and raised a family with a privileged economic situation. But, immersing himself in the experience of encounter with Christ, he sold all his possessions and distributed the money to the poor to live out his monastic vocation. Even when he was elected as the bishop of Caesarea (ca. 370), he continued embodying an austere life marked by poverty. His homilies offer a witness of a commitment to justice for the poor. With words and lifestyle, Basil invited the rich to do what he did—give their goods to the poor and fight for the social justice—and, in so doing, marked service to the poor as a priority for the Church that every member must embrace.[42]

Basil's homilies show the care of a Church pastor who was deeply concerned about his sheep, who suffered with them the burden of an unequal, unjust, and oppressive society.[43] Basil and his community experienced a period of crisis in the Roman Empire, with political, economic, social, and cultural impact.[44] It was within a context of an agricultural society suffering because of low production, that is, an insufficient harvest to meet the region's need. But this did not prevent the exploitation promoted by those who were richer to keep their privileges, making most of the population to suffer because of food scarcity and, consequently, hunger. One of Basil's homilies addressed the subject of hunger and thirst, a concern that was close to his heart.[45] The Church father managed to unite pastoral practice with theoretical reflection and denunciation of injustices.

Basil's homilies reveal that the Church's concern at that time (fourth century) was not only with heresies and the development of the theological doctrine,[46] but also with ethical and social issues, whose main moral concern was the poor and their lives.[47]

In his *Homily on Luke 12* or *On Greed*, Basil criticized the rich and their greed, which made them exploit the poor without mercy:

> Do not wait for a famine to open your granaries, for he who raises the price of grain is accursed to the people (Prov. 11:26). Do not take hunger in exchange for gold. Do not exchange common need for private abundance. Do not be a peddler of human misfortunes. Do not make the wrath of God an opportunity [to acquire] an abundance of goods. Do not scourge with a whip the injuries of those who have been afflicted.[48]

Basil denounced the greed of the rich and their attachment to goods as one of the reasons responsible for the existence of the poor. He called the rich "greedy" and "thieves":

> If each acquired what he needed to meet his own need and let the remainder go to the needy, then nobody would be rich, and nobody would be in need....Who is greedy? He who does not stop at what is sufficient. Who is the robber? He who takes for himself what belongs to another. Are you not greedy? Are you not a robber? Do you welcome and make your own private possession the things that are intended for distribution? Or again, he who strips someone of his clothes is called a clothes-robber, but he who does not clothe the naked, when he is able to do so—does he deserve a different name? The bread that you have belongs to the hungry. The cloak that you are guarding in your barns belongs to the naked. The shoes that are wasting away in your possession belong to the barefoot. The money that you have buried belongs to the needy. And so you have done an injustice to as many as you were able help.[49]

In the *Homily on the Rich*,[50] Basil preached about the text of Matthew 19:16ff. on the rich young man. He affirmed that following the Master, Jesus, consists in giving everything to the poor. Whoever does not carry out this request from the Master—the only one who can save us for the eternity—does not have Jesus as his Master.[51] The justification that a rich person needs to hold goods to survive is not acceptable when one becomes a follower of Jesus. Money and power always lead to desire to have more, to avarice. This causes the rich to create injustices, to oppress and exploit the poor to increase their wealth and, if necessary, even to practice violence, because wealth has become a vice.[52]

In times of hunger and thirst, Basil denounced the structure of injustice that led to such calamity. He exhorted to break with this structure and to live out the gospel teaching as the guide for ethical practice.[53] Hunger is the worst human misfortune, against which everyone must fight by sharing everything in common (Acts 3:32).

As a local ecclesial leader, Basil invited his community to embody a fraternal love able to feed the hungry by sharing what they have.[54]

In his homilies, one can clearly see what kind of poverty Basil refers to: social poverty, a fruit of an unjust society. This reality challenges Christians to live out the gospel teaching in an ethical life that begins with material sharing, and with a pointed call to those who have goods and wealth to give them to the poor.

Basil of Caesarea and John Chrysostom were examples of Church fathers of tradition who stressed the centrality of the poor for the proclamation of the gospel and for the ethical life of the Christian community. In a creative and reinvigorating way, they continued the mission of Jesus for the historical poor: concrete people, bent over by the weight of lacking basic goods to survive and by the oppression that prevents them from getting out of such a situation.

In the course of the Church's history, one also finds many people who embodied the centrality of the poor as privileged recipients of the proclamation of the good news of the kingdom, people like Francis of Assis, Ignatius of Loyola, Camillus de Lellis, Vincent de Paul, Mother Teresa of Calcutta, and so many others—publicly known or quiet servants in their communities—who are "distinguished models of social charity" (*Deus Caritas Est* 40). These servants of the poor also exist in our times, some of them among us, helping the poor in our communities, and many of them the poor themselves, helping each other by being grounded on a strength originating in their christological faith. Considering the context that I came from, the fresh air coming from the breath of the Holy Spirit through the renewal promoted by the Second Vatican Council made the Catholic Church in Latin America wake up to the reality of the crucified people, the impoverished people. It is for these that the Church must show a Jesus Christ alive in history, incarnated in their reality, pointing to the practices of liberation. Coming from the same reality and with an experience of serving the poor in Argentina, Pope Francis, who embraced the perspective of a Church of missionary-disciples as presented in the Document of Aparecida,[55] encourages us to be a field-hospital Church,[56] that is, a community of disciples of Jesus that is not afraid to go to the most challenging reality to serve those in need, namely, the poor and the marginalized (*Evangelii Gaudium* 24, 183).

THE POOR IN LATIN AMERICAN TRADITION AND ITS RELATIONSHIP TO THE GOSPEL

For many years, the Latin American Church was marked by historical colonialism whose consequences that are still felt today. The colonial model of evangelization was carried out by Church leaders until the Second Latin American Episcopal Conference (CELAM) held in Medellín, Colombia, in 1968, while most countries were experiencing brutal dictatorial regimes and an increase of poverty. In this context of oppression and poverty, a new model of being the Church and doing theology flourished, this being a new local tradition that I freely call the "Latin American tradition."

The CELAM Conference in Medellín was called to contextualize the innovations of the Second Vatican Council on the Latin American region. This Council was an attempt to renew the Catholic Church and, as such, it awoke the Church from a long period of inertia regarding actions in favor of the poorest. During the time that the Church closed itself down, cornered by the advances of modernity, it adopted a posture of self-defense and condemnation of everything from the modern world. Vatican II was a breath of the Spirit that presented to Church's leaders the importance of dialogue with the world and its secular developments. In a common expression used during the Council, it was necessary to make an aggiornamento, a word first used by Pope John XXIII that can be understood as *a time for updating*, to be open to read the *signs of the times*. Hence, the Catholic Church can present itself as a sign of life and salvation in the world.

The Second Vatican Council offered a perspective that included the importance and the need for the Church to turn to the poor. The text of Luke 4:16–30 that we have studied appears several times in the documents of the Council to support the Church's mission in proclaiming the good news to the poor, since it was to these little ones that Jesus preached and served in a privileged way.[57] As an example, I highlight the Dogmatic Constitution on the Church, *Lumen Gentium*, the Vatican II document about the nature and existence of the Church. *Lumen Gentium* stresses the Church as the people of God.[58]

This understanding of the Catholic Church, along with the concept of revelation in the history offered by the Dogmatic Constitution on Revelation, *Dei Verbum*,[59] and the theology of the signs of the times from the Pastoral Constitution on the Church in the Modern World, *Gaudium et Spes*,[60] offered the motivation and inspiration for the flourishing of a new theology, contextualized in the concrete reality of the crucified peoples of Latin America.

Lumen Gentium shows that the Church needs to be free from possessions and the search for earthly glory, to be an example of humility, austerity, and abnegation. As Christ was sent by the Father to evangelize the poor, the Church must serve Christ in them:

> Just as Christ carried out the work of redemption in poverty and persecution, so the Church is called to follow the same route that it might communicate the fruits of salvation to men. Christ Jesus, "though He was by nature God...emptied Himself, taking the nature of a slave," (Phil 2:6) and "being rich, became poor" (2 Cor 8:9) for our sakes. Thus, the Church, although it needs human resources to carry out its mission, is not set up to seek earthly glory, but to proclaim, even by its own example, humility and self-sacrifice. *Christ was sent by the Father "to bring good news to the poor, to heal the contrite of heart,"* (Luke 4:18) "to seek and to save what was lost" (Luke 19:10). Similarly, *the Church encompasses with love all who are afflicted with human suffering and in the poor and afflicted sees the image of its poor and suffering Founder. It does all it can to relieve their need and in them it strives to serve Christ.* (no. 8; emphasis is mine)

Despite being innovative, the Council's text could not be very daring and, due to many Council fathers fearful of assuming a poor Church for the poor, Vatican II was not able to explicitly state an option for them. (Such an option was verbalized by Pope John XXIII, the one who called the Council and became an important influence on Pope Francis who sees the concept of a preferential option for the poor linked to the legacy of Vatican II.) Realizing that the Council would not advance to a radical commitment to the poor, a group of bishops, mostly from the then known Third World, met in the Catacombs of St. Domitila on November 16, 1965, and made a commitment for a poor Church, servant of the poor.[61] Forty bishops signed a text making such a commitment, known as the "Pact of the Catacombs."[62] This pact became an initial draft for the Document of Medellín. The pact and the Council's renewal foreshadowed the Medellín Conference, where the ecclesial commitment to the poor would become explicit. The bishops who signed the Pact of the Catacombs wished that Vatican II had incorporated the concept of Church of the Poor, as John XXIII had requested. This did not occur at the Council, but it occurred in the Latin American Church in the 1960s. Ironically, today, we see Pope Francis calling for a Church for the poor.

In Medellín, Latin American bishops (those who were in the Council and new ones who received its documents with enthusiasm) began to be effectively concerned with the situation of Latin American *pueblos*, people who were victims of predatory economic power, injustice, and oppression from economic and state forces. The Church's leaders looked at that reality and listened to the cry of the poor. In light of the Word of God, it began an ecclesial movement of defending the poor, grounded on a commitment to their liberation from oppression and poverty. However, for the Latin American Church to be able to embody this commitment, later known as the preferential option for the poor with coherence in its ministry, it was necessary to be a poor Church, *with* and *for* the poor. Medellín embraced this commitment that was already lived out by many bishops in their local communities, such as Hélder Câmara (Brazil), Leonidas Proaño (Ecuador), and Samuel Ruiz (Mexico) among others, along with the experience of many priests and religious sisters and brothers who went to live amid the poor (an experience known as *comunidades inseridas*, that is, "inserted communities"), and to develop basic ecclesial communities. Therefore, the Document of Medellín not only expressed concepts, but embraced an ecclesial experience occurring in the Latin American land, and designated concrete practices for the pastoral and social ministry of the Church.[63] Medellín expressed this effervescence in a pastoral text, a manifestation of application of the aggiornamento proposed by

Vatican II, to promote and support the Church of the Poor and its struggle for liberation.

The Medellín Document says that a poor Church:

> Denounces the unjust lack of basic goods [for the poor] and the sin that sustains [this injustice]; preaches and lives the spiritual poverty as an attitude of spiritual childhood and openness to the Lord; commits herself to material poverty. The poverty of the Church is, in fact, a constant in the history of salvation.[64]

The Latin American Church wants to be a prophetic sign of commitment to free the poor from the bonds of injustice, misery, and oppression. That is why this regional Church takes on the commitment of a poor Church, as Jesus was poor, and for the liberation of the poor, as Jesus anointed by the Lord to evangelize the poor and free the captives (Luke 4:18–19):

> The Church in Latin America, because of the condition of poverty and underdevelopment of the continent, feels it is urgent to translate this spirit of poverty into gestures, attitudes, and norms that make the Church a lucid and authentic sign of the Lord. The poverty of many brothers cries out for justice, solidarity, witness, commitment, effort, and liberation to fulfill the salvific mission trusted by Christ.[65]

The commitment to the poor embraced by the Latin American Church as the core of its ecclesial manifestation and ministry has a theological meaning: an awareness of a commitment that locally manifests the continuity of Jesus's mission in the history of a people crying out for liberation. As the people in Egypt cried out and were heard by God, who sent Moses, so the crying of the outcast in Israel was heard by God, who sent his Son to proclaim the kingdom of God to the poor and bring eternal salvation. Eschatological salvation and historical liberation were bound together in Jesus's actions and teaching. The Church continues this liberating action in history assisted by the Holy Spirit until the eternal salvation is given, as a grace, by Christ.

In Medellín, it was clear just who the poor were. The Conference of CELAM spoke about the poor as being deprived of basic goods and suffering the brunt of misery, hunger, oppression, injustice, and marginalization. The poor for Medellín are the *anawim*, the same conception discussed earlier in this book, which is also the principal meaning of *the poor* used in Luke 4:18. The poor, to whom the good news of the kingdom of God was proclaimed by Jesus in the Gospel of Luke, are the same ones assumed by the Second Conference of Latin American Bishops for their liberation:

> The Lord's particular mandate—which includes the evangelization of the poor—must lead us in our distribution of efforts and apostolic personnel, which must preferably focus on the poorest and most needy sectors and people segregated for one reason or another, stimulating and accelerating the initiatives and studies that are carried out for this purpose.[66]

The liberation of the poor embraced by Medellín was linked to the economic, social, and political aspects of the continental reality. Only later, in the development of Latin American theology, other kind of oppressions and marginalization were added in order to be addressed by a liberating perspective, such as injustice and oppression because of ethnicity, race, culture, sex, and gender.[67] The meaning of *the poor* becomes broader, as it is understood as "those who are at the bottom of the heap in history and those who are oppressed by society or cast out from it."[68] In other words, the poor and the option for the poor today include all those who suffer any kind of injustice and oppression because of their socioeconomic condition and because of who they are.

The reception of the Medellín Document was warm and inspired the ministry of the Latin American Church to embody a truly liberating practice. In the theological sphere, the Conference made possible the systematization of Liberation Theology, which starts with the poor and the identification of Christ with them and moves toward a theology incarnated in history and committed to a liberating praxis.

Years later, the third CELAM Conference, which was held in Puebla, Mexico (1979), gave continuity to Medellín's ideal and textually stated its option for the poor:

> The Conference of Puebla assumes again, with a renewed hope in the vivifying strength of Spirit, the statement of II General Conference that made a clear and prophetic preferential and option for the poor in solidarity; nevertheless, the mistakes and interpretation that some made and misrepresent the Medellín spirit, showing the ignorance and hostility of others. We affirm the need of conversation within all of the Church for a preferential option for the poor in order to promote integral liberation.[69]

Moreover, in Puebla, one finds a maturing in the theological reflection gestated in Latin America since the 1960s until Medellín and raised between the two CELAM Conferences. In the 1970s and 1980s, liberation theology developed along with the liberating practice of its main proponents. The heart of Medellín's Christology consisted of following Jesus in his commitment to the liberation of the excluded. In Puebla, there was an unfolding of this Christology, in which the poor became identified with Christ. In situations of misery and suffering, one recognizes the face of Christ who challenges and questions this concrete situation.[70] In reference to Luke 4:18–21, Puebla confirmed the poor as privileged recipients of Jesus's mission, and consequently, as privileged recipients of the historical mission of the Catholic Church. "The poor are the first recipients of the mission, and their evangelization is *par excellence* the sign and the proof of Jesus' mission."[71]

In 1992, Santo Domingo hosted the fourth Conference of CELAM. It occurred in a context of ecclessial tension between the pontificate of John Paul II and the development of liberation theology. As a result, the Santo Domingo Conference was like a break in the liberating path of the Latin American tradition because, unfortunately, it did not offer an invigorating continuity in the social ministry of Church among the poor and their ecclesial initiatives (such as the basic ecclesial communities) as in the previous two conferences. However, even very timidly, the bishops gathered in Santo Domingo maintained the preferential option for the poor in their final document.[72] In addition, some consider that Santo Domingo offers a significant contribution on the theme of inculturation in the evangelization of Latin American *pueblos*. Much discussed during the conference was the role of the Church in the colonization of the indigenous people, in the context of the five hundred years since the arrival of Columbus at the same island, and the beginning of the domination of the "new world" named America. On the matter regarding the poor, this Conference added practically nothing. Its merit was in not openly rejecting Medellín and Puebla.

I like to see the Conference of Santo Domingo as a transitional meeting of the next generation of the Church's leadership, particularly among the Latin American episcopate. Santo Domingo was not led by any bishops who signed the Pact of the Catacombs or experienced, firsthand, the excitement created in the years following Vatican II. But Santo Domingo helped in the generational transition that opened the eyes of the Church to new realties and challenges in Latin America after the democratization of most of its countries, the rise of economic globalization, and the awareness of new forms of oppression. In this transition, new leaders appeared, such the archbishop of Buenos Aires, Jorge Mario Bergoglio; of Aparecida, Raymundo Damasceno Assis; of São Paulo, Claúdio Hummes; and of Tegucigalpa, Óscar Maradiaga, all of whom were among the leaders of the Latin American Church exercising a key role at the fifth Conference of CELAM in city of Aparecida, Brazil.

At the Conference of Aparecida in 2007, a deep discussion about the preferential option for the poor returned to the center of the Church's concern and commitment. In the immediate months after the publication of the Aparecida Document, some theologians argued that the preferential option for the poor did not appear in the Document with the same enthusiasm as it appeared Medellín and Puebla. The argument was that reflection about historical liberation and social commitment to the liberation of the poor was not the theme that ran through the fifth Conference.[73] Even so, it advanced in the comprehension of this option and its centrality for the Church's life and ministry, especially regarding the theological understanding of the identification between Christ and the poor. Therefore, the preferential option for the poor was embraced as an option of the christological faith:

> Our faith proclaims: Jesus is the human face of God and the divine face of man. Because of that, a preferential option for the poor is implicit in our christological faith in a God who became poor for us, so as to enrich us with his

> poverty. This option arises from our faith in Jesus Christ, God made man, who became our brother; an option, however, that is not exclusive neither exclusionary.[74]

The Document of Aparecida strongly emphasizes the personal encounter with Christ. It is from this encounter that the true christological faith shines. Moreover, it is from this experience of encountering Jesus that one goes to the poor, joining them in their reality. Among the poor, one contemplates the face of the suffering Christ in the face of their suffering—"the suffering faces of the poor are the suffering face of Christ."[75] We find here a theological account that reflects the gospel's teaching; for example, when Jesus says that, serving his little ones, he is served (see Matt 25:40).

In Aparecida, *the poor* acquires a broader meaning because the document considers the new realities and situation of the continent where the text was written. The bishops faced a different context from previous conferences, which encompassed newly excluded and oppressed people, whom the Church could not despise. With that, Aparecida offers a new dynamism for the preferential option for the poor that springs from its christological foundation. Therefore, this dynamism shows that the signs of the times are important for us to discover who are the poor, privileged recipients of the proclamation of the good news, today and always in the context of our local communities and realities. The *anawim* are also the socioeconomically poor, but globalization, which is one of Aparecida's core concerns, the ecological crises, the rise of intolerance, and the manifestation of old prejudices have given rise to new *anawim* who are in the underworld of history[76] due to the oppression, marginalization, and disproportional vulnerability that they experience.

The poor in the Latin American tradition have a deep relationship with Luke 4:16–30. Both the poor in the Gospel and the poor to whom the Church in Latin America has turned in its evangelizing and liberating action are those who suffer for not having access to basic goods and opportunities to survive and flourish with dignity. They are oppressed, placed in the margins of society. The preferential option for the poor is an evangelical option because it was for these that Jesus intended his action to proclaim the good news of the kingdom of God. Nowadays, however, the Latin American Church seems to be experiencing a paradox. On the one hand, the continental tradition presented above from the development of CELAM conferences continues to flourish, reaching beyond Latin America. It was brought to the central leadership of the Catholic Church by Pope Francis—the former archbishop of Buenos Aires and one of the main hands that wrote Aparecida—who clearly exhorts the ecclesial vocation of "a Church which is poor and for the poor" (*Evangelii Gaudium* 198) and states the preferential option for the poor as an "ethical imperative" (*Laudato Si'* 158). On the other hand, there are some Catholic groups and leaders, even among the episcopate, who distance themselves from the poor and, consequently, from Pope Francis's teaching. This kind of decision and the option for a pastoral approach of defending the Church from the attacks of the secular world stimulates division and weakens the Church's evangelizing vigor and prophetism among those who are impoverished and oppressed. This paradox also occurs in the Catholic Church in the United States. This is especially surprising considering that the Church, here, does not have a strong tradition related to the embodiment of a preferential option for the poor as embraced by the U.S. bishops as a collegial body. The poor are central to the life and action of the Church, which is the people of God united to Christ and assisted by the Holy Spirit in history for the promotion of life. I remember the words of Archbishop Oscar Romero, now *San Romero de America*. In a reality of the crucified peoples that he experienced, St. Romero paraphrased Irenaeus of Lyon with what seems an urgent call: *Gloria Dei vivens pauper* (the glory of God is the poor person who lives).[77]

A THEOLOGICAL STUDY OF LUKE 4:16–30

Perhaps it does not seem appropriate that a theological study of the biblical text that inspires this book begins only now, especially considering that our journey so far has been theological. It is part of the theological endeavor, as seen from the previous analysis, to focus on the textual understanding of biblical literature and history, whether biblical and/or ecclesial. However, I now shift my focus to what theologians call systematic theology to offer an account on fundamental themes for Catholic doctrine that emerge from reading and studying Luke 4:16–30.

The exegetical study of this Lukan pericope suggested some themes of systematic theology. As the Word of God is the soul of theology and this Word is particularly present in the Sacred Scriptures, it is not surprising that, starting from a biblical text, one can develop a comprehensive theological spectrum capable of making connections with different areas and themes of Catholic doctrine. The richness of New Testament texts is so great that, through a pericope, it is possible to make a broad theological reflection with dogmatic relevance and ethical implications.

The first part of this chapter focused on the question of who the poor are as privileged recipients of the evangelical proclamation. Jesus taught us this in the text of Luke and the tradition of the Church continued promoting this teaching throughout history. We have seen that, after the Second Vatican Council, the Catholic Church in Latin America clearly took on the preferential option for the poor, an option that comes from christological faith. However, Luke's text does not only reveal elements of Jesus's mission and points out the continuity of his mission by the Church throughout history, but it also reveals elements of the mystery of God. In Jesus, we have—as much as possible for humankind in their limited capacities to know—the maximum of God's revelation in his transcendental infinitude.

The Joint Mission of the Word and the Spirit

Access to God's revelation takes place in history through human mediation. God takes the initiative to reveal himself to the human being who, due to their limited nature, would not be able to know the unlimited transcendent reality. It is only by grace that we access the mystery of God, in an imperfect manner due to being imperfect human beings, incapable to comprehend all the perfectibility of the transcendent. The Holy Fathers had already said that we will never be able to know the essence of God. A complete and perfect understanding of God is impossible.[78] The inner "life" of God is far beyond any human attempt to comprehend and to express it with our language. The transcendental life of God escapes all human speech.[79] God reveals himself to human beings as grace, a movement of his love for humanity. It is up to us to accept the grace of revelation and seek to understand it logically and coherently, although imperfectly.

The maximum and definitive point of God's revelation in history happened with the incarnation of his Word, Jesus Christ, the Son of God: The Incarnate Word in history. In Jesus's life, death, and resurrection is the fullness of God's revelation for humankind. However, this grace is not a simple historical event that occurred in the past with all possible understanding of God's revelation coming from the past as a single act of apprehension of the mystery. Revelation in Jesus is an ongoing process led by the dynamism of the Holy Spirit who guides the Church. Therefore, the fullness of God's revelation in Jesus has been unveiled and understood over time in a never-ending process. Thus, God makes himself present in the history of his people and reveals himself through events and words (*Dei Verbum* 2), starting from his Son and continued under the guidance of the Holy Spirit. There is an immanent dimension to God (or immanent Trinity), that is, God in his relationship with himself and in the communion of divine Persons within the transcendent reality. Moreover, there is an economic dimension to God (or economic Trinity), that is, the revelation of God throughout history in his role as Creator, Savior, and Sanctifier in the economy of salvation. With this, God reveals himself as Father, Son, and Holy Spirit.[80]

In the Christian theological tradition, any understanding of God's revelation starts from the Scriptures in a dialectical relationship with history. This relationship is a result of a contextual encounter between God and humankind, that is local in the experience of a person or a community, but also points to the acontextual reality of God as grace. As history progresses, God makes himself present in the path of a people, shaped of communities experiencing concrete historical challenges. This dialectical relationship allows us—absorbing the experience of faith and enlightened by the Sacred Scriptures—to perceive aspects of revelation that are already in the Bible and in Jesus but have not yet been made as explicit as viewing the biblical text as a single historical event. As Joaquim Severino Croatto suggests: the biblical text has a *reserve-of-meanings* that provides new understanding and interpretations of God's revelation throughout history when a text is read by communities in their present historical context and challenges.[81] This is a creative process, possible because the community of faith and its reading of the Bible are always assisted by the Spirit of God.

Luke 4:16–30 presents Jesus's mission of bringing the good news to the poor, an aspect discussed in chapter 2. In doing so, the biblical author emphasizes that Jesus will carry out his mission under the assistance of the Spirit of God. Jesus says, "The Spirit of the Lord is on me, and he has anointed me to bring good news to the poor" (Luke 4:18). This reveals that the entire ministry of Jesus is exercised through the assistance of the Spirit. Luke's first book is the Gospel that most features Jesus being guided in his actions and words by the Spirit of God.[82] The same Spirit who guided Jesus to death and resurrection also led the apostolic Church in Acts (Luke's second book), and it is the Spirt that guides the Church throughout history.

Therefore, one finds in Luke a central aspect of the revelatory grace of God's mystery: the mission of Jesus, the Incarnate Word, takes place under the anointing of the Spirit. Every action of Jesus is the action of the Incarnate Word. Being the action of the Word, which is with the Spirit on Jesus, I argue that Luke contains elements of the revelation of the *joint mission of the Word and the Spirit*. Now, it is up to us to understand this joint mission, revealed by the Gospel, that has grown in its understanding throughout history in the development of the tradition of the Church and its explanation of this mystery. This joint mission is dynamic and, by the grace of the spontaneity of the Spirit, it has manifestations in particular contexts, such as the reality of the poor in Latin America, where God's mystery is concretized in their local struggles.

In Jesus's life, the presence of the Spirit is constant. Jesus is fully human, but the human is lived by the Son of God. Therefore, his humanity is holy because it is lived in the Spirit and does not mix with his divinity.[83] Hence, his sanctity is communicated to all humanity, who is called to live in the Spirit by the Son.

Jesus Christ is the Word who assumes humanity being, therefore, perfectly human and God. Because he is divine, he is radically different from the human and, being a human person, he is equal to us. But one can emphasize that his humanity is different from ours because it reveals the true human. Jesus, as a human, acts perfectly. His action reflects the action and desire of God. Everything that comes from Jesus is the action of the Incarnate Word of God, who was sent by the Father. Jesus Christ assumes everything of the human (except the sin) and his life is totally turned to the Father and to the love of the neighbor. Jesus's action is animated by the Spirit, qualifying his humanity. In other words, the quality of Jesus's action is the expression of love and of the Spirit, a *pneumatic Christology*. The same Spirit that qualified the action of Jesus was communicated by him to everyone so that we can also qualify our action. This communication is revealed in John's Gospel when the risen Jesus sends the disciples as the Father sent him and breathes the Spirit on them (see John 20:21–23).

Jesus's life in the Spirit is fundamental for developing a Christology from the Incarnate Word, as it allows us to understand the divine action of Jesus and his intimacy with the Father. The Spirit is the *atmosphere* that Jesus lives in from birth (he was conceived by the Spirit) until his death (he gives up the Spirit) and resurrection (sending his Spirit). Jesus places us within this *atmosphere* at Pentecost, by the sending of the Holy Spirit upon the Church. In this sense, the joint mission of the Word and the Spirit has a historical impact and a cosmic breadth. When the Father sends his Word, along goes his Spirit, the visible and invisible dimension of God who manifests himself in history:

> When the Father sends his Word, he always sends his Breath. In their joint mission, the Son and the Holy Spirit are distinct but inseparable. To be sure, it is Christ who is seen, the visible image of the invisible God, but it is the Spirit who reveals him. (*Catechism*, no. 689)

With the incarnation of the Word, humanity is assumed by God. In this regard, it is important to distinguish three points: First, *the being assumed humanity*: Jesus is God made human and the humanity of the Incarnate Word is autonomous because Jesus acts as a human person, sustained by the Spirit. Thus, Jesus is the Word of God and a perfect human. Second, *the act of assumed humanity*: Jesus acts from his birth to his death as a human, but he has at his root the Word, which is the root of all human participation in the life of God, the root of Jesus's holiness and of all holiness. By a perfectly human act, Jesus saved humankind because he died by an act of perfect love, an act of love animated by the Spirit.[84] Third, *the communication of the divine life* is made by Jesus through his holiness as a human person. In this way, Jesus shows not only the way of holiness, but also the truth and the life. This suggests that we are called to be fully children of God, dependent on Them, the Trinity. We are children of the Father, in the Son, animated by the Spirit.

The mission of Jesus, inaugurated in Luke's Gospel, in the synagogue of Nazareth, is the accomplishment of the work of the Father by the Son in the Spirit. Any act and teaching in Jesus's mission reveals the identity of the Son of God, who, being the Incarnate Word, assumes the human nature. In this sense, the action of Jesus is a *theandric action* in the order of the Spirit,[85] which first manifests herself in a historical moment with Jesus of Nazareth and continues to manifest herself throughout history in concrete realities experienced by communities of faith. Contingency and particularity of realities do not limit the Spirit, as she transcends history, being a transcendent reality, and makes us participants in the eternal trinitarian life in the order of the Spirit.

In the Spirit's anointing of Jesus in the synagogue, there is the manifestation of the joint mission of the Word and the Spirit. In history, the Spirit led Jesus to carry out God's work among the poor. This feature of Jesus's mission for the poor is an aspect of God's partiality in favoring them that, in realities such as that of Latin America and many other marked by oppression and poverty, must be highlighted with great emphasis. The poverty of most people in the Global South forces us to emphasize Jesus's mission as the liberator of captives and the evangelizer of the poor. Thus, starting from the reality of the oppressed, it seems to be an ethical mandate for the ecclesial ministry that springs from the joint mission of the Word and the Spirit. The mission of the Church must be an ethical manifestation of the transcendent joint mission, in the immanent historical reality where the poor cry out for justice and life with dignity.

The Spirit who guides Jesus's disciples in Latin America and any other reality marked by oppression leads them to serve the poor and the oppressed in a free movement of love. Thus, in the encounter with the poor, we encounter the face of Christ and our service to them takes place in the atmosphere of the Spirit, that is, by the grace of God. The Spirit is God's own grace present in the world, in lives of the men and women who welcome this grace. To know whether we act under God's grace, or to discern whether our action in the world is a fruit of the assistance of the Holy Spirit, we must look at the life and teaching of the historical Jesus, judging our actions from the lens of the gospel. Hence, the joint mission is manifested in the practice of a community when, in realities marked by poverty, injustice, and oppression, we focus our effort to bring the good news to the poor.

Communion with the Father

According to the *Catechism of the Catholic Church* (no. 27), the desire for God is written in the human heart and it is only within a search for the satisfaction of the most intimate desire for truth and happiness that the human finds in God because the human being was created by God and for God. Within this, the human being, since the most remote times, has established a relationship with a transcendent reality. This reality has been called God by many traditions and some have even established, by analogy, a paternal-filial relationship with God, calling God the transcendent Father. Israel's own tradition even calls God the Father of the poor. However, the distance between the human and the transcendent is preserved within a level of intimacy that only the Son, Jesus, had.

Jesus called God Father, but in a totally original and intimate way, unknown and even frowned upon by the religious authorities of the time. Jesus, when praying, called God Father (Luke 10:2–26)—*Abba*, my dear daddy—in a new way, one that conveyed that He was close to God, part of a communion in which one knows the other deeply. Reading Isaiah in the synagogue, Jesus means that the Lord is the Father who anoints his Son to carry out a mission among the poor: "The Spirit of the Lord is upon me."

I suggested above that Luke's Gospel places special emphasis on the presence of the Spirit in Jesus's life. Jesus is filled with the Spirit from the beginning to the end of Luke's narrative. The incarnation is presented as a work of the Spirit (see Luke 1:35). At the opening of his Messianic program, Jesus is under the Spirit of the Lord. Luke 4:1–30 offers an expression of the Trinity, as St. Irenaeus highlights: the one who anoints is the Father, the anointed is the Son, and the anointing takes place in the Spirit, which is the anointing itself.[86] In this trinitarian expression of God, the relationship of the divine Persons is manifested in the fulfillment of Jesus's mission in history, a relationship of communion and intimacy. Jesus, in the performance of his mission and in his teaching, reveals the Father, the Son, and the Holy Spirit.[87] The entire life of Jesus is in communion with the Father and in the Spirit. From his experience as a human and his intimacy with the Father, Jesus reveals the Trinity. The manifestation of the invisible mystery of God in historical reality is the experience of Jesus manifested by his words and deeds.

Jesus is the one who reveals the Trinity, a reality existing forever and ever, but made known to us in history through the experience of Jesus. In the bosom of God *himself*, the transcendent *is* always Trinity: Father, Son, and Spirit in communion, immanent Trinity. For the human being, the Trinity needed to reveal themselves, as an act of grace, to become known in history through the mission of the divine Persons: the Father with the creative gesture; the Son in his saving and sanctifying action of humanity; and the Spirit in the continuity and completeness of the dynamic action of the Son. This is the economic Trinity.[88] As a result, from the revelation contained in the New Testament and from human experience itself, a theology (and/or doctrine) of the Trinity has been developed, but the Trinity does not depend on any theology or doctrine. The Trinity is a revealed fact in history, and the human being can participate in the trinitarian communion, an opportunity offered by God's grace.

Jesus is the anointed of the Father to free the humankind by the action of the Son, in the Spirit, of bringing the good news to the poor. Through Jesus, we know the Father, the Son, and the Holy Spirit present in the history of human salvation. Discussing the revelation of God as Trinity, the *Catechism of the Catholic Church* offers a more spiritualized and dogmatic account on this mystery (nos. 238–48). Despite starting by saying that the Father is revealed by the Son, the *Catechism* greatly emphasizes the function of the Holy Spirit, considering that she reveals the Father and Son. The *Catechism* aims to stress the action of the Spirit in the history and life of each individual person because only in the Spirit can we profess the faith in the Father and in the Son and, thus, confess the faith in the Trinity. The *Catechism* seeks to base its argument on the New Testament, but its starting point is the faith given by tradition, so much so that the text quotes as a source of truth the Councils of Nicaea (325), responsible for the dogma on the consubstantiality of the Father and the Son, and that of Constantinople (381), which professes the faith in the Holy Spirit who proceeds from the Father and is God, equal to the Father and the Son.[89] The *Catechism* is a text for the Catholic faith community coming from the magisterium, but its language, when speaking about the Trinity, despite being objective, is very dense, especially for humble communities embodying their faith within a context of poverty and oppression. The question of language is perhaps today one of the greatest challenges for theology: How do we speak of the mystery of God so that everyone can easily understand the experience of this mystery?

In a reality such as the one in Latin America and most Catholic communities in the Global South, starting from the experience of the historical Jesus might be a good way to speak about the Trinity and raise awareness of a personal experience of trinitarian communion. The identification of the suffering of the poor—of my community in an impoverished country—with the suffering of Jesus has offered them an experience of walking as a community along with the presence of the Trinity. The one who revealed the Trinity to us lives united to the Father in an intimate relationship that strengthened him in the fulfillment of his mission carried out in the Spirit. The strength of the Spirit was sent upon all of us with the reality of Jesus's resurrection. This allows the people, in their historic march for liberation and suffering as a crucified people, to identify with Jesus in his liberating action of proclaiming the good news to the poor and freeing the oppressed. In this identification, the poor learn from him to be intimate with God, also calling him Father, and living in the Spirit according to the evangelical teaching.

Through the historical experience of Jesus and by an act of faith, the Christian community learns that God is Trinity, for he reveals the Father, the Son, and the Spirit. In the development of Jesus's life, we learn how God functions. Thus, Jesus tells us who God is and how God acts in the world.[90] His relationship with God reveals the relationship that human beings can have with God and with others: a relationship of communion. In the intimacy of the Son with the Father within the Spirit, that is, in love, Jesus reveals communion as a constitutive element of the Trinity. God is not simple solidarity among persons, but *communion* and *participation*. This becomes concrete in the action of Jesus with the poor. Luke 4:16–30 reveals that God the Father meets the poor through his Son in the Spirit.

The practice, teaching, and entire life of Jesus reveal a divine authority, not just because it comes from God, but because it makes God visible. That is why Jesus demands faith in himself for the one who seeks to be the beneficiary of a miracle. He constantly repeats, "Your faith has healed you." It is not only faith in the God of Israel, but faith in him.[91] Jesus acts as the holder of God's power and thus reveals himself to be the Incarnate Word of God.[92] The practice of Jesus is the practice of God's Word; therefore, it is the practice of God. Through his actions, Jesus reveals the privilege of the poor: communion with God is a communion that passes through the poor in bringing the good news to them. In following Jesus, we discover God the Son, who he is. Therefore, the profession of faith in the Son is united to an ethic, the one taught by Jesus and lived by his followers in discipleship.

The Spirit is revealed by Jesus through all his life and actions. The characteristic of Jesus's work is spiritual, lived-in a concrete context and, at the same time, beyond a historical reality.[93] The presence of the Spirit has always been in Jesus, from the incarnation to the resurrection. Anointed by the Spirit, Jesus launches his messianic program (see Luke 4:16–30) and the Spirit is the authority in the execution of the program and the strength to bear all the consequences, leading to Jesus's total self-donation to the human being out of love on the cross. There is a strength in Jesus that, at the same time, is both in him and different from him. This force is the presence of the Spirit, which becomes clear with the resurrection. The apostolic community will call it the *presence of the Holy Spirit*, which was in Jesus and continues in the Church.[94] In one sentence, Francisco Catão summarizes the revelation of the Trinity through the action of Jesus: "Jesus' work is the work of God, witness of the union of the Son with the Father, in the Spirit."[95]

The intimacy of Jesus with the Father is unique, but it is not a closed intimacy in its own transcendental reality. This relationship of intimacy opens itself for the participation of others, a movement of grace that allows us to participate in God's intimacy. God calls us to communion with him by sending his Son, loving us with the same love that he loved his Son because the Father loves us in the

Spirit and, through Christ in the Spirit, we enter into communion with God.[96] This is a call—the human vocation—to participate in the life of the Trinity, being assumed as children of God through the Son in the Spirit. Hence, our vocation is a life in the grace of being assumed as children of God, a filiation that Jesus has by nature and we by participation.

In history, the Son and the Father are revealed by the Spirit, as Leonardo Boff affirms, "The Spirit leads us to the discovery of Jesus as the Son of God and allows us to cry out, Abba, Daddy."[97] All access to God as Father and Son is through the Spirit, who places us in communion with God, a communion that is the love between the Father and the Son in which we also participate through love, which is the Holy Spirit herself.

The Spirit is eternally united to the Father and to the Son. In history, they are always found together through the constant reuptake of Jesus's message with its liberating force. Through the Spirit, we return to the life of Jesus to answer the questions of our current time and location. The Spirit is also sensitive to the signs of God's presence in concrete realities and to the crying out of the poor. This means that, in a reality marked by poverty and exclusion, the emphasis on aspects of Jesus's historical mission is necessary to promote a dignified life for all who suffer because of the lack of basic goods to flourish. Through the Spirit, we see in the face of the poor and the oppressed the face of the crucified Jesus. Because of this, we are impelled, starting from the privileged teaching of the gospel to the poor in the proclamation of the kingdom of God accomplished by Jesus, to embody the mystery of the Trinity in communion with them, who are not simply *them*, but *us*, our companions of faith and liberation.

Toward Resurrection

To close this chapter, I offer a short account of salvation. Luke's pericope shows us Jesus's concern to set the oppressed free, to restore sight to the blind (that is, to care for the sick), and to proclaim the acceptable year of the Lord, which, as we saw in the previous chapter, is related to Israel's tradition of the *sabbatical year* and *Jubilee year*. Luke 4:16–30 points to a salvific manifestation on a historical dimension, as it presents God fulfilling the promises made to his people in history, and, at the same time, it opens to a much broader perspective of salvation: the eternal salvation (eschatological dimension), that is, resurrection, the center of the Christian faith. The event of Jesus's resurrection is the lens from which the community reads Jesus's life; thus, the evangelist writes from the post-Easter experience with its historical and eschatological relevance.

Reading Isaiah 61:1–2 and 58:6 in Luke 4:18–19 and the following statement that today this Scripture has been fulfilled, Jesus declares himself as the Messiah-prophet, the Christ, that is, the anointed of the Lord who came to fulfill the promises of God. This has a soteriological aspect, coming from a writer who already experienced Jesus's resurrection. The terms *aphésai* (free) and *dektón* (acceptable) indicate that salvation in the eschatological dimension of the last day passes through a historical fulfillment of God's promises. Salvation is not only reserved for the resurrection after death, but it begins with a process of liberation of humankind in history. The proclamation of the good news to the poor, with the release of the oppressed and the acceptable year of the Lord, which has a socioeconomic connotation, are signs of the wonders of the kingdom of God, already present in Jesus, as an anticipation—albeit a limited, changeable, and contingent anticipation—of the eternal salvation in the resurrection. It is an eschatology that begins in history, in an incomplete way, and continues beyond time and space with final salvation in the eternal reality of God, then fully.

The Messiah-prophet also expands the scope of the fulfillment of God's promises. In addition to foreshadowing the wonders of the kingdom in history, these promises extend beyond the borders of Israel and the Jewish people. This is clear in verses 25–27, when Jesus quotes the prophets Elijah and Elisha, who were sent by God to alleviate hunger and to heal foreigners. It seems that Luke's theology has been drawn from Pauline sources, with the universalization of the proclamation of the gospel and the opening of salvation to all who adhere to the faith in Jesus Christ as common points of emphasis. The fulfillment of God's promises will not only fall to the people of Israel, but to all who accept his Son, Jesus Christ.

Salvation begins in history and affects personal existence. It is not enough only being a member of a group, or a church, it is necessary to be deeply touched by the mystery of Christ. This occurs not only in individual life, but also in a common life, in solidarity and in the social constitution of human historicity. Salvation begins in history with answers to the concrete questions of today sought in the mystery of Christ.[98] For this reason, Jesus touches on issues pertinent to his time, such as oppression, marginalization, and the importance of making the acceptable year of the Lord a social ethical practice. This is a social program able to restore justice. As we understand the liberating action of Jesus in history and embrace its practice in a deeply existential commitment to the poor, the sick, and the oppressed, we deepen the experience of faith centered on Christ as the Savior. Jesus Christ becomes an effective savior in history as people assume and practice his liberating revelation of God. Salvation does not exist apart from spirituality or the Christian moral life; and eschatology without the practice of faith has no existential content.[99]

Showing a God in the concrete history of people and Jesus as the Son who evangelizes the poor for their liberation, in any context marked by poverty, enables an existential experience of the salvific mystery of Christ. This is God in historical presence that allows us to find what gives meaning and a positive destiny for human existence.[100] In the suffering of the Latin American people, Christ is existentially found in a transcendent experience that returns to the concrete reality with meaning since such experience is realized within a sociocultural *locus*. This allows Christ to be seen in the features of the people who experience him in their locality, offering meaning for personal and collective existence. The Messiah-prophet Jesus becomes the Messiah-prophet Christ whose features become those of crucified peoples anywhere in the world.

As proclaimed by Jesus, "bringing the good news to the poor" means that salvation passes through the poor and, in a reality like ours, this encounter with the poor is essential for salvation, not a choice that can be rejected. According to Jon Sobrino, it is necessary to place salvation in relation to the poor, a reality with the potential of salvation. Consequently, Sobrino arrives at the formulation *extra pouperes nulla salus*, a strong and challenging statement, as it presents the reality of the poor as an environment capable of providing salvation, with the one who saves always being Christ:

> Strictly speaking, we are not saying that with the poor there is automatic salvation; we claim only that without

> them there is no salvation—although we do presuppose that in the poor there is always "something" of salvation. What we aim to do, ultimately, is to offer hope, in spite of everything. *From the world of the poor and the victims can come salvation for a gravely ill civilization.*[101]

Jon Sobrino stresses what we can learn from the poor. With them, we learn to have hope, not to give up in the face of pain and suffering, to show solidarity, and to realize that a new type of social organization is possible. The poor revive the utopia of a dignified life in a just society. That is why we can receive from them a sign of salvation for the constitution of a new civilization. Therefore, the preferential option for the poor is the differential of the disciple of Jesus Christ. God, through his Son, chose the poor. The option of liberation makes the reality of God themself to emerge in history. Grounded on an encounter with Christ, the option for the poor, for their historical liberation and eschatological salvation, is an expression of our deification, a work of God's grace.[102]

There is a dialectical relationship between God's salvific proposal and the human response. It is a relationship between the contingency of reality and the transcendence of human freedom.[103] As we are immersed in a limited dimension, which is touched by the unlimited, we cannot fully capture God's proposal with our historical responses. Through the revelation of God in Jesus, however, we have a safe way through which our answers to God must pass in order to achieve historical liberation and eschatological salvation. This path must pass through the poor in an encounter with them that creates a community of learning and solidarity. In this community, serving the poor, we shall attain, not by our own merits but by God's grace, salvation. In his homily on Matthew 25:31–46, St. Basil of Caesarea says, "Salvation depends on renouncing the wealth that you have for the poor and putting yourself at their service."[104] Basil was a living witness of his preaching; from a wealthy family, he left everything to live solely for Christ and for the service of the poor. His life synthesizes the salvation that begins in the historical dimension, serving the poor for their liberation, which extends to the eschatological dimension: the eternal salvation given in our resurrection within the mystery of God.

4

The Church Continues the Mission of Jesus Christ

The flourishing of Christian faith begins with a personal encounter with Jesus Christ. Anything related to the Christian faith comes after this encounter and is sustained by it in the atmosphere of the Spirit. It is an existential experience that offers meaning for life and guidance for personal and social practice. Narratives about Jesus, theological books, liturgical celebrations, and morality based on Jesus's teaching are not the beginning of the faith, but a consequence of this encounter, although one can encounter Jesus for the first time through these secondary elements offered by the Christian community. The New Testament is a good example of this. These texts were written by people and communities who first had a transformative encounter with Jesus, whether the historical Jesus or the risen one. This encounter changed their lives, impacting all aspects of their existence from self-understanding to moral practice, to eschatological hope. Some of these first followers of the man of Nazareth felt, for many different reasons, the need to write about this man. They did so from the lens of their encounter, considering the challenges of their reality. These texts became so relevant for Christian faith that they expanded beyond the communities and realities to which they were written. Thus, they are texts through which many encounter Jesus in their personal lives. Although the

Bible contains the Word of God where one can encounter Jesus as his/her first experience of faith, other texts and Christian practices, such as liturgy, popular religiosity, and moral examples, can also function as mediations to encounter Jesus, an experience that is personal as a result of grace.

In continuing to unfold our christological essay from a biblical text and its reading from the lens of a particular historical experience of faith, it is now time to profess this account by unfolding the relevance of Luke 4:16–30 and its Christology for the pastoral and social ministry of the Church, as a community of faithful disciples who continue Jesus's mission in history.

After an invigorating paschal experience and the sending of the Holy Spirit, the first disciples of Jesus continued to perform, inserted in a concrete reality, the mission initiated by the historical Jesus, who announced the kingdom of God to the poor. The disciples came together in groups and formed communities of followers of Jesus Christ. As their central axis of faith, these communities had Jesus Christ himself, who died on the cross, but rose and was alive amid the life of his followers through the Holy Spirit. The kingdom of God, which was announced by Jesus, continued to be proclaimed but with a new element: Jesus also became identified with the kingdom, which is why one can affirm, "Jesus announced the kingdom, and the community announces the risen Jesus."

Throughout the history of Christianity, the Catholic Church has always announced Jesus Christ under the assistance of the Holy Spirit, sometimes more faithful to the gospel, sometimes less. Being a historical reality, even having a transcendent aspect, the Church has a human dimension that carries the weight of its contingency and the failures originated from human limitations and fragilities. "The Church is both holy and sinful."[1] Thus, the Church, especially its hierarchical leaders, sometimes enjoyed the benefits of joining powerful elites more so than the challenge of serving the oppressed. For example, after the exciting years of primitive Christianity, Catholic clerical leaders, such as bishops and priests, joined the Roman imperial power that opened the door for Christianity to have political benefits. Church leaders were co-opted by this power, assimilating court ceremonials, privileges, and the status quo. As a result, they distanced themselves from the vitality and prophetism of proclaiming the gospel to the poor and advocating for their justice.[2] However, at the same time, the Holy Spirit inspired individual prophets who questioned the institutional Church by remaining faithful to the spirit of the gospel and its central demand to proclaim the good news preferably to the poor, which is the kingdom of God identified with Jesus Christ incarnated in history to promote life to the *anawim*, that is, those bent under the weight of the lack of basic needs. This movement of the Spirit led, for example, to the emergence of new forms of religious experiences grounded on a life of austerity and medicant orders in the Middle Ages, of which Francis of Assisi and his companions are great examples.[3]

At moments in the history of Christianity, the institutional Church, seduced by the benefits of temporal power, distanced itself from announcing the *aphésai* and the *dektón*, that is, liberation and acceptance. The Church also distanced itself from *the privileged recipients of the proclamation of the good news*, unlike what the Lord's Anointed, Jesus did. This proclamation was the core of Jesus's missionary program offered in the synagogue in Luke 4:18–19 and then carried it out in the course of his ministry. The Holy Spirit, however, never failed to raise up saints and prophets within the Church, the people of God, to keep alive the mission of Jesus among the poor for their liberation. Even in great moments of crisis in the ministry of the Church and in the world, the Holy Spirit never abandoned the people of God (both laity and clergy).

Currently, one might suggest that we are living a moment of crisis in the world and in the Catholic Church,[4] which seems to leave us unmotivated, beset with scandals, such as the sexual abuse crisis, and some ecclesial institutions and leaders that seem far from the poor and other marginalized groups. For those who directly experience these issues, there is a sense that the flame of prophecy has been extinguished. However, faith in Jesus Christ and the assistance of the Spirit raise hope, allowing us to see the sign of prophecy, such as those in the ministry of Pope Francis in his call for caring for the earth and the poor. In moments of crisis, the gospel always shows its dynamic and revitalizing force, and the Holy Spirit acts to sustain the faithful and inspire prophets within the people of God.

Now sixty years after the Second Vatican Council, the Catholic Church is going through a moment of reorganization of its pastoral practice based on the new world conjuncture. In this reconfiguration, according to João Batista Libanio, four Church scenarios stand out and, according to the prevalence of one over the others, it will be the path that the Church will follow in the coming decades.[5] Libanio, a great Jesuit theologian from Brazil, wrote these scenarios before the pontificate of Pope Francis and died a little after the beginning of the ministry of the first Latin American pope, but Libanio's analysis presents different ministerial postures of the Catholic Church in its service for the world that coexist today (and an argument could be made that they always have coexisted), often enough with conflicts and divisions. In each historical period, one scenario appears more than others and/or different realities within the same period, highlighting one more than the others in their local ministry. For instance, what is highlighted by Francis's ministry is not the same as that highlighted by the U.S. Conference of Catholic Bishops. Therefore, it is worth understanding these scenarios. They show the diversity of the Church's perspectives of pastoral ministry and understanding of its historical mission.

According to Libanio, the scenarios are (1) the Church for the institution, (2) the charismatic Church, (3) the Church of preaching, and (4) the Church of liberating praxis. The title given to each scenario offers a sense of what each one represents. Currently, these four scenarios coexist with their own tensions. Perhaps the prevailing one should not be the best historical embodiment of their dynamism, but rather the interrelationship among all, based on the concrete challenges of each local church, and marked by openness to adaptations according to the concrete realities of particular communities. This would give room for an ecclesial flexibility in which different perspectives share a healthy coexistence, accepting that local and historical challenges would play a key role in determining which scenario would be highlighted to respond to specific challenges. However, to be faithful to Jesus's mission, it seems that nobody can deny that the announcing of the good news to the poor is central to any historical manifestation of the Church. Moreover, contexts marked by oppression and marginalization, as the one in Latin America and in most countries in the Global South, demands a greater focus on the proclamation of the good news to the poor through a liberating praxis against institutionalized oppression and toward social justice.

Although I recognize the value and relevance of the two first scenarios, I stress the last two because they follow a natural development of the reflection offered in this book and because they better correspond to the reality of most Latin American people and the challenges of impoverished communities there and elsewhere.

In the Church of preaching, "catechesis, theology, evangelization, and missionary proclamation will play a central role."[6] This is a scenario of a Church that focuses on the proclamation of God's Word. Biblical study is the main axis, and dialogue with modern sciences has significant relevance. For Libanio, this Church has a great chance of being the leading characteristic of the Catholic community because it will meet the need of a society that searches for knowledge, but against the "spiritualist, charismatic surge" of some Catholic groups. In this case, Catholic communities will be a representation of a Church of minorities, that is, a small community and not a Church of mass numbers because of the high demand for deep knowledge about the foundations of the Catholic faith and tradition. Libanio wrote it before the advent of social media and didn't predict how this would impact Catholic committees. I would add to his view that this Church of preaching would function as a response to the superficiality and conflicts created by social media because this Church would be grounded on the communitarian experience of small communities where people gather to listen to, study, and understand the Word of God from the lens of their local reality. This serves as a response to the lack of personal encounter and dialogue created by virtual environments and their superficiality of knowledge. Thus, it will be a small Catholic Church, as Libanio suggested.

The Church of liberating praxis is founded on the preferential option for the poor and stands on the side of the oppressed and excluded, fighting for liberation and justice. This Church will be formed by communities guided by social ministry and an experience of socioeconomic austerity and simplicity. It will be organized in small communities, in the model of basic ecclesial communities, and ordained ministers, that is, priests and bishops, will not be the center of the Church as canonical authority and the source of decisions. Priests and bishops will be guides, pastors who help in the liberation process. The laity will have great autonomy and agency for leading decision-making processes. In this scenario, the reading of the Bible will be focused on concrete life, on the real people's problems, valuing hermeneutics and exegesis. It will be a Church that uses modern sciences as an instrument, including social and health sciences, to analyze society and take a stand in the face of oppressive systems. Its chances of success lie in the tradition of Medellín-Puebla, which took a position in favor of the poor, a position later confirmed by the Conference of Aparecida. This Church of liberating praxis will also attract and motivate the faithful by witnesses of martyrs, such as Oscar Romero, Dorothy Stang and many other known by local communities, because they were killed by oppressive systems due to prophetic activity on behalf of the gospel. The martyrs will be signs of hope and anti-idolatry of the world powers. However, the crisis of the left and sociopolitical activism can generate a strong shock in this scenario, opening space for the growth of a postmodernism contrary to any liberating praxis,[7] such as the growth of the far-right political movements with great support by conservative Christian groups.

Libanio wrote this well before the world that we are experiencing today with the rise of far-right movements, intolerance, and the spread of misinformation through social media. This phenomenon impacts the Catholic Church, including many Catholic leaders and faithful being part of its promotion. At the same time, the Catholic Church has seen the humble practice of Pope Francis, who embodies a liberating praxis through his humility and prophetic voice on behalf the poor and the oppressed. Francis's call for a synodal Church where the faithful have an opportunity to participate in the decision-making and against clericalism are examples of his effort for a liberating Church as people of God. However, Francis's view suffers resistance inside his own community, a resistance that is aggressive and closed to dialogue.

Pope Francis believes that "unity prevails over conflict" (*Evangelii Gaudium* 226–30). Unity is not a uniform Church, but rather a community that embraces diversity in which all are supported by the same foundation: faith in Jesus. This christological faith means that the Church cannot excuse itself from the mission of proclaiming the good news to the poor. Fulfilling this mission, the Church is a prophetic community in the world that remains faithful to the New Testament tradition of freeing the oppressed, proclaiming the acceptable year of the Lord, and bringing the kingdom of God—that is, the good news—to the poor as the privileged recipients of the gospel message. In its pastoral action and social ministry, the Church considers the reality in which the community is inserted as a starting point for the proclamation of the values of the gospel and the defense of life in the light of Christ under the assistance of the Holy Spirit. In any present or future scenario of the Church, this evangelical truth cannot be rejected, otherwise the christological faith is restricted to an abstract individualist spirituality that does not demand an ethical practice that reflects the teaching and the life of the historical Jesus, the main source of revelation.

THE HISTORICAL ACTION OF THE COMMUNITY UNDER THE GUIDANCE OF THE HOLY SPIRIT

The Church is made up of disciples and missionaries of Jesus Christ who, by meeting Jesus personally, become his disciples and assume, in community, the task of continuing the historical master's mission throughout all times. This view on the origin of Christianity is highlighted in the final document of the Aparecida Conference (2007), which emphasizes the fundamental importance of the personal encounter with Christ that leads to seeing in the face of the poor the face of the crucified Jesus.[8] According to the document, following Jesus means being permanent disciples in an ongoing process of discipleship of learning new ways to live out Jesus's mission in the midst of different historical contexts and times. Therefore, being a disciple of Jesus is also being a missionary in the current reality of the faithful, where they concretely embody an ethics in continuity with Jesus's historical ministry.

Jesus's ministry in Galilee cannot simply be transported in time and space into the present to be lived out anywhere. Our time and space are very different, marked by their own challenges and crises, such as the ecological one, resulting from our dominant model of production and relation to nature. Our context or the contexts of our communities are increasingly diverse and plural, with global interconnections and local impacts. The COVID-19 pandemic is an example of this, a global-health issue that is felt in the lives of individual people in their local realties, with disproportional impact on the lives of the poor and most vulnerable. Even the context in which the Document of Aparecida was written—fifteen years ago—

has significant differences from today. However, insights from this Document are still relevant.[9] Aparecida does not absolutize the particularity of challenges of the first decade of this millennium, but rather offers a lens to read the historical reality from one foundation: the christological faith reflected in the Catholic tradition as it is expressed in the Vatican II. This lens and foundation are found in Pope Francis's teaching, which expands the vision of Aparecida to read the current global challenges.[10]

The Document of Aparecida takes up the theology of the signs of the times from *Gaudium et Spes*,[11] considering this theology from the need of a true personal and pastoral conversion:

> Personal conversion awakens the ability to submit everything to the service of building the kingdom of God. Bishops, priests, permanent deacons, consecrated men and women, lay men and women, are called to assume an attitude of permanent pastoral conversion, which implies carefully listening and discerning "what the Spirit is saying to the Churches" (Rev 2:29) through of the signs of the times when God manifests himself.[12]

Following Jesus includes being challenged by the reality and its pastoral needs and particularities. Conversion is not an isolated act that occurs once, constituted by a single, personal transformation. Rather, conversion is an ongoing process that Jesus's disciples experience when they let the historical reality, with its social and pastoral challenges, question the posture and practice of the disciple. This questioning comes from the signs of the times and demands an ethical response that would not be possible without a conversion to open us to ministerial and social service as an integrated aspect of Jesus's mission to respond to our crisis. An example is the ecological crisis that, in accord with Francis, requires from all "an ecological conversion, whereby the effects of their encounter with Jesus Christ become evident in their relationship with the world around them" (*Laudato Si'* 217). This conversion takes place in a historical context, from which its questions cannot be ignored:

> The pastoral care of the Church cannot be fulfilled without considering the historical context in which her members

> live. Their life takes place in very concrete sociocultural contexts. These social and cultural transformations naturally pose new challenges for the Church in her mission to build the kingdom of God. Hence, in fidelity to the Holy Spirit who guides the Church, the need for ecclesial renewal arises from the historical context, and this need implies spiritual, pastoral, and institutional reforms.[13]

Aparecida Document presents a desire to continue the mission of Jesus in actions that contribute to the construction of the kingdom of God. For this to happen, an interaction between human and divine—imminent and transcendent—in history is necessary. The Catholic Church's journey is under the assistance of the Spirit. Because she is incarnated in a specific context, she exists only as an incarnated community in specific times, contexts, and existential situations.[14] Therefore, the universal Church should consider local realities—their own problems, dilemmas, challenges, and pastoral needs. Within history, God's revelation, which has its maximum point in Jesus Christ, is revealed by events and actions within the interaction between Jesus's proposal and human responses. All this takes place under the aegis of the Spirit, who is the soul of the Church and guides it in discerning the signs of the times.[15]

The faith community has the mission to continue the mission of Jesus. To carry out this task, Jesus himself did not leave his disciples at the mercy of the world. He placed them under the assistance of the Spirit, under the one who anointed Jesus to carry out his historic ministry.

The Holy Spirit is the soul of the Church. The Spirit is the communion of people gathered in community. She guarantees the unity of Church in her pluralism and differences, even with the existence of conflicts, because the unity of the Church is communion in the dynamism of the Spirit and not in the immobility of uniformity and structures. What builds the Church is this communion—an imperfect mirror of the trinitarian communion—in the mission of bringing the good news to the poor for the construction of the kingdom of God. This truth, when encountered with the Latin American reality, gives birth to a new spirituality, a new life in the Spirit, marked by the option for the poor in the struggle for liberation, an option from the christological faith.

The Church is the people of God gathered in community by the power of the Spirit to continue the mission of Jesus. In any reality marked by inequality and oppression, the breath of the Spirit, following Jesus's actions in favor of the poorest, encourages the struggle for liberation. The community of Christian believers is embedded in history, within concrete contexts that, in the case of Latin America and many other regions in the world, are oppressive and sustained by structures responsible for marginalization and poverty. The action of the Holy Spirit is not outside history, for God reveals themself in history through the journey of a people; therefore, the Spirit, the soul of the Church, leads people in communion to be authentic witnesses of the love of Jesus, a *love-service*[16] that frees his disciples from their selfishness, leading them to proclaim the good news to the poor and to fight for liberation and the acceptable year of the Lord.

In the book *The Holy Spirit and Liberation*, José Comblin offers a pneumatological account (that is, a theology of the Spirit) of the Holy Spirit as the one who guides the historical action of the Church in continuity with Jesus's mission.[17] Comblin's thesis is that the Holy Spirit is the soul of the Church who gathers a communion of people in their struggle for liberation. The Holy Spirit is in the communion of people as a community that builds the Church. In other words, the Holy Spirit builds the Church that is shaped by communities of followers of Jesus in concrete realities.[18] Considering Latin America, Comblin sees that a new spirituality was born, a new life in the Spirit, marked by the preferential option for the poor.

Inspired by Vatican II, especially *Lumen Gentium* 7, and aware of the experience of the Latin American Church after Medellín, Comblin reaffirms the Council's thesis that the Holy Spirit is the soul of the Church and presents the liberating experience of the Spirit within the historical praxis of the poor in Latin America. The Church does not exist without the Holy Spirit. It is the people of God gathered in community by the power of the Holy Spirit in continuity with the historical mission of Jesus Christ. In a reality of inequality and oppression, the breath of the Spirit, in continuity with Jesus's actions in favor of those who were poor and marginalized, leads and strengthens the struggle for liberation.[19]

Pneumatology and Christology are closely related in the life of the Church. After the resurrection, Jesus Christ did not send the

Holy Spirit to the constituted Church and then, just after the experience of Pentecost, begin an entire new mission. Rather, the Spirit constitutes the Church in continuity with the historical mission of Jesus. The Church exists in the segment of the directions of the Spirit in an intrinsic relationship between them—the Spirit and the Church—under the grace given by God to embody the mission of his Son. Therefore, the Holy Spirit is the soul of the Church that unites it to the Father and the Son in a historical movement.

The Holy Spirit is in the community, as communion among the people in the following of Jesus, which is the Church. For a long time, however, the influence of the theology of Robert Bellarmine, a respected Jesuit theologian and cardinal, prevailed, being embedded in the Council of Trent (sixteenth century), which understood the Church as an institution founded by Jesus and directed by the ecclesiastical hierarchy. The Spirit would assist the clerical hierarchy, giving them legitimation, holiness, and authority to lead the Catholic Church. Bellarmine's theology prevailed in theory and practice until Vatican II,[20] which brought about a change that, in practice, is still difficult to achieve. This change was possible because the Council appealed to the most ancient tradition of the Church and the New Testament to support Vatican II's ecclesiology.[21]

The New Testament does not offer many explanations about the relationship between the Holy Spirit and the Church, but it offers texts about the relationship between God and his people, and between the Spirit and the community. Some examples include the promises of the Spirit in the Johannine writings that were made to the Church (see John 15:26; 16:7), for she will lead the Church toward the truth; in Paul's letters, the Church is a concrete community animated, gathered, and guided by the Spirit (see 1 Cor 12:13; Rom 6:15; 1 Cor 10:17; 1 Cor 12:27; Rom 12:5). In the Acts of the Apostles, the Spirit raises up the apostles, who raise up communities, which were born from the experience of the Spirit and thus experience a new reality of living under the Spirit.[22]

Generally, the doctrine of the Church fathers from the first centuries of Christianity closely follows the teaching of the New Testament. St. Irenaeus, for example, said, "Where the Church is, there is the Spirit of God, and where the Spirit of God is, there is the Church and all grace. Thus, the Spirit is the truth."[23] They present a communitarian experience of the Spirit, linked to Baptism and the

Eucharist. However, there appeared in the fourth century an understanding of a pneumatology oriented by a more individual conception of the experience of the Holy Spirit that was not necessarily linked to a community. The two conceptions coexisted without major problems, as they were complementary. "The Spirit is a gift, that is received, welcomed, dwells in the Church. The Spirit guides, directs and enlightens the Church."[24] However, in the West, the Latin Church, the experience of the Spirit was increasingly linked to the ecclesial hierarchy. The Catholic Church moved from being a reality of salvation to being a means for salvation. This perspective covered up the spiritual experience of people in community. The inversion in the understanding of the experience of the Spirit remained dominant, particularly among the clergy, until the Second Vatican Council, which did not develop nor systematize a doctrine on the Spirit, per se, but opened a new perspective on the relationship between the Spirit and the Church. Although some argue that Vatican II defines the Church as people of God, it does not offer an articulated final definition. The Council highlights the role of the Spirit in the Church, presenting her as the soul of the Church. The Spirit moves the Church to be a sign of Christ in the world, unites the faithful, and continues the mission of the Son of God.

Vatican II stresses very emphatically that the Church is the people of God (*Lumen Gentium* 9) and takes up the Pauline metaphor of the body: the Church is the mystical Body of Christ. The people of God is a Body whose head and guide is Jesus Christ. What unites the members and moves them in the exercise of Jesus's mission is the Holy Spirit:

> Giving the body unity through Himself and through His power and inner joining of the members, this same Spirit produces and urges love among the believers….
>
> He [Jesus] has shared with us His Spirit who, existing as one and the same being in the Head and in the members, gives life to, unifies and moves through the whole body. This He does in such a way that His work could be compared by the holy Fathers with the function which the principle of life, that is, the soul, fulfills in the human body. (*Lumen Gentium* 7)

This conception of the Holy Spirit in the Church has great practical relevance. There is a fundamental presence of the Spirit in the Church. The theology of a spiritual Church does not deny the historical reality, contrary to any form of institutionalization, because the Spirit would be contrary to the institution. Denying the Church as an institution is difficult because the Church is part of human reality. Thus, the Holy Spirit does not deny the human and its historical-material matter. A true spiritual Church is not without an institution and, as such, the spiritual Church is not alien to the historical material reality because the Spirit calls the Church to carry out the same work that Jesus was called to perform as God's anointed and incarnate *Logos*, that is, the Word of God made human in the history of the world.[25]

The presence of the Holy Spirit in the Church is the guarantee of the continuity of Jesus's mission within human history. Comblin says, "The Spirit penetrates the inner sanctuary of the human being and makes their action spring up."[26] Being from the Spirit, the Church is formed by human beings guided by the Holy Spirit herself, but what gathers the community is not the human power or something institutional created by an individual. The gathering is the communion of people in community, originated from the people gathered in a communion of love, that is the Holy Spirit, the Creator of the Church. In this communion, which includes diversity and conflicts, the Spirit is always present because she is love, and the Church is there.

The Church is in history, suffers its influences, and influences it. Nothing is historically predetermined. The Church changes when necessary and remains the same when it does not need to change. Yet, changes in the Church do not follow the manner of secular transformation, what can frustrate many people. As Pope Francis says, "Time is greater than space" (*Evangelii Gaudium* 222–25). The Church is dynamic within the dynamism of its own history, led by its soul, the Holy Spirit. The Spirit guides, leads, and energizes the Church through communities that build their history, in processes of creation and re-recreation, between mistakes and successes. Within time, the Church is always called to carry out the mission of the Spirit in continuity with the mission of Jesus Christ. Thus, the Church acts in the world by the Spirit and communicates her charisms, gifts given to the Church to serve the world.

"The Holy Spirit shows herself through the actions she performs in people's life."[27] For this action to happen, the Spirit leads them to search for a new spirituality, one that corresponds to the circumstances of the current cultural context of those who, guided by the Spirit, realize that traditional models may not correspond to the historic moment and its specific challenges.

Two fundamental models of spiritual journeys, consolidated through people's experience, are offered by Eastern Orthodox and the Western Latin Church traditions. In their classical forms, both spiritual models face challenges in our contemporaneity. The Eastern model has deification as the work of the Spirit in the person: "God became man so that man could become God, and it touches the heart of orthodox spirituality: man becomes by grace what God is by nature."[28] This model is profound but lacks greater scope and historical reference. Many times, it sounds too abstract and distant from contemporary Christian audiences.

The Western model has received great influence from St. Augustine's theology: sin is the fundamental experience, and the Holy Spirit is the origin of the path to liberate from sin through God's grace and justification. This perspective considers people in their individuality, in which everyone is in sin and begins a process of individual salvation by the gift of the Spirit. This model also sounds far from people's concrete faith experience today because its heavy metaphysical understanding of the human nature and its relationship with God.

For José Comblin, these models are in crisis. They are in themselves insufficient for today's culture. We need new models that are closer to the historical conditions and people's concrete social and ecclesial experiences. "Historical experience has shown that the Holy Spirit raises models that correspond to the fundamental frameworks of a culture."[29] Sometimes, these models face questioning and rejection by leaders of the charismatic Church as, for instance, occurred with the medicant movement led by the Franciscans and Dominicans in the Middle Ages. This is also the case of many mystical experiences. Mystics questioned structures and even suffered persecution within their communities, such as the case of St. John of the Cross and Meister Eckhart. The charism, a grace from the Spirit, is always ahead of institutional structures of power. Charism reforms structures.[30] Comblin's pneumatology is developed within the Latin American context and the charisms raised by the Holy Spirit on that continent. In this context, the main concern is with this underdeveloped reality and poverty that were oppressing and killing vulnerable people. Thus, the Holy Spirit raises a model corresponding to this historical context, a model of a spirituality of liberating praxis.[31]

Like the historical Jesus, the Church is at the service of humanity,[32] especially the part of humanity wounded by poverty, misery, and oppression. The Church's actions are historical and anthropological efforts for the liberation of human beings from all bonds that prevent them from flourishing. Whatever the Church does toward this goal as a response to the gospel's call to bring the good news to the poor is led by the divine, that is, by the Spirit present in the Christian community.

In the Latin American reality, the starting point for Catholic social ministry is an alienation that the people of this continent experience. This oppressive integral alienation—impacting all dimensions of the life of the poor and historically marginalized groups—demands a transforming and liberating experience that takes place in the community, as a space for solidarity and collective efforts. This experience is a spiritual journey, during which the transcendent touches the imminent existence, creating the atmosphere of the Holy Spirit. This spirituality impacts peoples from different socioeconomic conditions who will converge to one single foundation, the crucified Jesus, and the option for the poor. On the one hand, there are the poor who are awakened to liberation; on the other hand, there are those who enjoy a privileged life. Transformed by the Spirit in the encounter with Jesus, they leave their privileges and join the poor in a liberating praxis. A life in the Spirit accepts the challenges of struggling for liberation, for the Spirit herself animates and sustains this struggle. She brings the community together and urges it to act with love, however difficult it may be.

This spirituality returns to biblical texts and makes Jesus's option for the poor its spiritual itinerary. This spirituality does not let those living under the atmosphere of the Holy Spirit see history from a fatalistic predetermined perspective nor run away from historical responsibility to re-create the world. In this spiritual experience, history is embraced through a commitment to transform it according to the gospel's teaching for the construction of the kingdom of God.

The challenge in Latin America is "to live according to the Spirit in the midst of the liberating struggles of oppressed Christian peoples."[33] Actually, this is the challenge that Catholics face in any context marked by injustice and oppression. This challenge calls for an incarnated spirituality, regardless of individual human wishes resulting from our human fragility and vulnerability to be seduced by material possessions. The Holy Spirit blows where she wants and when she wants, a spiritual air of liberation and detachment.

The Spirit unites and leads a community within the context in which it finds itself. The Holy Spirit raises important charisms to the historical reality, charisms of prophesy and creativity able to respond to our current challenges. In Latin America, a context that cries out for justice and liberation, the Spirit leads us to *liberation* and what is *acceptable*, just as Jesus conducted his ministry after the anointing in the synagogue. A spirituality of the poor emerges in the awakening of a new action, an action that makes the rich renounce their privileges and join the poor for justice. Seemingly new, this spirituality is not as novel as it seems because it is the spirituality of the New Testament, the spirituality that led Jesus to live among the poor and marginalized. This spirituality is the Spirit given by the risen Christ to his apostles and disciples, who animated and guided them to offer their lives to Jesus by bringing the good news to the people and serving the poor. The liberating spirituality takes us out of our comfort zone, causing us to be uncomfortable with injustice, and, therefore, leads our efforts to build a poor Church for the proclamation of the good news to the poor as privileged recipients of the kingdom of God.

THE COMMUNITY BRINGS THE GOSPEL TO THE POOR

Following Jesus Christ takes place under the Holy Spirit, who is responsible for the constitution of the Christian community, the Church—the people of God who walk in history together with the Lord. This is a community of priestly people who, as disciples and missionaries of the master Jesus, who is ever such, embrace the mission of bringing the good news to all humanity and, in a preferential way, to the poor, its privileged recipients. Thus, serving the poor, Catholic communities are a sign of life, offer hope, and represent the possibility of the kingdom of God preached by Jesus for the world.

The Catholic Church is always called to be a poor community and to announce the good news to the poor, that is, a humble community inserted in their midst and working with them for the construction of a more just, equal, and fraternal society. In this way, the Church's communities—local churches with the presence of the universal Church within a global institution—become a witness of the values of the gospel to humanity and, at the same time, invite people from other beliefs to dialogue with values for the promotion of human life and care for the earth.[34]

The text of Luke 4:16–30 shows the centrality of the poor in the ministerial activity of Jesus. The gospel, the liberation, and the acceptable year of the Lord are announced to them. This centrality is essential for all those who meet Jesus and become his disciples. The full revelation of God is in Jesus, everything he said and did. He revealed himself through being poor as a poor Messiah,[35] and his poverty enriches us with his greatness. Salvation is manifested through the poor Jesus Christ who, inserted in the most suffering reality, carried out the Father's work in history for the salvation of all. The Church continues the ministry of Jesus in all times and, just as Jesus was a sacrament of the Father manifested in history, the Church is a sacrament of Jesus. In this way, this sign of Jesus is even more visible when the Christian community is closer to poverty and to the proclamation of the good news, preferably to the poor, as did the Lord.

The Gospel narratives present Jesus as sharing the fate of the poor. He inserted himself into the world of the poor, assuming this reality in all its social, religious, and human vulnerability, with his weak and fragile flesh. Inserted into this milieu, Jesus defended the cause of the poor. Because of this activism, serving the outcast and speaking against oppressive authorities, he was arrested and condemned to die on a cross. As a result, Jesus had the same fate as the poor: dying unjustly on the margins.[36] As its inheritance and mission, the Church receives this insertion into the history, cause, and destiny of Jesus. Therefore, it is sent on a mission to announce the good news to the poor and, when it fails to do so, the same Spirit sent by Jesus at Pentecost inspires prophets who raise their voices[37] within the Church, pointing to the center of its mission: being poor, with the poor, and for the poor, looking at the utopian horizon of the kingdom of God.

During Vatican II, the Holy Spirit raised prophetic voices that pointed to the need of a Church for the poor, focusing preferentially on the little ones, those who are poor, oppressed, and marginalized. The formulation "preferential option for the poor" did not appear in the Council, but it certainly allowed the emergence of this premise as a fundamental axis of theology and pastoral ministry of the Church in Latin America. The Pact of the Catacombs was (and still is) a prophetic voice because many bishops, especially the Latin Americans led by Bishop Hélder Câmara,[38] through this pact committed themselves to live according to the luck and destiny of the poor. They understood that this commitment was necessary to proclaim the good news of liberation and the construction of the kingdom of God in history. Among other things, the bishops specifically committed to the following:

> We shall seek to live in the ordinary way of the people around us as regards accommodation, food, transport, and everything that follows from this....
>
> We renounce forever the appearance and the reality of wealth, especially in dress (rich vestments, striking colors) and in symbols made of precious metals (these signs must certainly be evangelical)....
>
> We shall give all that is required of our time, thought, heart, resources, and so on to the apostolic and pastoral service of people and groups that are workers and economically weak and underdeveloped, without letting this prejudice other people and groups in the diocese. We shall support the laity, religious, deacons and priests whom the Lord calls to evangelize the poor and the workers.
>
> We shall do everything possible to ensure that the leaders of our governments and public services adopt and put into practice the laws, structures and social institutions that are necessary for justice, equality, and the harmonious and complete development of

> the whole human being and of all human beings and thereby for the coming of a new social order worthy of human children and children of God.[39]

It is important to rescue the Pact of the Catacombs because it offers a *model* of a Church committed to poverty and to the poor. One can say that this model reflects key aspects of Lukan community, as presented in the second chapter. The model of the Lukan community was committed to embody a humble lifestyle—a poor Church—focused on the poor, a Church for the poor. This primitive community was mostly made up of members from a privileged economic situation who were called to renounce everything in favor of the poor, after their encounter of faith with Jesus Christ. On many occasions throughout history, the Church allowed itself to be attracted by power, prestige, and wealth, moving away from its liberating mission among the poor. The poor became objects of charity and not agents of liberation in the community. In these occasions, the Catholic Church, particularly its hierarchy, lost its prophetic voices, moving from a Church of the poor to a Church of the status quo.[40] The Pact of the Catacombs was emblematically a chorus of prophetic voices for the Church to return to its humble and servant origins.

The Latin American and Caribbean bishops' Document of Aparecida brings hope when it says that the community of the faithful is called to be "a dwelling place for fraternal peoples and a home for poor of God."[41] The Church is called to take up the virtue of poverty as a way of life[42] and to make a concrete option for the poor,[43] embracing the cause of the poor,[44] and standing beside them on their way.[45] Together with the poor, the Church lives out its evangelizing ministry *with*, *for*, and *from* them. Their reality and experience become the lens to read and re-create the world. Aparecida is an invitation to be a poor Church and to offer something from this condition.[46] This text stresses that "the poor are the privileged recipients of the Gospel,"[47] and evangelizing them is a sign of the presence of the kingdom of God.[48] Jesus chose to be poor and, as such, announced the kingdom of God, assuming the destiny of his social condition and liberating action. The Church must do so in the continuity of the mission of Jesus, obedient to the Spirit, rooted in the gospel, incarnated in reality, and attentive to the "signs of the times."

Fifteen years after the Document of Aparecida and six decades since the Pact of the Catacombs, their renewed christological call for a poor Church as a community for the poor is still relevant. This call has been embraced by Pope Francis through his witness as a humble servant and his writings, which highlight a humble, servant Church to be a universal call. In some of these texts, he even used the Document of Aparecida to remember this christological call. While cardinal of Buenos Aires and an active member of the CELAM (Conference of Bishops of Latin America and Caribbean), Pope Francis was one of the main contributors behind the final Document of Aparecida. In addition, I risk affirming that he knew the Pact of the Catacombs, considering the impact of this text in Latin America since the Conference of Medellín, a tradition that Francis knows well.

It is not clear the total number of bishops who signed the Pact of the Catacombs. There is a list with the names of the participants that is now at the Université Catholique de Louvain, Belgium. But this list is not official. Some of the bishops included Hélder Câmara; Antônio Fragoso; Francisco Austregésilo Mesquita Filho; João Batista da Mota e Albuquerque and his assistant Fr. Luiz Gonzaga Fernandes, who was ordained auxiliary bishop in Rome days later; Jorge Marcos de Oliveira; Henrique Golland Trindade, OFM; José Maria Pires from Brazil; Manoel Larrain from Chile; Marco Gregorio McGrath from Panama; Leonidas Proaño from Ecuador; Alberto Devoto, Vicente Faustino Zazpe, and Juan José Iriarte from Argentina; Alfredo Viola from Uruguay; and Tulio Botero Salazar from Colombia. It is also known that a few bishops from Europe, Asia, and Africa also participated in the meeting committing to the pact.[49]

Several Latin American bishops, as well as many other Christian missionaries, priests, religious and laypeople, committed themselves to this poor Church, lived this pact and were true prophets in their communities and social reality. They suffered persecutions and great injustices, such as bishops Hélder Câmara, Pedro Casaldáliga, and Leônidas Proaño. Others took up martyrdom for the evangelical cause of the poor, such as Archbishop Oscar Romero, who was canonized by Pope Francis, Archbishop Enrique Angelelli, and Archbishop Juan Gerardi.[50] This shows that taking on Jesus's mission for the cause of the poor means being willing and ready to suffer the same fate as Jesus. The readiness is strengthened by a spirituality in which, intimate with the Father, one finds the face of Christ in the poor and serves them as a real gift for others in the Spirit:

> The readiness to give of one's own life, and actually give one's life, for love, is a central element in Christian spirituality. But in the context of the reign, this readiness cannot be either purely idealistic or merely intentional. It must be real readiness. After all, persecution and death are real possibilities, as current history attests.[51]

A community of faith that embodies its discipleship in an experience of poverty and proclaims the gospel to the poor naturally becomes a prophetic community, as it goes against the established order and breaks with the apathetic complacency of our times. Conscious of its mission and united to Jesus, the community of faith embraced martyrdom for love.

With Jesus as the foundation of faith and historical partner, the community learns that all action must be based on compassion and solidarity with those who suffer. At the same time, inserted amid the poor, the Church learns that there are important values in this world where we find elements for collaboration in the project of building a "civilization of solidarity."[52] The world of the poor has a lot to offer. Without wanting to glorify this context and aware of its limitations, the reality of the poor, their suffering, and experience of faith show the need to work for the construction of a new civilization: the one of "austerity and solidarity," which must be preached as a prophecy against the accumulation of wealth, social inequality, and the greed of human beings. Thus, it is a work that goes beyond a verbal announcement of a new reality, to foster concrete actions toward the construction of this new civilization, a historical manifestation of a social experience within the current world and its injustices. This is a path carried out by the ministry of the community of faith to renew and transform the world from inside, moving forward in the direction of the utopia of the kingdom of God.[53] Only in this way, we can begin to move from a globalization of indifference toward the globalization of solidarity, one of our biggest challenges today remembered by Pope Francis.[54] Following

Jesus means walking toward this utopia, being signs of the kingdom of God for the world. From and with the poor—from vulnerable bases of society—it is possible to transform the current global order structured in a system of human and environmental exploitation. A movement grounded on a christological foundation shows compassion and solidarity as liberating values capable of improving human relationships according to justice and equity. These values come from Jesus Christ and are present in the struggle of every community of faith that is marked by oppression and marginalization.

Certainly, one of the great motivations that led Jesus to live with the poor and to dedicate his life to them was compassion. "What made Jesus different was the unrestrained compassion he felt for the poor and oppressed."[55] When we speak of compassion, we speak of a very strong feeling, in which the other becomes the destination of our love and our gratuitous action. Compassion led Jesus to live among the poor, and it moved him to act in favor of the dignity of the other. Jesus asks everyone to have the same feeling of his compassion toward others in their suffering. Thus, compassion must be the basis of the Church's action and all forms of solidarity. Compassion was like an impetus for Jesus's action in the Spirit, so it must also guide the Church's action in the Spirit.

Compassion guided Jesus's practice. Today, it becomes a key element in the struggle for justice and solidarity with the poor. In a context of crucified people, compassion needs to be placed as the engine of an action capable of defending the lives of these people. Solidarity with others in their moment of suffering becomes an imperative to live out as a disciple who follows Jesus. Loving your neighbor, united to God's love, is the greatest commandment, as Jesus says to a teacher of the law (see Mark 12:29–31). Serving the other with a *love moved by compassion* makes you detach from yourself and go to meet the other as Jesus did and taught when telling the story of the Good Samaritan (see Luke 10:25–37). In this text, we find Jesus saying that the Samaritan was *moved with compassion* (v. 33). The term used in Greek is *splanchnisthéis* (past aorist tense of the verb, *splanchnízomai*),[56] the same used when referring to the compassion Jesus has for little ones. Something very deep made the Samaritan come to the aid of a wounded man.

Compassion calls for a concrete commitment to the other, real people who are suffering as victims of any kind of violence. In the

Latin American experience, the poor are victims of a *life without life*, that is, forced to an existence without dignity, left to their own fate within the historical vulnerability of not feeling the satisfaction of freedom and the joy of life. So, moved by compassion, any intervention for the benefit of life seeks to touch the roots of injustices responsible for hurting the dignity of our people. In an encounter with the poor in their reality, *we enact solidarity with them*, being poor against poverty in the commitment to justice, so life can flourish. As Gustavo Gutiérrez says, "Solidarity with the poor means entering into their world, a long and difficult process, but necessary for a true commitment."[57]

Amid the poor, being a Christian means commitment to the liberation and life of the vulnerable. In the humble environment, among the poor, sick, the oppressed, and the marginalized, one contemplates in them the face of the crucified Jesus, a spirituality that truly hears the cry of the unfortunate in their experience of injustice and defends the values of the kingdom of God.

According to Catholic social teaching, solidarity is a principle with two complementary aspects: a *social principle* and a *moral virtue* (*Sollicitudo Rei Socialis* 38–39). These two aspects of solidarity encourage people in their relationships, lead them to commit themselves to transforming unjust structures that harm the dignity of others, and guide them in the struggle for the common good. Solidarity must be complemented by concrete actions, that is, by transformative charity. "Jesus of Nazareth makes the connection between solidarity and charity shine brightly before all, illuminating the entire meaning of this connection."[58]

Solidarity is a "way of making history" (*Fratelli Tutti* 116) that builds the possibility of justice for societies and their people. In Catholic social teaching, the virtues of solidarity and justice are closely related to social justice and peace.[59] Pope Francis says,

> Solidarity finds concrete expression in service, which can take a variety of forms in an effort to care for others. And service in great part means "caring for vulnerability, for the vulnerable members of our families, our society, our people." In offering such service, individuals learn to "set aside their own wishes and desires, their pursuit of power, before the concrete gaze of those

> who are most vulnerable....Service always looks to their faces, touches their flesh, senses their closeness and even, in some cases, 'suffers' that closeness and tries to help them. Service is never ideological, for we do not serve ideas, we serve people." (*Fratelli Tutti* 115)

Solidarity is the basis for a fair society. For that, solidarity must be a part of our ways of operating in the world and the structure that sustains political, social, and economic institutions. Thus, solidarity goes beyond sporadic acts of generosity to be a means of creating justice.

Solidarity and justice are united as virtues for the promotion of people and opportunity for the poor and the oppressed to flourish. Together, these virtues are enriched by the practice of charity as an expression of Christian love beyond the mere philanthropy that most of the time complies with systems of oppression. Charity marks justice with love in relationships between people. For this reason, Pope Benedict XVI affirms that even in a just society, charity—love—is necessary. "Love—*caritas*—will always prove necessary, even in the most just society. There is no ordering of the State so just that it can eliminate the need for a service of love" (*Deus Caritas Est* 28). We still need to do a great deal to reach this long-awaited fair society, however. The conjunction of solidarity—justice—charity is fundamental for the increasingly globalized world that gives rise to new poor and victims of oppression. Starting with its witness, the Church is called to embody charity in its communitarian relations and to embark on the struggle for a just society in which all human beings have access to the necessary means to flourish and live with dignity. The *Compendium of the Social Doctrine of the Church* states,

> It is undoubtedly an act of love, the work of mercy by which one responds here and now to a real and impelling need of one's neighbor, but it is an equally indispensable act of love to strive to organize and structure society so that one's neighbor will not find himself in poverty, above all when this becomes a situation within which an immense number of people and entire populations must struggle, and when it takes on the proportions of a true worldwide social issue.[60]

The Church's prophetic mission requires all members of the mystical Body of Christ to embrace charity/love as a fundamental aspect of daily practice toward those who cry out for immediate help. Moreover, this practice should be united, without fear, to a commitment to changing the structures that generate poverty, oppression, suffering, and premature death. Following Thomas Aquinas's perspective that love is a movement toward others resulting from God's grace and this is charity, Pope Francis affirms, "Love, then, is more than just a series of benevolent actions….Our love for other, for who they are, moves us to seek the best for their lives. Only by cultivating this way of relation to one another will we make possible a social friendship that excludes no one and a fraternity that is open to all" (*Fratelli Tutti* 93). For Francis, love/charity means commitment to justice in a society that fosters solidarity and social friendship among its citizens. The poor and the oppressed are marginalized from this friendship by structures that create and sustain their poverty and oppressions. Therefore, to live out the commitment to love the other, the neighbor demands a Church that manifests its social face through evangelizing zeal in favor of the poor and the oppressed, expressed in the Catholic social teaching as a preferential option for the poor. Making this option for justice in favor of those victims of injustice, and living it prophetically, means being faithful to the gospel.

The social ministry of the Catholic Church challenges us to be world prophets for justice, fighting for equity against the inequities that prevent people from flourishing and society from development. Peoples massacred by injustice and great social inequality, such as the impoverished and marginalized communities in Latin America and minorities in the United States, challenge the social ministry of the Church and all of us to embody practices and attitudes focused on social issues, that is, actions oriented toward the most vulnerable people in our societies. This ministry can impact social, economic, and political spheres in the defense of the poor, revealing and awakening a deep reflection on social inequalities, injustice, and oppression. It is therefore necessary and urgent to work on the concept of equity as a practical principle that reflects the preferential option for the poor, so that society can move toward justice.[61] Treating the unequal as such, prioritizes them so that they leave the underworld of exclusion and misery and are inserted into a dignified life. In a prophetic Church—shaped by active small ecclesial communities with active social ministry—that defends the interests of populations socially excluded from all historical development, equity is placed as a starting point and not equality, as this is the point of arrival of social justice.[62]

The concept of equity has been used a lot in the context of health inequalities of global and public health. For instance, the World Health Organization (WHO) affirms that promoting "equity and people-centered care" when developing health policies are essential for population health.[63] According to the WHO, health is a right and it needs to promote thought and action "maximizing equity and solidarity while being guided by responsiveness to people's needs."[64] All this needs to be done with intersectoral actions, that is, other socioeconomic actions that support people's well-being and opportunities, such as access to education, transport, jobs, clean water, and so on. Equity is, therefore, a pragmatic concept that leads us to see and act to address injustice and inequalities. Thus, we can turn to social interventions focusing on the weakest and most fragile individuals and population of society. The preferential option for the poor complements the concept of equity in many ways, but above all, it shows that those who are most vulnerable and marginalized because of injustice are not simply objects of social actions coming from the top but, rather, partners in the endeavor of building justice.[65] The unequal reality and the realization that poverty, as well as anything related to it that causes impoverishment, such as racism, sexism, and ecological degradation, is what most threatens the lives of human beings, and justifies Christian social activism in favor of the poor and the oppressed, as a double positive response to the christological call to bring the good news to the poor and to the historical appeal of the "signs of the times."

Catholic social teaching guides us in the direction of the globalization of solidarity, as emphasized by Pope Francis.[66] However, it is necessary to be clear that this teaching is not a mere theoretical argument, but rather a call to embody concrete actions reflecting Jesus's mission as it is presented in the gospel. The social teaching is not a static doctrine to believe, but a guide for actions that translate into history what you learn from what you believe: the mystery of Jesus, the Incarnate God. José Comblin affirms, "Jesus did not enunciate a doctrine, but performed significant acts—of high symbolic value—that denounced the lies of his opponents and awakened people's hope."[67] It is not enough to announce a theoretical teaching, but it must be lived out. It is not enough to say that we need a new social order, it is necessary to make this new order happen in concrete relationships in the daily life of our communities, being living witnesses of the values of the kingdom of God.

A Church of the poor is detached from the ostentation of everything that goes against poverty and a humble sustainable lifestyle. The preferential option for the poor is a radical commitment and an "ethical imperative" (*Laudato Si'* 158) that reveals the inequality and injustice existing in the world against those who are most vulnerable. There is partiality that is difficult to deny. To reach a world of equals with fairness, it is not enough to preach about equality and justice. As Jon Sobrino highlights, "In a world made up mainly of poor people, not even equality (if they had it!) would ensure that they would be taken seriously. They must be placed at the center in order not to be 'expelled' from social and ecclesial citizenship."[68]

The community of faith that proclaims the gospel to the poor as privileged recipients is a community marked by poverty, that is, a poor Church, home of the poor. This is the Church! It follows Jesus, who went to live with the poor and proclaimed the gospel to them. As the apostle Paul states, "He became poor for your sake, so that you should become rich through his poverty" (2 Cor 8:9).

INCARNATION AND THE INCULTURATION OF FAITH

The Word of God is not incarnated in the world in a generic or extra-cultural way, in order not to be a property of any restricted space or nation, but rather universal. This is not the universality of God's Word. Jesus came within a culture, in a particular socioreligious context as part of a historical period, but this does not restrict his message or eliminate his universal character. God's incarnation in history respected the limits of time, space, and humanity, so that it can be open to being universal with different faces.

The incarnation of the Word in a particular context shows us the interaction between God and humanity. The self-revelation of God to human beings does not hurt the specificity of a group to which the transcendent manifests. Human freedom, local construction, and cultural heritage are respected by the action of God who, by making the Divinity present in history, manifests the transcendent in a dialectical relationship with human culture to elevate human beings to a more fully human existence.[69]

Returning to the historical Jesus and seeking to understand his local context are opportunities to realize that he assumed all the elements of the culture where he was born and raised. He took to himself the fragile and weak humanity of the poor to be *with* and *for* them, promoting liberation by announcing the good news. In this relationship, Jesus shared with the poor the experience of their insecure life and, at the same time, the local traditions, especially religious ones, such as going to the synagogue and celebrating Easter. The entire ministry of Jesus, whose mission was to announce the kingdom of God, did not take place outside a culture, but within a sociocultural context. Jesus announced values capable of elevating a specific group in the fulfillment of its humanity. The values of the kingdom of God are proclaimed within a culture to elevate it and to denounce what dehumanizes it.

The first ones who encountered the Christ of faith and professed that he was the risen Lord arrived at this proclamation from the experience they had with Jesus of Nazareth, listening to, and witnessing his teaching and action. All this occurred within the *locus* where "the real Jesus," the historical person, was revealed.[70] Even the experience of the resurrection took place within a context, well situated in time and space. The Christ of faith was interpreted within a local experience, the reality of early Christian communities. According to each specific situation, the interpretation of Jesus as the Christ of faith followed different directions but was united by a common point: he was risen and alive, he was the Savior. Our faith is the result of a tradition coming through the witness of those who knew Jesus and first interpreted him, as a person, and his words and deeds, in the light of the paschal experience. As Andrés Torres Queiruga stresses, "The deep meaning of inquiry into the 'historical Jesus' consists precisely in moving beyond this interpretation in order to attain, through it, the *same experience* and to interpret it in *our* culture."[71]

God revealed the transcendent mystery in Jesus inserted into a culture. Thus, Jesus's actions became a paradigm for every culture in an *intracultural* way, not to destroy cultures, but to elevate them by promoting their people. Jesus embraces his full culture and context as his own historical existence and so the cultures where we experience Jesus in our time and space. He does not deny the local specificity but is a prophet with a message against what dehumanizes.

After the paschal experience, Jesus's disciples looked back to the life and teaching of their master with a different perspective, now provided by the encounter with the resurrected. The entire experiences with him were felt with another sense after the resurrection, gaining a new meaning. In addition, particular situations and challenges faced by each faith community (believers in Jesus as the risen Christ) contributed to the understanding of Jesus's life and teaching, in a process of construction and consolidation of who Jesus is and his relevance for people's existence. This is relevant for those parts of the New Testament that were written having as a starting point the interaction between the experience of faith and the concrete situation of communities. Each text portrays a Jesus reflecting the concrete context of a community, considering its internal and external conflicts, with the joy and hope of being a follower of Jesus and dialoguing with converts from different religious backgrounds and nationalities. This is one of the reasons for Luke's text being concerned with the universality of Jesus's message and emphasis on issues related to poverty and helping the poor. This aspect is quite unlike Matthew, who wants to show Jesus as the new Moses, the true interpreter of the Scriptures, a Jesus in constant conflict with the Pharisees. Luke sets this tone for his text because his community was made up of many Christians who were coming from the Hellenistic culture and religions (with many gods), while Matthew was part of a community formed by Jews in a period known as Formative Judaism, during which there were a great conflict with the Pharisees.[72]

The New Testament offers a plurality of christological interpretations, precisely because the experience of the risen Christ and the interpretation of Jesus's life are incarnated in a particular context. Each community has its experience of salvation within its *locus*, which "provides grounds for various christological interpretations."[73] This diversity of views in the New Testament prevents us from an absolutization of dominant christological perspectives and reveals the richness that a plurality of christological interpretations has to offer to our experience of faith. According to Roger Haight, the diversity of Christologies is a gift for the Christian tradition, but interpretations cannot be made simply considering individual subjectivity. They must obey certain criteria within a faith intelligently understood from the commitment to Jesus as the salvific mediator between God and the human being:

> If it [Christology] accounts for the data of scripture, is intelligible in terms of a contemporary understanding of reality, and empowers Christian life after the pattern of Jesus' own preaching, it is an orthodox christology. That there can be several irreducible christologies that fill those criteria is proved by the New Testament itself.[74]

These Christologies must be developed to promote a greater incarnation of faith in particular cultures, so they can elevate them to be more fully human. A Christology that considers the local reality presents the face of Jesus with the features of the people who listen to and accept his message. For example, Jesus Christ has a face marked by poverty in an impoverished community, an indigenous face among the indigenous people, a black face in the faith experience of Afro-communities, even a woman's face among women's groups who fight for gender equality from their encounter with Jesus. An enculturated and dynamic Christology with features of local cultures and struggles highlights aspects of Jesus related to his liberating ministry among the poor and marginalized.

Guided by the Holy Spirit, each generation and people (*pueblo*, *povo*) find Jesus Christ and God's Word spoken within their context and time. This encounter inspires human beings in their own history, within local traditions, customs, and liturgical feasts enlightened by the gospel message that becomes part of people's lives. Each Christology appears in a specific context within the horizon of different experiences to answer its own questions, facing the concrete problems of a people. "[Christologies] result from a re-reading of the Gospels from a particular location."[75] This is part of the dialectic between God and the reality of people in each geography and historicity.

The geographic place I develop this Christology is Latin America and the historical time is the beginning of the second decade of the twenty-first century. The place is inhabited by great plurality of peoples (*pueblos* who share the lands of a same continent, with an experience that constitutes the existence of the Latin American *pueblos*), having a strong Christian presence, but also wounded by poverty and oppression contrary to the Christian ideal. In other words, *pueblos* of this land are a diverse and crucified people. Whether considering a broad view such as Latin America generally and its inequalities, or small contexts of historically marginalized groups in a country (for example, Black and immigrants in the United States), Christology must be a theological endeavor that reflects Jesus incarnated in concrete realities to respond to historical challenges.

The Document of Aparecida says that Latin America has a great wealth and cultural diversity of peoples. "There are diverse indigenous, African-American, mestizo, peasant, urban, and suburban cultures in our region."[76] Each culture with its richness coexists with unequal conditions within the so-called globalized culture.[77] In addition, the document recognizes that these cultures offer values in the face of the anti-values of (postmodern) culture that are imposed through mass communication vehicles. Aparecida spoke about Latin America, but its message goes beyond that region because many other parts of the world share the same challenges with Latin American people. Everywhere, one finds rich cultures struggling to survive amid socioeconomic injustice and exploitation of powerful forces, operating in a paradigm of prejudice and economic greed. Pope Francis shows the expansion of this view when he states,

> Destroying self-esteem is an easy way to dominate others. Behind these trends that tend to level our world, there flourish powerful interests that take advantage of such low self-esteem, while attempting, through the media and networks, to create a new culture in the service of the elite. This plays into the opportunism of financial speculators and raiders, and the poor always end up the losers. Then too, ignoring the culture of their people has led to the inability of many political leaders to devise an effective development plan that could be freely accepted and sustained over time. (*Fratelli Tutti* 52)

When Francis chose the parable of the good Samaritan as the foundation for his proposal of a society grounded on fraternity and social friendship,[78] he offers a social teaching that flourishes from a historical encounter with Jesus, oriented to answer socioeconomic challenges afflicting people's lives, especially the most vulnerable.

Christology, as a reflection of an incarnate faith through culture and social challenge, exposes what does not serve to promote and elevate the humanity of the human being. Francis believes that fraternity and social friendship (as an expression of solidarity) help human beings in their social organizations to grow in their humanity. Thus, evangelization has, as a primary goal, the proclamation of the values of the kingdom of God, summarized in Luke 4:16–30: *liberation and the acceptable year of the Lord*. This proclamation is first to the poor in a preferential option for them because Jesus addresses them in a privileged way.

Roger Haight suggests that the Catholic Church is in a new global situation with three tensions: between the local and the global, between rich and poor, and the relationship between the Church and other religious traditions.[79] He speaks from the context of North America—that has particularities and differences compared with the Latin American one—but he thinks these tensions are global. In a globalized world, therefore, Haight offers insight on some issues for the global Church and its local manifestations in realities across the globe, especially considering that communities anywhere are part of the macro reality of the Catholic Church, and they suffer the influences of what he calls postmodern culture.

Within these three tensions suggested by Haight, there is no doubt that the tension between rich and poor draws our attention regarding the existing inequality in Latin America, marked by concentration of income and assets in the hands of a few, while much of the population suffers from poverty and marginalization. The reality of socioeconomic inequality is growing around the world, including the United States, where Black and Latino communities are disproportionally impacted. This tension also exists in the relationship among Latin American countries, wounded by underdevelopment and victims of the neoliberal market, and rich countries, which dominate the capital and control the international economy. These local and global contexts demand a Christology that is prophetic and announces the values of the kingdom of God through the preferential option for the poor for the promotion of the human being as a whole, that is, an integral development, to use the language from Catholic social teaching.[80]

The Church's mission must closely follow the footsteps of Jesus's ministry. The kingdom of God is what Jesus preached, living with the poor and against their oppressors. It was not a proselytizing practice or a preaching of conversion from one faith to another, but rather a preaching of values capable of elevating the human being and building a new world order. This does not prevent conversions from happening, but, in the first place, there is the struggle for human life, for justice, and an experience of love, that is, showing the message of the liberation and life of the kingdom of God proclaimed by Jesus:

> The reign of God is God's will being done. Christians read this will of God in the teaching and action of Jesus. It manifests itself in his call for repentance and conversion, in his parables of a reversal of selfish human values, in his healing of the sick, in his association with the poor, in his concern for the dignity, personhood, participation, and the human flourishing of the marginated, in their instinctive siding with the oppressed and underdog. These things which seem so earthly in the telling are of God; they are God's reign; they are God's and Jesus' mission.[81]

Consequently, inculturation becomes prophetic and leads us to face everything that contradicts the values of the kingdom of God. To proclaim the good news is to defend what Jesus defended and, therefore, to respond with careful attention to the specific questions raised in the context of each people. Marked by a crucified people, inculturation in Latin America and Latino communities elsewhere must respond to the aspirations of its people.

The ministry of announcing the good news should be done from the perspective of dialogue to better respect the freedom of the other and contribute to the realization of a collective construction of a just society. The values of the kingdom of God must be presented in a dialogical perspective; thus, the relationship with the other—from another religion, from another culture, and from different mindsets and identities—does not become a relationship of hardening on both sides, but rather a search for common grounds that permit the construction of bridges able to sustain a collective and sustainable promotion of the human. This would be a prophetic endeavor. From the Church's perspective, there is not an explicit formal desire to build a uniform Christian society and to overcome other traditions. Uniformity does not match with the plurality of Christologies in the New Testament nor with the anthropological reality of peoples. Instead, there is a desire to spread the values of the kingdom of God along with other traditions toward the common goal of human flourishing.[82] Hence, the Church becomes a witness of the kingdom of God, a partner in a common cause, and a sign of life for the world.

In Latin America, a markedly Christian continent, a dialogical perspective necessarily involved a relationship with the cultures of its peoples, which have a history of more than five hundred years of evangelization and thousands of years of religious ancestry. The incarnation of the Christian faith springs from a dynamic relationship among gospel, culture, and the ancestry of original people (older than even the incarnation of the Word in a local culture and a land in Israel). From this relationship originated Latin American Christianity, which, despite many existing attempts to make it to look similar to a European manifestation of faith, has its own identity, with the brown and the black faces of La Virgen de Guadalupe and Our Lady of Aparecida. It is not the Christianity of Europe brought by the colonizers, but a faith resulting from a dialectical relationship among the universal gospel, the transcultural transcendent, and the autochthonous cultures existing across Latin America. (This dialectic is also the origin of European Catholicism, as one manifestation of the faith in a local reality.) Within this relationship, we also have a dialectic between the faith initially brought (and many times imposed) by European colonizers and missionaries and the culture they found in the "foreigners"—the peoples of the so-called New World.

All this dialectical interaction gave birth to the Church in Latin America, which is the same universal Church of Jesus Christ, but with the face of inculturation, because the gospel is alive, historically incarnated by the power of the Holy Spirit.

Despite all the problems and abuses that existed in the evangelization process of Latin America, history shows that the Spirit sowed her seed in a new land. The *authentic inculturation* took place at the bottom, starting from the humble people of the land themselves, especially from the poor and marginalized. It has been a process from below in which the incarnate Jesus becomes uniquely present in popular religiosity, an expression of faith with great existential and theological meanings for Catholic communities.

Mariological manifestations of faith in Latin America help us to see this process of faith inculturation from below more clearly.[83] Much before the arrival of the Christian faith in Latin America, many original peoples of this vast land had a powerful connection with a spiritual experience of a female transcendent reality. This is very connected with the earth, having a strong harmony with nature. *Pachamama*, the mother-earth, is perhaps the most known manifestation of this spirituality. In many regions of Latin America, its peoples have great proximity to the Blessed Virgin Mary, mother of Jesus, with a huge diversity of Mariological devotions, in which Mary gained the face of each people, particularly the oppressed people, such as Our Lady of Aparecida in Brazil, a Black Virgin Mary, and Our Lady of Guadalupe in Mexico, with an indigenous face. *El acontecimiento guadalupano* (the Guadalupian event) is an example and proof of an authentic inculturation and incarnation of the gospel in the culture of a people made by the poor, since the Virgin of Guadalupe stands alongside the indigenous people marginalized and impoverished by the process of colonization.[84]

In the original *Nican Mopohua* text of this event—the text with the story of the apparitions of the Virgin in Tepeyac, Mexico—one finds a paradigm of an authentic inculturation of faith. A process carried out by the poor people themselves, not by the ecclesiastical authorities, which gave rise to the deep faith of the Mexican people and conferred a national identity. The text brings a message of liberation, addressed to the poor as its privileged recipients, a result of the dynamic interaction of the gospel and the action of the Holy Spirit within a culture, a worldview, and lives of the poor. The Guadalupian event offers the message of the kingdom of God proclaimed by Jesus, placed under the protection of the Blessed Virgin Mary, the Mother of God, and our Mother, as the *Nican Mopohua* text refers to Mary.[85]

According to Richard Nebel, the message of *Nican Mopohua* is currently becoming a model of an enculturated evangelization for Latin America.[86]

Popular religiosity is one of the greatest riches of Latin American peoples, as expressed in the Document de Aparecida and supported by the magisterium of Pope Francis.[87] This religiosity is the result of the incarnation of the Christian faith in the customs and traditions of these peoples, with elements of traditional Catholicism. The inculturation originates in a dialogical interaction (sometimes more tense, sometimes less so) that gives rise to something new and original. The Guadalupian event is a paradigm of faith inculturation. In popular religiosity, one finds Christ suffering in the face of the poor, the indigenous, and the oppressed, but also finds the merciful Christ, compassionate and servant, in the relationship between the poor and a God who is close to them. This expression of faith manifests a living gospel in relationships among the poor, united by the disfigurement that the situation of poverty and oppression causes. There, Jesus Christ has been incarnated in a culture from which we learn to live in solidarity and to trust God through faith, charity, and hope.

A CELEBRATION OF FAITH WITH THE FACE OF LOCAL PEOPLE

If we have a Christ with the face of the people who welcome him and assume him as a way of life and salvation, the liturgical celebration of these people will correspond to this Christ, who is incarnated in the local culture. The celebration of the Paschal Mystery is existentially experienced and ethically embraced by all who place their faith and hope in Jesus Christ.

The Second Vatican Council's document on the liturgy, *Sacrosanctum Concilium*, aims to encourage greater participation of the faithful in liturgical celebrations and, thus, provide them with a deep identification with the Paschal Mystery celebrated with their existence and daily lives. This perspective allowed the Catholic liturgy to undergo some adaptations,[88] such as the celebration of the Eucharist in the vernacular, that is, the language spoken by local communities.[89] The proximity created by these adaptations is essential so the gospel can be incarnated in a culture and provide an authentic encounter with Jesus Christ and meaning for people's lives. The faithful now hear the Mass in the language they speak at home, the same one they express their personal and cultural identity, the same one that they now listen to the Mystery of God.

Liturgical and sacramental celebrations have an anthropological-existential foundation because, in celebrating the Memorial of Christ, the life of the human being rescued and loved by God's grace is celebrated. The experience of life is sacramental and ritual. The sacraments of the christological faith are linked to the life of the community and to the entire existence of a person in her key moments. The seven sacraments are not only understood at their historical-conscious level, in which one can date their establishment, but also at their structural-unconscious level, which translates the fundamental axes of human life. The sacraments accompany the life of the believer, from birth linked to Baptism; to food for existence, the Eucharist; and to illness and death, Anointing of the Sick. "The external rites flesh out the deeper, underlying experience that may even be unconscious. Where life is personally experienced in a radical way, there God is experienced."[90]

Worship is existential and inseparable from the concrete life of a community.[91] When we celebrate Easter, it happens in our lives, and we harvest the fruits of liberation. For the harvest and the food (in the rite), is the remembrance of a fact, Easter, which was an agricultural festival in its remote origin. We give a theological meaning to this feast, a paschal event, and celebrate it as a memorial of *passion, death, and resurrection* in our lives (the union between the theological and the anthropological). This fact ritually occurs in the memorial today and this allows the faithful to be present in the fact, that is, the people are included in the Passover of Jesus.[92]

The celebrated liturgy requires a commitment from all who participate in the sacrament to others among us here (in the liturgical community) and elsewhere (in the broad social community). The social dimension is in the nature of the Catholic liturgy, as there is no liturgical celebration without a gathered assembly. Considering her particular Church, Ione Buyst stresses that "the Latin American Church, in the effervescence of the conciliar renewal, has learned to live and interpret facts like these [the Council and Latin American Episcopal Conferences] and the entire social and political life of the continent, as an Easter process. In them God is at work, Christ is actively present."[93] The paschal fact is actualized and realized in the concrete reality of the people. The memorial of the passion, death, and resurrection of Jesus is not celebrated as a distant historical fact, but in the present, in a specific reality, with its pains and joys. This realization of the existential paschal experience is possible thanks to the Spirit, who enlightens, drives, and guides the people in their historical reality.

Christian worship unites the sacred with the "profane" life, that is, everyday existence is united within a sacramental worship. True Christian worship takes place in the concrete life and has as its principle the life of Jesus Christ, a pleasing worship—the only and final sacrifice—to God, the Father. This makes all Christian ritual christological and existential.[94] Thus, the liturgy celebrated in Latin America, especially in impoverished communities, is united with the life of the people and their suffering because Christ is present, *Emmanuel—God with us*, in the historical context.

In their worship, Catholics offer their existence to the Father, and in the sacramental liturgy, they remember the mystery of Christ in their own existence. The memorial is current and present in the concrete life of each believer, transforming it in an ongoing process between the transcendent and the immanent. Existence itself gives consistency to the liturgy that is sacramental and not simply to a rite of repetition. Worship and life are not separate, because the life of the believer is the first liturgy. The rite helps in this union, when a "ritual sacramental memory" is made, within a christological ritual. "The liturgy is an expression of the definitive action that God carries out in history through his Son Jesus."[95]

A sacrament takes place in an encounter between God and the human beings who welcome what is transcendent. Moreover, the encounter occurs within a historical reality, involving the specific context of each culture where the sacrament is celebrated. Incarnated in a reality, God makes a proposal (the initiative is always from God's grace) and expects a free answer from the person, made with her own identity and questions originated in her *locus*. Offering a positive answer, the individual accepts God's proposal, and thus, the grace is completed (the grace of God's initiative and the grace of personal positive answer). This encounter, between God's proposal and the personal acceptance, is celebrated sacramentally. However, the celebration is not just a rite, but rather the high point of a sacramental life, in which human beings discover God and the trinitarian grace through gestures of life. The poor know how to perceive the wonderful gestures of God in their lives, even within the tragic situation in which they live. After the celebration, there is an extension of the sacramental grace in the ethical life that has been supplied to embody the liberating project of Jesus Christ. The sacrament leads to an existential commitment to change practice into *praxis*, starting from conversion and hoping for liberation through Jesus Christ. Therefore, anyone who eats, that is, receives the eucharistic communion, is to become communion for the other.[96]

Sacramental actions express and manifest a reality united to our life: our life in Christ's existence. Sacramental liturgies are linked to our reality, so in Latin America, a reality marked by social injustice, the sacraments become more sensitive to social reality and the prophetic mission of Christians. The kingdom of God acquires a prophetic tone, a christological prophetism, that will be part of the sacramental celebration of any community marked by the cross of oppression.[97]

In Christian communities across the world, every struggle of the people for liberation, in its political and social fight in search of better living conditions to flourish, is based on faith in the Paschal Mystery of Jesus Christ, confident in his active presence in the historical reality, as a companion in the suffering of oppressed people.

Considering the Latin American community, the celebration of the Eucharist is linked to the struggle of their poor people. Ione Buyst, who breaks the bread in these communities and writes about their experience, stresses,

> We announce the death of the Lord which continues to take place in the passion and death of the poor. We proclaim the resurrection of the Lord who projects himself in the resistance and organization of the poor for better living conditions, for participation and citizenship, for a civilization of love, for a society where there is no more misery or oppression, but rather equality of conditions for all.[98]

In Latin America, the existential aspect of the liturgy enters the life of the people in their struggle for liberation. The people's passion and Christ's own passion in resistance through prophetic struggle for the construction of life is Christ's own resurrection; the people's Easter is Christ's Easter. This is Jesus Christ within the life and culture of Latin American peoples in search for realizing the liberating project that Jesus announced in the synagogue of Nazareth. It is a Catholic Church, the people of God, a sign of God's kingdom under the anointing of the Holy Spirit, and the continuation of the historical mission of Jesus Christ.

5

The Centrality of the Sick and the Poor in Jesus's Mission

The last three chapters were a comprehensive theological account, presented based on the central biblical text: Luke 4:16–30. Theological contents were discussed from an experience of faith in Latin American communities marketed by poverty and oppression. They offered the theological *locus* to read the Gospel and interpret theological themes in Luke 4. Chapters 2, 3, and 4 followed the methodology and theological perspective discussed in chapter 1. Now, we continue the development of a Christology by focusing on a specific field that relates theology and health-care ethics, precisely in global health and theological bioethics. The context for a theological approach of this chapter and the following ones will be global public health and its ethical challenges.

Catholic communities have developed many projects and created uncountable institutions to serve the sick. Historically, the Catholic Church—through its religious orders, devoted Catholics, and lay and clerical organizations—has always acted in the field of health care, primarily caring for the destitute and the sick. In many places, the first "hospitals" were created by the Catholic Church and its members. Thus, when one considers global health as an international collective endeavor to address health disparities and promote health and well-being particularly in regions marked by poverty—a term of secular origin—it is fair to recognize that Catholic institutions and communities have been very active in this field, so much so that the care for the destitute and the sick is regarded as a key element of the mission of the Church.

In my experience in the field of global health from a theological approach, I often highlight the mission of the Catholic Church to care for the sick by directly addressing where this care should be delivered, and then how to promote this care, as well as who must be partnered in providing it. In the context of global health, we are faced with the reality of the poor and those most vulnerable to illness suffer due to of lack of proper health care. This leads us to focus on the need for a preferential option for the poor[1] in health care, a Catholic social principle that serves as a guide for efforts in promoting health and well-being for the most disadvantaged of our societies.

It is a fact that the main cause of health issues, diseases, and premature death is poverty.[2] This single cause creates a vicious cycle[3] that begins with injustice and ends with death. Poverty is *not* a natural phenomenon, but a socioeconomic creation that makes people *vulnerable to illness*. Once sick, a poor person does *not have access to necessary medical care*. This leads to *more suffering*, making the person poorer and sicker. Consequently, the poor *person dies* through a denial of his/her dignity. Even rich countries suffer with this reality, with poverty and lack of access to proper health care impacting marginalized, impoverished communities. (The way that the COVID-19 pandemic disproportionally impacted African American and Latino/a communities in the United States reveals this connection among poverty, socioeconomic injustice, and health care.)

Therefore, the preferential option for the poor guides us to a perspective that places the poor at the center of global health efforts to break this vicious cycle. This Catholic social principle inverts the most common logic of global health governance from a top-down to a bottom-up approach. Therefore, we look at global health challenges from the social *locus* where these victims of structural violence are *from below*. This approach recognizes value in the experience of the poor and includes their voices at the center of our discussion and actions in global and public health.

Regardless, I must make a self-criticism that applies to many works in theological ethics and Catholic bioethics. This criticism concerns presenting Catholic social principles, such as the preferential option for the poor, as important resources for global and public health, especially in a reality marked by poverty. These presentations often show the pragmatic aspect of these principles but sometimes forget to present their foundations, most notably their biblical foundations. The goal of this chapter is to reflect on the biblical foundation of the option for the poor and the Christian mission of caring for the sick and poor. We conclude this chapter by offering key elements of a liberation approach to global health grounded on this biblical foundation.

BIBLICAL FOUNDATIONS FOR CATHOLIC MISSION IN GLOBAL HEALTH

Biblical studies and those related to pastoral care have significant scholarship about the healing aspect of Jesus's historical mission, and how the Church has continued this mission throughout history. It is common to see Catholic health institutions state that their mission is to continue the healing ministry of Jesus. This is seen, for example, in the mission statement from the Catholic health institution, Christus Health: "Our mission [is] to extend the healing ministry of Jesus Christ,"[4] and that of the Catholic Health Association: "Catholic health care is a ministry of the Catholic Church continuing Jesus' mission of love and healing in the world today."[5]

Gospel passages with Jesus caring for the sick are regularly presented to illustrate the biblical foundation for this health-care mission. There are many of these passages in all four Gospel narratives. Jesus healed people with skin diseases, a woman with a hemorrhage, blind men, and a child. He even brought his dear friend, Lazarus, back to life. Perhaps the most repetitive action of Jesus in the Gospels is related to his ministry to the sick, most of them poor and marginalized. In addition, Jesus told stories to show the importance of caring for those who are sick. These stories include the parable of the Good Samaritan (Luke 10:29–37) and the allegory of the Last Judgement: "I was sick, and you visited me" (Matt 25:36).

There is no doubt that the historical ministry of Jesus has the care for the sick, particularly the impoverished and marginalized sick, at the center of the mission.[6] This care is, in turn, placed at the center of the mission of his followers. The connection of the sick and the poor was present in the ministry of Jesus, and most Catholic health institutions highlight this connection in their mission statements, for example, Ascension Health states, "Rooted in the loving ministry of Jesus as healer, we commit ourselves to serving all persons with special attention to those who are poor and vulnerable."[7]

One can say the option for the poor is clearly present in Jesus's ministry for the sick. Continuing this ministry means an option for the poor in health care. We need to observe the action of the historical Jesus to understand this option in his actions and the relevance of it for the ministry of the Church.

Considering Jesus ministry, the choices that he made—going where life was most threatened to help the poor, the sick and the suffering—and his cry against all forms of injustice and oppression that hurt people's dignity, it is possible to know, concretely, that Jesus chose to promote all human lives beginning with those who have been prevented from flourishing with dignity. Moreover, he was killed because of this choice of promoting the life of the oppressed and marginalized. It was a redemptorist death, freely accepted, that united historical and eschatological salvation. Therefore, the eschatological salvation is a continuation of a historical life with dignity sustained by justice. Where this has been broken by oppression, poverty, and marginalization, the mission of the Church is to work to rebuild justice to sustain human dignity. Inspired by Jesus's deeds and teaching, the historical mission of Jesus's disciples includes the defense and the promotion of life with dignity from those bearing the burden of oppression and its consequences, such as the impacts of health inequalities. Following Jesus means making his choices and going to where the poor and oppressed are crying out for help, health, and dignity.

The Beatitudes in Luke 6:20–23 (see also Matt 5:1–12) show how blessed are the poor, the hungry, and those who weep. They will have the kingdom of God and will be satisfied and comforted. Happy are also those who are persecuted for Jesus's sake, that is, for being Jesus's disciple following in his footsteps in proclaiming the good news to the poor as privileged recipients (see Luke 4:16–19). Catholic health ministry must understand that its mission is to go to where the poor, the hungry, and those who weep are. This is a Samaritan solidarity (see Luke 10:2–37), marked by a union between physical care (for example, medical assistance) and a social care (for example, fight against health inequalities). As a social virtue stated by Pope John Paul II,[8] solidarity is unified by these two aspects of caring for the sick—practical action and social activism.

The Episcopal Conference of Latin American and Caribbean Bishops (CELAM) presents that Jesus's actions communicate his mission of promoting the value of life to the Church:

> Jesus, the Good Shepherd, wants to communicate his life to us and to place himself at the service of life. We see how he approaches the blind on the way (Mark 10:46–52), when he dignifies the Samaritan woman (John 4:7–26), when he heals the sick (Matt 11:2–6), when he feeds the hungry (Mark 6:30–44), when he frees the demon possessed (Mark 5:1–20). In his kingdom of life, Jesus includes everyone: he eats and drinks with sinners (Mark 2:16), regardless of being treated like a glutton and a drunk (Matt 11:19); he touches lepers with his hands (Luke 5:13), lets a prostitute anoint his feet (Luke 7:36–50) and, at night, receives Nicodemus to invite him to be born again (John 3:1–15). Likewise, he invites his disciples to reconciliation (Matt 5:24), to love the enemies (Matt 5:44) and to opt for the poorest (Luke 14:15–24).[9]

Although the Gospels present Jesus discoursing about his ministry, it is through his own actions that his teaching gains meaning and concrete relevance, pointing out the value of life and where his disciples should promote it.

Jesus had a posture of total gratuitousness, with unconditional acceptance of the other. He was not afraid of criticism and made his life an expression of love in total self-giving to the other, to the point of offering his own life. Jesus's life reveals an authentic existence and rescues us from the slavery of an individualistic world, so we experience the mystery of communion with God and our neighbor. This mystery is capable of leading, by the power of the Holy Spirit, the Catholic health ministry to serve the sick who are not only suffering because of an illness, but also the impoverished sick who cry for justice, revealing that their illness is a result of injustice and health inequalities. "Faced with exclusion, Jesus defends the rights of the weak and the dignified life of every human being. From his Master, the disciple has learned to fight against every form of disdain for life and exploitation of the human person."[10]

Jesus's ministry was marked by caring for the poor and the sick. This is clear in the Gospels. Grounded on the gospel's message, Catholic health ministry has no choice but making its health-care service a work for the poor who are disproportionally vulnerable to fall ill and then prevented from finding proper medical assistance. In many cases, this leads to premature death. Catholic health ministry cannot pick and choose where and who to serve, especially if the choice is playing in a health market for those patients who can pay. Guided by the christological faith, Catholic health ministry is, above all, for the impoverished and marginalized sick. Thus, the option for the poor is at the center of this ministry.

In the Document of Aparecida, CELAM's bishops state that the preferential option for the poor is an option from "our christological faith."[11] Pope Francis reaffirmed this (see *Evangelii Gaudium* 198) and added, "We need only look around us to see that, today, this option [for the poor] is in fact an ethical imperative essential for effectively attaining the common good" (*Laudato Si'* 158). The option for the poor is necessary for attaining the common good, a condition for human flourishing. The common good includes health care and well-being, including decent living conditions and access to opportunities that allow people to flourish. Therefore, care for the sick, including global health initiatives that promote social justice for population health, embraces the preferential option for the poor as an ethical imperative originated in our christological faith for attaining the common good.

What does "attaining the common good" mean in this health and well-being context? It means that continuing the healing ministry of Jesus is not simply providing health care for those who are sick. It is not simply designating some health-care resources to those who are poor as an act of charity, or as a humanitarian effort to help suffering impoverished people. This is only a part of the ministry that addresses a small piece of the problem and does not "effectively" lead impoverished and oppressed populations to "attaining the common good." The preferential option for the poor that continues the healing ministry of Jesus is also fighting against the system and the structures responsible for creating poverty and oppression. These are the very systems and structures that make people vulnerable to illness and dying prematurely because of the lack of good living conditions, opportunities, and access to health care.

Continuing the healing ministry of Jesus in history does not mean playing with the socioeconomic system, maintaining the status quo (sometimes even promoting it), and providing some care for the poor who are sick. The healing ministry of Jesus is prophetic because it provides a comprehensive perspective in caring for the sick. This includes the option for the poor and liberation from oppression for the "year acceptable of the Lord," a jubilee year when all can attain the common good. There is no care for the sick detached from a commitment to the liberation of the poor and oppressed. This comes, as CELAM and Pope Francis stress, from the biblical roots that shape our christological faith.

THE INTEGRAL HEALING MINISTRY OF JESUS

As previously stated, Gospel narratives about Jesus's healing of the sick are frequently used to highlight his healing ministry and are often presented as the foundation for the Church's mission in health care. Sometimes, however, there is a narrow understanding of these narratives, which lacks consideration for the entire ministry of Jesus and the privileged recipients of the good news. This understanding fails to present the link between the healing ministry, the poor, liberation, and the common good. The healing ministry of Jesus is part of an integral program (I use the word *integral*, referring to the perspective of *integral development* as presented by Pope Paul VI in his encyclical *Populorum progressio*), which is clearly present in the Gospel of Luke when Jesus launches his program of actions in a synagogue in Nazareth, known as "The Galilean Ministry" (see Luke 4:16–30).

The previous chapters offered a detailed exegetic–hermeneutical analysis of this Lukan text and its christological value for our faith and the ecclesiastical mission of Jesus's disciples. Considering this analysis, I will note again some key christological elements of this text, since they form the foundations for our historical mission of continuing the healing ministry of Jesus.

Although this text has parallel texts of Jesus in a synagogue (cf. Mark 6:1–6 and Matt 13:53–58), this Lukan text displays a unique aspect of its author and his/her communitarian experience of faith and social challenges. As developed in previous chapters, Luke 4 is a unique creation of the Lukan community, a diverse group of Jesus's followers committed to austerity and supporting the poor and oppressed. It is worth noting again that Luke presents Jesus reading a text of the prophet Isaiah in the synagogue, something unique in the entire New Testament. In this scene of Jesus reading the words of the prophet and his message, we find the core of Jesus's ministry:

1. *to bring the good news to the poor* (the poor are the privileged recipients of the gospel);
2. *to proclaim liberty to captives* (new opportunities and freedom are given to those who made something wrong, that is, mercy);
3. *to give sight to the blind* (healing the sick and the disable);
4. *to free the oppressed* (promoting liberation from oppression); and
5. *to proclaim the year acceptable to the Lord* (building a new time and new society based on God's justice).

According to Luke, the ministry of Jesus is centered on these five core aspects in an internal equilibrium. This equilibrium matches the dynamism of human societies in which all aspects of its development are interconnected. Hence, Jesus's ministry reveals actions for an integral development that is stressed by Catholic social teaching. This teaching suggests that the mission of the Catholic Church to continue the healing ministry of Jesus is not limited to care for those who are sick. It also includes a prophetic praxis, which includes the poor, toward attaining the common good and freeing the oppressed from the structures of oppression and injustice that are responsible for the vicious cycle: poverty; vulnerability to illness; lack of health care; and premature death. Bringing the good news to the poor and proclaiming the year acceptable of the Lord in health care includes caring for the sick and freeing the oppressed. That is liberation, a truth from our christological faith. Any care for the sick that ignores systemic structures responsible for creating poverty and oppression limits the healing mission to a palliative role. This facilitates keeping, and in many cases promoting, these structures of oppression. This partial ministry is not the healing ministry or mission of Jesus.

Moreover, Luke 4:16–30 goes beyond this practical teaching about Jesus's mission. It also forms the source for a theological understanding of our faith in God based on a christological account developed in the Gospel. The passage reveals the mystery of God and the mission of Jesus's disciples in a profound depth of interaction, with the concrete historical experience of a community and its struggles for liberation. This demonstrates a harmonic circular relationship between the Scriptures and the experience of a community in history.

In Luke 4:16–30, Jesus is anointed by the Spirit to lead a mission entrusted by the Lord God, the Father. In this mission, the poor are presented as the privileged recipients of the gospel message. This New Testament pericope indicates a search for understanding the joint mission of the Word (Jesus) and the Spirit in communion with the Father, revealing the trinitarian mystery of God. At the same time, the Lukan text suggests the Church's mission is to continue the work of Jesus in history under the guidance of the Holy Spirit. Thus, Luke 4 allows us to realize the actions of Jesus in history guided by the Spirit. The same Spirit empowers the Church to continue the ministry of Jesus throughout history. Announcing the gospel of liberation (the good news) to the poor was a central part of Jesus's ministry. Within the liberating gospel, the healing of the sick occurs with no contradiction to practices of medical care and justice in health care, but rather being complementary to them. Thus, the earthly journey of the Catholic Church is to continue Jesus's mission of liberation and healing in history assisted by the Holy Spirit. The christological understanding of Luke 4 has theological trinitarian implications (the trinitarian mystery revealed by Jesus) and ecclesiological enlightenment on the Church's historical mission for integral development.

These previous two paragraphs summarize the theological thesis developed in chapter three with ecclesial and social implications. Hence, Luke 4:16–30 reveals the pivotal event that provides a Christology that unifies all interconnected aspects of Christian life and the Church's mission in history. This mission is to bring the good news to the poor, care for sick, free the oppressed, and build a new realty for "effectively attaining the common good." Catholic health institutions and actions in global public health that aim to extend the healing ministry of Jesus cannot excuse themselves from their responsibility to promote justice and address health inequalities created by poverty and structures of oppression. The healing ministry of Jesus is a ministry of care for the sick and liberation. It is a ministry in which the poor can attain the common good.

A LIBERATING APPROACH TO HEALTH CARE

Being rooted in the christological faith that inspired the Catholic healing ministry as a historical continuation of Jesus's mission means embodying Jesus's actions and teaching in the practice of Catholic health institutions. This includes a preferential option for the poor in health care. The journey of this book demonstrates the centrality of this option in the Church's life. Now, we add the centrality of this option to a specific portion of this life: the ministry for the sick that is not exempted from operating without a preferential option for the poor.

A liberating approach in health care inverts the most common way we see and address health issues.[12] First, as noted earlier, the common way is a *top-down approach*, that is, from health "experts" and leaders distant from the reality of the people and which prevents these experts from an authentic and productive dialogue with local communities and their vulnerable populations. These people are the victims of injustice, marginalization that impact on their well-being and access to medical services, creating health inequalities and disparities. The second is *health contexts* dominated by a strong competitive health market under neoliberal rules, such as health care in the United States that conditions health care as a privilege accessed by particular social groups, mostly those who have access to pricey health insurance and can afford medical services. In addition, neoliberal health markets focus on offering medical services with high potential of financial gains, that is, it is a profit-based health care.

Top-down approaches and neoliberal health markets work well together. As a result, patients and communities are excluded from an active participation in decision-making process, and the poor and historically marginalized groups are also excluded from accessing health care. The focus on medical services with more potential for financial gains dismisses a comprehensive view of heath, that is not only health care delivered by providers and medical institutions, but rather part of a social system including, for example, the social determinants of health. Poverty and social injustice are determinants of health that cannot be addressed only by clinicians in hospitals.

Catholic health systems are not immune from these two aspects of health care. These systems often operate in a top-down approach playing inside the health market. When this happens, they narrow the service for the poor to some health assistance provided to individual poor without challenging structures responsible for health inequalities. This creates a separation between structural mechanisms, which, in turn, creates the vicious cycle presented at the beginning of this chapter, and the care offered by a health system. In this scenario, caring for the impoverished sick becomes restricted to a mere act of philanthropy without a concrete commitment to justice and the participation of the poor in the common good, while endeavoring to maintain the neoliberal health market and its method of health-care delivery as a privilege rather than a right. Considering all this, one can conclude that this was not Jesus's approach to caring for the sick and the poor.

Such health-care philanthropy does not address the structural violence that is responsible for creating poverty and injustice with their consequence for the lives of the poor and historical marginalized communities. It does not challenge structural injustice and create opportunities for people to attain the common good needed to flourish with independence and dignity. Without challenging unfair structures, this approach treats the poor as passive recipients of certain forms of assistance, only available for some individuals lucky enough to find a clinic that delivers free medical care. In global health, this kind of assistance with a top-down approach often functions to keep the poor in a reality of dependency, far from any kind of agency and socioeconomic development. It reproduces forms of colonialism with very sophisticated mechanisms. The poor are infantilized, with a friendly form of management of poverty through dependency and a "charity" that prevents the individual from dying but does nothing to raise the person from poverty to independence.

Any action that aims to help the poor and dismisses their contribution as agents of transformation reproduces oppression in a new and sophisticated form of colonialism. This is a veiled evil because it provides bread to the poor so that they do not die hungry and love those who offer the bread. The poor in their historical agency are not recognized, however. They are prevented from realizing their own knowledge of the human condition and their reality. Consequently, the poor do not become aware of the structural forces that create the poverty they live in and the paths to fight against these forces. For those who provide the bread, it is good that the poor are still there, otherwise how could they be seen as good or even saints back home? Helping the poor so that they realize they are agents of their own history, and asking why they are poor and what we can do together to change this reality, does not please people from an upper social class who are the beneficiaries of the current socioeconomic structures. This is well represented in a famous phrase of Hélder Câmara, the Brazilian bishop, who was persecuted during the dictatorship in Brazil: "When I feed the poor, they call me a saint. When I ask why so many people are poor, they call me a communist."[13]

Feeding the poor without asking why they are poor, struggling for their independency within their own reality, contributes to what Paul Farmer calls "management of poverty."[14] Managing poverty provides gains for many people, even for those who say they are working for the poor. This also manages a false historical determinism of being controlled that Paulo Freire affirms is imprinted in the mind of the oppressed so that they do not believe in their capacity of rebuilding the reality and making history. Paulo Freire understands this as a source of oppression inside everyone's mind.[15] For him, justice begins with a process of liberation of the mentality from this historical determinism that decides who is rich and who is poor. History is made by the human being who is always challenged to create and re-create the world. The poor have the ability to re-create their world every day to survive in their impoverished reality and oppression. They are not and cannot be seen as passive recipients of our actions "for them," in a colonial paternalism already a fruit of a supposed historical determinism.

The poor have power in history that, once it is recognized and empowered, we have what Gustavo Gutiérrez calls "the irruption of the poor in history."[16] If we want to act to build justice for the poor, it must be made *with* and *from* the poor. We do not liberate the poor; they liberate themselves and us, among them. As Paulo Freire suggests in his book *Pedagogy of the Oppressed*, that liberation and justice can only happen from the poor. The poor not only liberate themselves but also the oppressor because the oppressing class does not liberate and cannot be liberated by its own action.[17]

The christological option for the poor empowers Catholic health ministry, both at home and abroad, to be a ministry of mutual learning and liberation whereby the poor and their partners work together toward justice. The option for the poor leads us to join the poor for a process of learning from them and the social *locus* where these victims of structural violence—those responsible for health inequalities—are to be found. The option for the poor is a perspective *from below*, from the experience of the poor, that places their voices at the center of discussions and actions for the common good in global health through their participation in decision-making processes.

In this liberating approach, the preferential option for the poor is an *existential* and *operational* principle for Catholic health ministry. First, this option is an existential commitment as a response to Jesus's call to be his disciple and to continue this historical mission as presented in the gospel. Leonardo Boff suggests that the historical reality of the poor is the *theological locus* of a new way of doing theology.[18] Therefore, it is only amid the poor that one can recognize the human condition and the historical situation that reveals the experience of suffering of those who are victims of injustice. At the same time, this is an encounter with the crucified Jesus, who died poor, and was also a victim of socioeconomic and political injustice. This double encounter, with the poor and Jesus, guides the mission of the Church. Consequently, it is an encounter that should guide Catholic health ministry.

As noted earlier, Pope Francis stresses the option for the poor as "an ethical imperative for effectively attaining the common good" (*Laudato Si'* 158). In doing so, Francis points out the operational aspect of this Catholic social principle that is necessary to lead us to develop the common good so that all can participate in it. Francis believes that only the market forces are incapable of promoting a care that can respond to the cry of the earth and the poor (see *Laudato Si'* 49, 109, 190). Therefore, he argues for an integral perspective of development in which all participate, including the poor who are not only recipients of actions, but active agents of transformation (see *Laudato Si'* 179). Their voices matter, and they have a knowledge that counts.

As an ethical imperative, the preferential option for the poor means allowing ourselves to be poor (whether spiritually and/or materially) to learn from the poor and their suffering, from their reality, and their beauty. Quoting the Document of Aparecida (no. 398), Francis highlights, "Only the closeness that makes us friends can enable us to appreciate deeply the values of the poor today, their legitimate desires, and their own manner of living the faith. The option for the poor should lead us to friendship with the poor" (*Fratelli Tutti* 234). The preferential option for the poor suggests an ethic of personal commitment, friendship, and collective effort. It is an option for poor against poverty to break the cycle of violence against the dignity of human beings vulnerable because of socioeconomic oppression.

Considering health care as a common good, the option for the poor becomes necessary to attain this good, something that any health system playing within the forces of the free market cannot achieve. Therefore, to be coherent to Jesus's mission, Catholic health ministry must embrace the preferential option for the poor as an ethical imperative based on our christological faith for attaining the common good and with prophetic praxis that includes promoting social justice for population health.

Finally, this liberating approach is *from below* grounded on a Catholic principle of a preferential option for the poor in health. Although a principle from a religious tradition, it is an inclusive concept with an operational aspect that creates encounters, encourages dialogue, promotes learning, and offers directions for global and public health strategies in local realities. Therefore, this principle has also a secular value. Sociologically, the preferential option for the poor leads us to where injustice occurs, to see the faces of the poor, to listen to their voices, and to learn from the stories of those who carry the burden of injustice and suffer its consequences, that often include premature death. In this reality, therefore, seeking the causes of injustice and death becomes a natural movement. The preferential option for the poor is a perspective that creates partners who listen to one another and work together to address the roots of injustice to create independency, breaking the vicious cycle of violence and structures that make people vulnerable to illness and premature death because of a lack good living conditions, opportunities, and access to health care.

CONCLUSION

> *The spirit of the Lord is on me, for he has anointed me to bring the good news to the poor, to proclaim liberty to captives, and to sight to the blind, to free the oppressed, to proclaim the year acceptable of the Lord.* (Luke 4:18)

Jesus read this text from the Prophet Isaiah in the synagogue in Nazareth, presenting it as a project of his public ministry. This narrative shows the centrality of the sick, the oppressed, and the poor in the mission of Jesus that was led by the Holy Spirit. Therefore, care for the sick, the oppressed, and the poor are part of the mission of his followers, also guided by the Holy Spirit in a project of integral development. The promotion of health and well-being is an effort that needs to combine medical care for the sick and practices to build justice with the participation of the poor as agents of historical change. This is done by liberating the oppressed and raising the poor from their poverty. It also includes their active participation to attain the common good.

6

Leadership from the Poor in Global Health for the Common Good

> *"Who touched me?" When all denied it, Peter said, "Master, the crowds surround you and press in on you." But Jesus said, "Somebody touched me; for I noticed that power had gone out from me." When the woman saw that she could not remain hidden, she came trembling; and falling down before him, she declared in the presence of all people why she had touched him, and how she had been immediately healed. He said to her, "Daughter, your faith has made you well;*[1] *go in peace."* (Luke 8:45–48)

> *Jesus stood still and ordered the man to be brought to him; and when he came near, asked him, "What do you want me to do for you?" He said, "Lord, let me see again." Jesus said to him, "Receive your sight; Your faith has saved you."* (Luke 18:40–42)

These two episodes in Jesus's ministry offer insights for the global health challenge that we address in this chapter. As we saw in previous chapters, bringing the good news to the poor and care for the sick are central to Jesus's mission. The destitute and the sick are not simply recipients of care, but active agents in the process that leads them to be healed. This is a challenge that must be addressed in global health. It is a question of governance and leadership in the context of health-care delivery and policies marked by top-down approaches that relegates the poor to a passive and submissive role.

There are common dynamics in the above two biblical passages. First, *sensitivity*: Jesus is among a crowd, going to a destination.[2] Jesus is on his way to some commitment. The first narrative is clear on this point: he was going at the request of a man named Jairus to see a twelve-year-old girl who was dying. The second only says he was going to Jericho but does not mention his commitment there. Second, *struggle*: the two destitute persons, a woman and man, seek Jesus for help. The crowd around him was not enough to discourage them to struggle for what they wanted. Third, *engagement*: Jesus was sensitive to realize these two people in need and engage with them. Even in his busy schedule, as one would say in our contemporary language, Jesus stops to speak with two people in need. The first passage affirms that Jesus hears the story of the destitute and sick woman, and in the second passage, Jesus asks the blind man what he wants. Jesus could have simply helped these people and moved on. What they needed may seem obvious, but Jesus chose to let them take the lead and present their voices. Finally, *protagonism*: Jesus says to both persons that their faith and not his power, saved them. A conclusion that one might have about these stories is that the main agents and the leaders that achieved the healing were the two destitute persons and not Jesus. He functions as a secondary agent who offers what is missing to complement the struggle these two people were having to live better and healthier lives. One could critique this interpretation, noting that Jesus had the cure, the goal of these poor people; therefore, he is the center. It is legitimate to understand the passages in this way, and it is not my intent to challenge that view and thereby diminish the importance of Jesus's miracle. However, Jesus would not deliver this cure, the miracle, if they did not struggle to find Jesus. Moreover, Jesus, a leader with the ability to deliver care, gives space for the destitute to engage with him as people with agency.

The four dynamics presented in the Gospel—*sensitivity*, *struggle*, *engagement*, and *protagonism*—can be seen as ethical attitudes able to sustain an approach toward global health, especially in matters of health-care delivery and policies in impoverished areas. They point out the embodiment of the preferential option for the poor in health as a practical orientation in which the destitute, sick, and the poor are agents in processes of health-care delivery, contributing to a model of global health governance that begins at the bottom, with the agency and active participation of the poor.

Global health governance is a challenging interdisciplinary field featuring a variety of nongovernmental organizations, governmental institutions of international development, academic centers of formation and research, and community and religious initiatives.[3] This plurality of independent organisms and global health actors has very little coordination to favor collaborative efforts, and sometimes, they even compete for space, funds, and especially local and international prestige. Global health governance is criticized for two main defects: a "lack of coordination among stakeholders," that is, among the institutions, organizations, and initiatives mentioned above; and a "lack of inclusion and participation of local communities."[4] To address these defects, some global health leaders and scholars suggest a centralized approach in which a larger organism, such as the World Health Organization,[5] would be the centralized guider for all initiatives in global health. This only deepens current top-down approaches, taking decisions for health-care delivery, policies, and research even further from local communities that global health actions aim to serve, solidifying the passivity and the dismissal of the local voices of poor and marginalized populations, as well as their culture and experience in acting within their own community. Here, there is an ethical issue related to the mentality that runs through most global health leaders and the structure of global health organisms.

Global health is a new discipline and action, and a Western invention that primarily focuses on bringing some health care to low- and middle-income countries. As almost everything from the Global North, global health is shaped by a modern Western epistemology—developed since the great navigations of Europeans to conquer other continents—that works to sustain the capitalist structures of our current globalized world.[6] One feature of this structure is that Westerners, that is, white people from a few Western European countries and North America (the United States and Canada) are the ones who could save the world's poor from their own poverty and misery. And this must be done in their Western way and without any intercultural and epistemological collaboration. The ethical issue is the diminishing of the human being and everything related to them when they interact with the West, its people, and its technology. In addition, this dominant perspective in global health prevents its stakeholders, leaders, and many people delivering care in poor, culturally diverse communities to see structures that contribute to creating the problems global health aims to address. According to Eugene T. Richardson, "The continuation of disproportionate amounts of suffering and death from infectious diseases in the Global South is not the result of an intractable problem thwarting our best efforts to prevent and cure disease; we have the means. However, as an apparatus of coloniality, public health manages (as a profession) and maintains (as an academic enterprise) global health inequity."[7] Richardson's analysis on coloniality[8] in global health shows contradictions that impact the way health care is delivered in impoverished regions and the ineffectiveness of most global health efforts in promoting sustainable care and local autonomy.

Top-down approaches and centralized governance are expressions of an ethical confusion that, instead of empowering local communities and voices from poor and marginalized people, disenfranchises them from their experience and capacity to contribute. Therefore, actions that are aimed to benefit the destitute and the sick are misguided. On the one hand, the poor are worthy to receive care from initiatives led or funded by foreigners; on the other hand, they are not worthy to help to inform any strategy of health-care delivery and policies in their own context, being relegated to a passive and often submissive role of being lucky to be recipients of international charity. Nothing changes their reality. The structure of the capitalist world will continue creating the poverty that makes marginalized populations vulnerable to sickness and premature death, while the wealthy nations that fund global health will continue to be wealthy, most of the time with the essential help of the natural resources coming from the nations where global health projects take place.[9]

The preferential option for the poor is a principle that challenges top-down approaches and the centralization of global health governance. This principle, which is an option in terminology but from a christological perspective is an imperative,[10] leads to practices that reflect an ethics in which the poor are active agents of collaboration and transformation, with a governance originating from the bottom in a dynamic process of participation and local leadership characterized by *sensitivity*, *struggle*, *engagement*, and *protagonism*.

After this long introduction that has presented the problem that needs to be addressed (top-down approaches and global health governance) and the ethical perspective to face it (a christological ethics), we will now develop the Catholic social principle of the preferential option for the poor as an ethical principle that helps us to address this problem and offers a different way to approach global health: one that is *from below*, with the *sensitivity*, the *struggle*, the *engagement*, and the *protagonism* of the poor. As the title of this chapter suggests, "leadership from the poor" means a shift of perspective. This shift of perspective is what I think the preferential option for the poor calls us to do when we engage in actions that promote justice for the poor and the oppressed, whether in global health or any other social area. Therefore, the goal of this chapter is not to offer a suggestion about what we can do for the poor, but rather present a framework for what we can do with the poor from their perspective and way of life. Hence, I emphasize a process of mutual learning that is developed from a belief in the agency of the poor who have a core contribution to offer to any global health initiative so that their partners, those who join them, are open to listening to the poor and learning from their experiences, struggles, and worldview. At the same time, the poor also learn from their new partners, in a dialectical movement of collaboration with the technical knowledge, skills, and resources offered by their partners who, as with Jesus in the gospel, create a space for the poor to be *protagonists*.

COLONIAL PATERNALISM AND THE POWER OF THE POOR

In my experience of serving in global health, I have seen many occasions when people with good intentions to serve the poor have contributed to keeping the reality of the poor dependent and far from developed. This reproduces forms of colonialism with very sophisticated mechanisms. The poor are infantilized through a soft form of poverty management that fosters dependency and a charity that prevents them from dying, but this does not do anything to raise them from poverty to independence. In some cases, these actions for the poor can result in tragedies, such as one in Jinja, Uganda, where 105 children died in a center for malnourished children created and led by a U.S. missionary with no medical training.[11] This case shows a mentality of serving the poor, without believing that they have anything to offer, without accepting that they know their own reality and recognizing that they can be active partners in a global health effort. Furthermore, this tragedy in Jinja simply presents a colonial mentality (or coloniality), in which the colonizer believes that he/she, who comes from a rich nation, is enlightened with all the knowledge of somebody else's reality, having all solutions for their problems. The locals, then, are simply poor, culturally primitive people who need Western help to survive. A phrase used to express this reality, especially in universities in the United States that offer global health opportunities for their students, is the "white savior complex."

Uganda, the place of this tragedy, is a country in which I have firsthand experience. Therefore, I want to bring a voice of a Ugandan friend to continue this discussion. Once while I was serving in Jinja, my friend said,

> *I am a Buganda*[12] *person and I don't think like you. Foreigners and missionaries come here to help us, like you. They do a good work, but they do not trust us. They treat us as if we are incapable of doing anything right. All the good work is attached to foreign missionaries and their international groups of people. They make us to be dependent on them and accept everything they are saying. We are helped when we are sick, in our immediate need, but we never advance to an independent life and to grow in a Buganda way.* (Archelo)

Archelo's statement reveals a way that most of us, when serving the poor, especially in a different culture, treat those who are locals within their own reality. We deny their agency and their capacity to help us beyond the use of their physical labor. Here begins the oppression, even in an action that aims to help those in need, because this denial inhibits the poor and the marginalized within their own reality—home—from being aware of their agency and ignoring the relevance of their struggle and their creativity in handling hostile living conditions. One of the results is the self-belief in the mind of the poor that they do not have the capacity to collaborate beyond physical work or obeying the direction of those who come from the Global North.[13] In other words, this approach reproduces an advanced epistemological and ethical colonialism that a priori sees everything coming from non-Western views as inferior; therefore, the knowledge and the culture of the poor in the Global South can be ignored.[14]

Simone Weil's philosophy helps us to understand the knowledge of the poor, developed from their experience of suffering. She developed an anthropology of the human condition from her concept of *malheur* and her experience among the *malheureux* of her time.[15] *Malheur* is a very specific concept created by Weil that any English translation cannot fully convey. Affliction is the most common translation. But *malheur* goes beyond that. It represents a kind of suffering that impacts all dimensions of human existence. The *malheureux* are those who experience *malheur* and feel abandoned in the world of suffering and oppression, as Jesus felt in the cross when he cried out, "My God, My God, why have you forsaken me?" (Matt 27:46; Mark 15:34).[16] This experience opens one up to receive God's grace, an aspect of Weil's thinking that I discussed in a different work.[17]

According to Simone Weil, the *malheureux* or, simply stated, the unfortunates, are experts in the human condition because of their experience of oppression, suffering, and abandonment. Most of the time, they do not realize the anthropological knowledge they have because of the experience of oppression in their daily lives. Therefore, Weil suggests joining the oppressed to learn from them and help them to move beyond their oppression, a process in which the oppressed are agents of their own liberation.

Among the unfortunates, Weil realized their oppression is a result of the separation between manual labor and intellectual work, that is, a disconnection between practice and contemplation.[18] The oppressed—the working class, the main unfortunates of her time—are prevented from the intellectual exercise of contemplation. This keeps them away from understanding social structures and systems that sustain their oppression, with no aspiration or imagination to build a new reality. Consequently, they are not aware of their knowledge of the human condition and become vulnerable to the oppressor. Simone Weil even criticized the labor movements and leaders of her time for not understanding this source of oppression, limiting their struggles only to achieve better wages.

In the context of Latin America, Paulo Freire understood this source of oppression to be present inside everyone's mind. The fight of the poor cannot be so reduced that the only goal is to raise them to be part of an upper socioeconomic class. Otherwise, they will continue being the oppressed who now can oppress by reproducing the same structure of injustice and exploitation.[19] I think this was one of the mistakes of the leftist governments in Latin America in the first two decades of this millennium. When leftist leaders created social policies to help the poor to leave their poverty, they stopped the work of conscientization with the poor. When the poor achieved better socioeconomic living and working conditions, they reproduced the same system of oppression and moved against the social policies that helped them to leave poverty. They never experienced liberation.[20]

For both Weil and Freire, liberation begins through a process of unifying practice and contemplation (or manual labor and intellectual exercise). Joining with the poor is an unavoidable part of this process. Weil tried it, but she was unable to develop a way to work with the poor for this process of liberation. Freire advanced this perspective with his experience of education for critical consciousness.[21] Conscientization is the key concept developed by Freire that leads us to work with the poor for the reconciliation of practice and contemplation, in which the poor are agents of a liberating praxis (*praxis*, here, in its real meaning: practice and theory functioning together.)

Weil's and Freire's insights are resources for actions in global and public health. First, Weil's anthropology reveals the human condition and its main experts: the unfortunates who show to all who we are. This places all in the same condition of need for care, particularly health care. Second, Weil and Freire demonstrate that the unfortunates, or the poor and the oppressed, have something to offer and teach us. At the same time, we can work as facilitators to help them to engage in a process of unification of practice and contemplation. This will put them on a path for liberation where they are agents and leaders of their own history. Third, with Freire's insights for working with the poor for conscientization, we create a process of mutual learning from below, led by the agency of the poor with us being among them.

This process in global health is a movement for justice in health, creating and re-creating health systems that serve all that is grounded on an anthropology of the human condition. It will be a fight against current health systems and perspectives dominated by the illusion that capitalism and its push for health care under a free market are the solution for health disparities. For example, the Brazilian public health system (the SUS, a Portuguese acronym for Unified Health System) that offers universal coverage grounded on the right to health has been suffering attacks in the last years by political leaders and private health companies, with strategies that prevent the poor from understanding the actual meaning of a health-care system dominated by the free market. At the same time, these attacks are translated into policies that dismantle the public system by favoring private investment to benefit only the top 20 percent richest of the country. Keeping the poor far from contemplation is the goal of the entire private health market and neoliberal economic forces that daily attacks the SUS, creating the illusion among the poor, and the population in general, that a public universal health care system does not work and never will. The free market cannot solve the health care problems in Brazil and in the world. The health disparities and inequalities in the United States, where health care is dominated by private systems on a profit-driven model, is proof that private health systems do not work for population health, but for themselves.[22] Free health market is a lie to manage poverty and inequality,[23] with a historical determinism imposed in the minds of the poor.[24] Weil's and Freire's accounts help to reveal the incoherence and intellectual manipulation of structures of oppression, such as the neoliberal free health market. At the same time, their account points out the *protagonism* of the poor as historical social agents, a historical power that must be considered by global health initiatives.

In his project on the epistemologies of the South, Boaventura de Sousa Santos suggests that the modern Western paradigm—the one that creates free markets—is a large part of the problem we live in today, with very limited opportunities to offer solutions to address our challenges.[25] He thinks that "there is no global social justice without global cognitive justice."[26] The knowledge and creativity coming from populations historically marginalized, such as the poor, oppressed minorities in developed countries (for example, Black and immigrants in the United States) and populations in the Global South, must be recognized and their holders empowered, so that "the irruption of the poor in history"[27] guides the work to build justice. Hence, we act *with* and *from* them, that is, with and from the poor.[28]

In the context of global health, our work with the poor must be for their historical agency and independency to break this vicious cycle created by the relationship between poverty and illness.[29] Top-down approaches and centralized models of global health governance and initiatives often provide bread, but do not ask why people are hungry. In doing so, they dismiss the agency of the poor in their own reality, and do not really join them in a project of independency from the perspective of the local suffering, with the collaboration of non-Western epistemologies. Frequently, global health initiatives simply provide bread (some medical care) in a soft form of colonial paternalism. This is one of the main ethical challenges for any global health effort coming from outside local realities. To face this challenge and to break this vicious cycle, Catholic social teaching offers important resources to cultivate/promote leadership from the poor in global health. The preferential option for the poor—the christological principle that has been deeply developed in this book—is one of these resources that leads us to shift our perspective from a top-down to a bottom-up approach, in which the poor are agents of history.[30]

The poor, who are experiencing a vicious cycle that is responsible for creating the vulnerability of many victims from violence against their dignity, are victims of structural violence, a social sin that creates oppression and hurts their dignity, impacting not only their living condition, but also their way of thinking and acting in the world. They are not poor because of any form of historical determinism, rather they are people who were impoverished. They were made—by years of colonial history, oppression, and exploitation of their resources—to believe they are inferior, with no capacity to lead any effort of development. If we do not change this colonial paternalistic way of helping the poor, we are also contributing to the maintenance of structural violence that manages poverty and inequalities according to the fallacy of historical determinism.

The option for the poor leads us to join the poor in a process of learning from them and to realize the social *locus* where these victims of structural violence are. The option for the poor is a perspective *from below*, from the experience of the poor, that places their voices at the center of our discussion and actions for the common good in global health, with *sensitivity*, *struggle*, *engagement*, and *protagonism* being ethical attitudes that empower the poor.

LEADERSHIP FROM THE POOR IN GLOBAL HEALTH

The preferential option for the poor is not only an inspirational motivation, but also an *existential* and *operational* principle. First, this option is an existential commitment in response to Jesus Christ's call to be his disciple. This commitment has always been present in the history of the Catholic Church as we noted in chapter 3. Although the expression *preferential option for the poor* only appeared in Latin America in the 1960s as part of a theology developed from the Conference of Latin American Bishops in Medellín (1968) and the experience of basic ecclesial communities, the poor have always had a privileged place in the Judeo-Christian tradition. This has been going on since the Exodus, led by Moses, to free the oppressed poor in Egypt; it is present in the prophetic tradition and its call for justice; and the poor were presented as the privileged recipients of the good news by Jesus (see Luke 4:16–18).

As discussed in chapter 3, the early Church was also crying out for justice to the poor, in the preaching of voices of Christian leaders, such as John Chrysostom and Basil of Caesarea. Even when the Church's hierarchy distanced itself from the poor in the Middle Ages, people like Francis of Assisi and Dominic of Guzmán were raised by the Holy Spirit to show that the Church's place was with the poor. However, it was in the flourishing of liberation theology, from the practice of Christian communities in Latin America, that the preferential option for the poor gained the status of a theological concept fostering a new way of doing theology. The option for the poor was then accepted as a concept of academic theology based on the practice of Christian communities, in which many professional theologians were inserted, lived, and operated.

Even among controversies, the option for the poor became the heart of liberation theology as an expanded theological notion. In other words, the concept of option for the poor only makes sense if there is a commitment to the poor through a historical praxis situated in the reality of the oppressed. Theology is done among the poor within their struggles. As we noted in the first chapter, the historical reality of the poor is the theological *locus* of a new way of doing theology. Consequently, it is only in the midst of the poor that one can recognize the human condition and the historical situation that reveals the experience of how victims of injustice suffer. At the same time, this is an encounter with the crucified Jesus, who died poor, also a victim of socioeconomic and political injustice. This double encounter, with the poor and with Jesus, leads us to reread the Christian theological tradition, which acquires a new meaning within the contemporary historical experience of the poor.

Pope Francis argues that the option for the poor is "an ethical imperative for effectively attaining the common good" (*Laudato Si'* 158). In other words, there is no way for societies to move toward justice in which all can participate in the common good without a serious consideration of those marginalized from accessing the good needed to flourish. Among these marginalized are the poor, who demonstrate the global reality of suffering and injustice. The current order of the world that is dominated by a capitalist system ruled by the market forces is not able to lead the world toward justice with the poor and the earth. In fact, these forces have created the global injustice we see today. Therefore, for Francis, the preferential option for the poor is necessary to help us in a collective effort to create an inclusive common good, a goal that the market forces have failed to promote in order to answer the cry of the earth and the poor (*Laudato Si'* 49, 109, 190). Hence, the option for the poor is not only a principle that leads us to join them, but also an operational foundation to guide us in the inclusion of the marginalized voices in our decision-making processes, offering them an opportunity to be agents of transformation (*Laudato Si'* 179). The option for the poor is the *sensitivity* to recognize the *struggle* of the poor as source of dynamic force and knowledge. It fosters an *engagement* in which we listen to their voices, expressed in their narratives and creative actions of survival that guide us to recognize their historical *protagonism*. This is a new way of global health governance, in which the voices of the poor matter, and their knowledge and historical force count.

Listening is the first practical attitude that, after joining the poor as their partner, is embodied in the operational incorporation of the option for the poor in global health. From a Christian perspective, listening is a prominent aspect in the teaching of the gospel that Jesus, living among the poor, displayed by showing sensitivity to their problems and suffering and by listening to them. Pope Francis understood the importance of listening to create any action and project that can lead us toward a world with justice for the poor and the earth. Listening is one of the pillars of his theology, suggested by many as a theology of encounter and dialogue.[31] In practical terms, this theology sustains Francis's view of a synodal Church, in which synodality—understood as the primacy of listening—means the active participation of all in the Catholic Church, doing so through a broad communitarian process of discernment and decision.[32] We can learn lessons from this view of ecclesial participation for use in global health. Although synodality is oriented for the life and organization of the Catholic Church, this is not isolated from socioeconomic and ecological issues that afflict the world. Vincent J. Miller argues that Francis's proposal of synodality expands "listening and discernment beyond the ecclesia to the entire human community, facilitating attention to the cries of the poor as well as marginalized cultures and degraded ecosystems."[33]

Furthermore, when the International Theological Commission published a document on the Theology of Synodality, a text previously read and approved by Francis, the theologians of that commission also highlighted the social aspect. For this commission, synodality is part of the Church's *ethos*[34] that expands the spiritual, listening, and prophetic basis of social *diakonia*. Synodality aims to foster a "spirituality of communion" and "practices of listening, dialogue and communal discernment." This is relevant "for the ecumenical journey and for prophetic *diakonia* in building a social ethos based on fraternity, solidarity and inclusion."[35] With this, the internal life of the Church and its governance point to external life:

> The practice of dialogue and the search for effective joint solutions by which we commit ourselves to peace and justice are an absolute priority in a situation where there is a structural crisis in the procedures of democratic participation and a loss of confidence in its principles and inspirational values, with the threat of authoritarian and technocratic aberrations. In this context, it is an important obligation and a criterion of all social action of the

> People of God to hear the cry of the poor and the cry of the earth, and to draw attention urgently, in determining society's choices and plans, to the place and the privileged role of the poor, the universal destination of goods, the primacy of solidarity and care for our common home.[36]

Thus, it is recognized that the synodality of the Catholic Church has an *ad intra dimension*, focused on the internal issues of the Church, and an *ad extra* one, oriented to the challenges of justice that impact people's lives, especially marginalized peoples and the environment. The synod on the Amazon presents these two dimensions very clearly, as Agenor Brighenti and Stefano Raschietti point out, "As in the [Second Vatican] Council, the first reference, 'new paths,' was addressed to the Church *ad intra*; the second, 'integral ecology,' to the *ad extra* perspective. The Amazon, as a theological place and subject, invited an 'integral conversion,' in all its dimensions, which had exactly as its horizon and paradigm an 'integral ecology.'"[37] Moreover, it is worth remembering that Pope Francis's integral ecology is a perspective that listens to the "cry of the earth and the poor" (*Laudato Si'* 49), in which "every ecological approach must integrate a social perspective that takes into account the fundamental rights of the most disadvantaged" (*Laudato Si'* 93).

Francis stresses the necessity of listening to create a dialogue able to understand the other, especially the other who is poor, oppressed, and marginalized. This listening has a social and operational aspect that could be understood as a principle of Catholic social teaching, alongside other established principles such as human dignity, solidarity, subsidiarity, the common good, and the option for the poor.

Listening, as presented by Francis in his account on synodality and social ethics, corresponds to the teaching presented in the Gospel passages earlier, where Jesus lets the destitute be the protagonist of the action of transformation, with a struggle and a voice recognized and listened to by Jesus. This evangelical teaching is very clear when Francis, through a great engagement with peoples from the Amazon, stresses that their reality and their voices must guide our dialogue and actions among them:

> The Amazon region ought to be a *place of social dialogue*, especially between the various original peoples, for the

> sake of developing forms of fellowship and joint struggle. The rest of us are called to *participate as "guests"* and to seek out with great respect paths of encounter that can enrich the Amazon region. If we wish to dialogue, we should do this in the first place with the poor. They are not just another party to be won over, or merely another individual seated at a table of equals. *They are our principal dialogue partners*, those from whom we have the most to learn, to whom we need *to listen out of a duty of justice*, and from whom we must *ask permission* before presenting our proposals. Their words, their hopes and their fears should be the most authoritative voice at any table of dialogue on the Amazon region. And the great question is: "What is their idea of 'good living' for themselves and for those who will come after them?" (*Querida Amazonia* 25; emphasis mine)

Although Francis is directly talking about the Amazon region, with its original peoples and challenges, he offers an operational way to engage with impoverished and suffering communities in culturally different contexts and fields, such as global health. First, the discussion about health issues, challenges, and strategies of health-care delivery and policies cannot be made far from where the problems occur. Local communities are the *place of social dialogue* with broad participation of those who live in these communities and feel in their skin the suffering resulting from injustice and poverty. Second, in this dialogue, the poor are the hosts, and we join them to participate *as guests* who want to partake in their struggle and not suppress their voices and creativity that have sustained their lives amid hostile conditions. Third, they are not only people whom we invite to join our conversations to have representation at the table; rather the poor are the *principal dialogue partners*, without whom nothing can be done. Fourth, their voices are the first and most important voices to be listened to, as a *duty of justice*. In other words, there are no possible paths for justice if we begin a global health initiative with the injustice of not listening to the voices of the poor in their local communities. Fifth, it is a call for humility and respect. It does not matter how poor a community is and how objectively visible is its need, we must *ask the community permission* to present everything we bring, regardless of whether we think it might help it. Our proposals will be a resource to build effective help if they are humbly presented to the poor as collaboration in a dialogical process of mutual learning that creates a collective project of development.

In Francis's thinking and in my framework for global health leadership from the poor, the preferential option for the poor becomes an *ethical imperative* that allows ourselves to be poor (spiritually and/or materially) to learn from the poor and their suffering, from their reality, and their beauty. The preferential option for the poor suggests an ethic of personal commitment and collective effort. It is an option for the poor against poverty to break the cycle of violence against the dignity of human beings vulnerable because of socioeconomic oppression.

As discussed in the previous chapter, Francis views the option for the poor as necessary for attaining the common good through a process that includes an engaged listening. The common good includes health care and well-being, within decent living conditions and access to opportunities for people to flourish. Therefore, global health initiatives that aim to promote social justice for population health must embrace the preferential option for the poor as an ethical imperative. Although the option for the poor originated in our christological faith, it has a value beyond the life of the Church, that is, an *ad extra* dimension to guide us toward attaining the common good.

"Attaining the common good" includes global health initiatives that emphasize the participation of the poor as agents of transformation, protagonists of history. This means that actions in global health cannot simply provide health care for the destitute and the sick. It is not simply a matter of designating some health-care resources to those who are poor as an act of charity, or as a humanitarian effort to help suffering impoverished people after a specific disastrous event. This kind of effort only addresses a small piece of the larger problem and does not "effectively" lead impoverished and oppressed populations in "attaining the common good," neither does it create development and sustainability. Being limited by this kind of action, we subconsciously promote colonial paternalism and the historical determinism presented above, thereby contributing to the management of poverty.

The preferential option for the poor inverts the logic of serving the poor, offering a new perspective from their reality and knowledge.

It creates opportunities for mutual learning, that is, an experience of encounter in which both the poor and their partners among them learn from each other in a process of collaboration for action in global health.

Although the preferential option for the poor and other aspects of this framework from below in global health—*sensitivity*, *struggle*, *engagement*, *listening*, and *protagonism*—are ethical and methodological guiders from a religious tradition, originating in the christological faith, they represent an inclusive perspective of an operational framework that creates encounters, encourages dialogue, promotes learning, and offers directions for global health strategies in local communities. Therefore, this framework also has a secular and interreligious value. Sociologically, the preferential option for the poor leads us to where injustice occurs, to see the faces of the poor, listen to their voices, and learn from the stories of those who carry the burden of injustice, suffering the consequences that often include death. In this reality, therefore, seeking the causes of injustice and premature death becomes a natural movement of justice. The preferential option for the poor is a perspective that creates partners who listen to one another and work together to address the roots of injustice to create independency, breaking the vicious cycle of violence and its structures that make people vulnerable to illness and premature death because of a lack of appropriate living conditions, opportunities, and access to health care.

CONCLUSION

Speaking from the context of global health, I cannot forget to mention the COVID-19 pandemic and how it made the relationship between the local and the global in health care and in the socioeconomic structure of the world explicit. All challenges related to the pandemic point out the structural issues of the current socioeconomic system that dominates the world, issues grounded on individualism, competition, and exploitation.[38] Pope Francis is perhaps one of the few voices who has identified this profound crisis in the dominant system, even before the pandemic, and who continues to speak prophetically to the world.[39] His teaching offers resources to rethink our priorities and our way to engage with the other, particularly the poor and those who are not like us. Early in the pandemic, Francis suggested that we will not be the same after this pandemic. The question we need to answer is whether we want to get out of this pandemic "better or worse."[40] Nevertheless, we departed from the COVID-19 pandemic without learning much from it. Global health, as an international, intersectoral, and pluri-organizational and institutional effort, has not learned much from this pandemic either. The poor and the most vulnerable, those who most suffer from any adverse health event, are increasingly more distant from any participation in global health initiatives that are aimed at their reality. Global health governance discussions are still restricted to the doors of offices and conference rooms in the Global North. Grounded in a christological foundation for a global health perspective from below, this chapter hopes to bridge this gap with an approach that includes the voices of the poor in global health as an opportunity for leadership from the poor.

If we want to build an effective global health field for those who are in poverty and dying prematurely because of their disproportional vulnerability and lack of medical assistance, we must rethink the way we engage with the poor, especially with national or international initiatives led by people from the Global North or people with power and privilege. The Catholic social principle of the preferential option for the poor offers an alternative way of leadership with and from the poor. Considering it is an opportunity to rebuild the way we serve the poor, seeing them not simply as objects of our philanthropy, but active partners of governance in a historical journey to attaining the common good.

7

The End of Life in a Global Health Perspective

The poor are the people who best represent the experience of the people at the bottom of societies and Christian communities. The shift from a view that begins at the top—represented by theoretical approaches or by looking at problems that impact rich nations—to a perspective originating from below, significantly impacts the way we do theological bioethics and see end-of-life challenges. To illustrate this shift, I present a short anecdote, that also works as a bridge to introduce some narratives of the experience of the poor with end-of-life issues in global health.

In September 2020, during the COVID-19 pandemic, I was part of a panel in a health-care ethics conference in the United States. It was a virtual panel on death and COVID-19. My presentation highlighted the situation of indigenous people in the Amazon region in Brazil, who were getting infected by the coronavirus and dying in isolation without access to medical care. The other panelists presented ethical issues in the United States about people dying in intensive care units (ICUs) without seeing a family member and with no spiritual care, the possibility of rationing ICUs, and questions regarding CPR (cardio-pulmonary resuscitation) and DNR (do not resuscitate). These issues are very relevant in the U.S. health context, and the audience engaged with the panelists with questions and comments. At one point, the discussion moved to issues of euthanasia, medical futility, and death with dignity in the United States, considering the challenges in the physician-patient relationship, particularly within this pandemic and how it questioned the decision-making processes regarding resource allocation and scarcity. With apparent ease, they began to address end-of-life controversies related to biomedical ethics. My talk about indigenous deaths—because of their disproportional vulnerability to be infected by the coronavirus and deaths due to the lack of access to minimal health care needed to save most of their lives—was lost in the conversation, until, close to the end of our time, the convener of the panel asked what I thought about the discussion taking place. My answer was simple: you are only talking about challenges in this rich nation, the ones that impact those who have access to health care, with the privilege to choose between CPR or DNR, and to refuse care at the end of life if they want. In the reality of the poor where I serve, most people do not have a chance to see a physician or a nurse. Many of those who see a health professional find a person overwhelmed with his/her work and lacking adequate resources to serve the sick, and this health iniquity did not begin with the pandemic.

The shift mentioned above—from a top-down to a bottom-up perspective—reveals that, in the reality of the poor and the oppressed, the biggest challenge for the end of life is not the ability to choose and refuse certain medical services to have a peaceful death, or a death with dignity, but rather it is in dying prematurely without proper care or far from access to any medical assistance. Considering global health from the reality of the poor, euthanasia, medical futility, advance directives, CPR or DNR, and healing care or palliative care for terminal patients are not the most prominent and urgent ethical questions. Most people do not have an opportunity to arrive at this stage of care with the privilege to choose or refuse specific treatments or measures of care. Poverty and structures of oppression that perpetuate injustice and marginalization are making people vulnerable to diseases. Furthermore, when sick, there is no proper health care for them, and the result is more suffering until death, most often resulting in a premature death.[1] Three narratives can illustrate this reality at the bottom of global health.

THE SCANDAL OF INJUSTICE IN GLOBAL HEALTH

Many scholarly studies show that poverty, oppression, and injustice are the main causes of sickness and premature death in the world. They are social determinants of health that impact people's lives, making them vulnerable to fall ill in a reality that lacks good or strong health systems. The poor disproportionally fall sick and die because of bio-socioeconomic factors and no access to health care. I will not discuss studies and the data that show this violent reality of injustice and oppression in global health, but I do recommend further reading.[2] Although numbers shock, we can get used to them and fail to see the faces and the stories behind them. This begins to occur with the numbers of the COVID-19 pandemic, especially when these numbers start to be far from us in time and space. All people suffering and dying are not merely numbers; they are human persons, with stories and dignity. Theologically, they are crucified people, in whose faces we are invited to contemplate the face of Jesus on the cross. Jesus identifies himself with the suffering of the poor, as we clearly realized when reading the Gospel of Luke and developing the Christology offered in the previous chapters.

As an invitation for imagination and contemplation, I present three stories to illustrate this reality of injustice and death. At the same time, they are the lives of three people to be contemplated and identified with the suffering of the crucified Jesus. This process will guide us in becoming aware of the end-of-life challenges faced by the poor.

José Manuel da Silva, a twenty-year-old, died at the emergency room (ER) at Hospital Ipiranga, after being shot by police officers who thought he was part of a gang of drug traffickers of a *favela* (slum) in São Paulo, Brazil. I do not know the details of this persecution and killing, nor why José Manuel was targeted, but I learned later that it was proven that he was not part of this gang. He never used drugs and worked at a supermarket, but José was a Black, poor guy who was mistakenly targeted by a police force with historical records of brutality and bias against Afro-Brazilian men. The story of José illustrates many stories of Black, poor, and young people who are victims of police brutality and the structural injustices of the Brazilian criminal system.

I interacted with José only for a short time, but I never forgot his last minutes of life. In the early 2000s, I was serving as a nursing student at the ER of Hospital Ipiranga, a public hospital near the *favela* where José lived. On a Thursday evening, about 5:00 p.m., police officers arrived at the ER with two young boys whom they had shot. I was part of a team in charge of caring for José who had two bullets near his chest, was unconscious, and had gone into cardiopulmonary arrest. We immediately began CPR. I was the person doing compressions. Police officers were yelling bad words at us that we could not allow this "criminal" to die. What was already a very tense situation in an overcrowded hospital, with many people waiting for assistance in the ER, became more stressful with the attitude of the officers. Unfortunately, we were not able to save José's life. He died. My team were speechless while a police officer said, "This son of a bitch is lucky, better die here than suffer in the hands of other prisoners." I did not know what to think. The physician leading the team asked a colleague and me to take care of the body and bring it to the hospital morgue where a forensic doctor would examine the body. José was only three years younger than me. I couldn't see any evil in him, but I saw so much evil in the situation of police officers yelling while we were trying to save him. Even if he was guilty, I thought he deserved better. I thought José must have a mother and a family who loved him. He couldn't only become one more police killing statistic, but he became yet another number of the structural violence of a system against Black and poor people: a young innocent man who lost his life in a very undignified and unjust way. Poverty, racism, and violence killed one more person whose story and dreams for a better life I never got the chance to learn, but I knew that they existed. José Manuel da Silva's face was once again the suffering face of Jesus on the cross, also an innocent person who was killed by a system of oppression, injustice, and violence.

Many years later, I was serving in a hospital in Haiti, where I met Michelin, who died while I was by his side. He was a twenty-six-year-old man in the final stage of his young life because of cancer. Michelin's life ended prematurely after a long saga searching for health-care assistance until he arrived at our hospital, where he died peacefully. Michelin, as with any person his age, had dreams and plans for his life. Pursuing his dreams amid poverty and lacking opportunities for education, as is the reality in Haiti, Michelin managed to buy a small motorcycle and became a moto-taxi driver. His passion for motorcycles was furthered with the possibility of making some money to survive. One day, already feeling weak, Michelin had a motorcycle accident with a truck that severely damaged his left leg, especially his knee. (Haiti has many young people working as moto-taxi drivers and the accident rate average is significant.) Michelin's friends took him to a public hospital in Port-au-Prince, and no physician was there because medical doctors were on strike. He received some care from nurses who stopped the bleeding and made a bandage. They knew he needed specialized care that they could not offer. His friends took him and searched for another place where they could find a physician. Their search ended with frustration. Michelin returned home where he lived with his mother in a small village about two hours from the hospital where I was serving. A few days later, someone told Michelin that the University Hospital of Mirabalais (supported by the NGO Partners in Health) had doctors working there. He went to the hospital and was accepted at the emergency room. He finally finds care, but later than ideal. Michelin received the necessary care for his leg, but his doctors also discovered that cancer had spread into his bones. I arrived at Mirabalais about a month after Michelin had begun his cancer treatment and he was already in palliative care. My relationship with him (and his mother, who was with him all the time) was short but meaningful. We provided the best care available so that he could die with dignity and be comforted by his mother. I learned a great deal listening to him and his mother, a strong woman who had to travel two hours to be with her son. She was a widow and had no other children. She did not have money to make this trip every day. She basically stayed all the time in the hospital and often had to sleep on the ground outside the hospital because she had no other place nearby to go. Neither did she have money to buy food. She ate what the hospital provided, which was not enough, and what other people shared with her. After her son died, she said, "I am sad because my son passed away. But I am thankful for all the care you gave to him and for seeing us as human beings who deserve your attention."

The final story is about indigenous people in the Amazon region in Brazil and their suffering due to COVID-19. The indigenous people are perhaps those who have most experienced the devastations of their communities because of infectious diseases brought by outsiders (mostly white people). Since the arrival of the Portuguese in Brazil, infectious diseases brought by them and previously nonexistent in South America, such as the flu, smallpox, measles, chickenpox, tuberculosis, and some STDs, were weapons used along with their guns to kill indigenous people in their own lands. It is estimated that in the sixteenth century, Brazil had 1,422 different indigenous peoples, with 40 linguistic families and 33 isolated languages with a total population of forty million. Today, these people are approximately 800,000, divided into 225 indigenous peoples, with 21 linguistic families. Most of these peoples live in the Amazon region.[3]

The COVID-19 pandemic's attack against these original peoples was not a new story for them, it was only one more cruel page against the historically oppressed original people of Brazil, people who have lived in this land with their culture and tradition for centuries before the Western invasion. The bitter memories of previous outbreaks and epidemics had been reawakened by COVID-19. According to anthropologist Carlos Fausto, "since the beginning of colonization, [indigenous peoples] had to learn the meaning of 'epidemic' in their own bodies." He reports the words of this friend from the Kuikuro people: "[COVID-19] is like the measles of my grandfather's time." (A reference to the deeply traumatic account of the measles epidemic that swept the region in 1954.) "[The disease] was sudden and swift, killing entire families without even leaving time to bury the dead properly. With everyone sick, no one was left to provide food, much less tend to the bodies."[4]

Numbers from Brazilian Health Ministry's Special Secretary for Indigenous Health show that COVID-19 mortality rate among indigenous people is 52 per 100,000 while among the general nonindigenous Brazilians it is 21 per 100,000. Indigenous individuals living in urban areas are five times more likely to be infected by the coronavirus and need hospitalization than nonindigenous individuals.[5] Santos et al. affirm,

> The crisis caused by the COVID-19 pandemic clearly exposes indigenous peoples' greater political, social, and environmental vulnerability. Experiencing daily violence and discrimination, indigenous people in Brazil live in precarious housing and sanitation conditions; face invaders and the damage caused to their territories; deal with food insecurity and lack of safe water, high infant mortality, invisibility of the indigenous families living in cities and towns; childhood marked by chronic malnutrition (25% of under-five children), and infectious and parasitic diseases such as diarrhea and pneumonia, the main causes of illness and death in indigenous children.[6]

The original peoples of Brazil have been suffering great attacks against their lives by farmers and gold miners who invade and exploit their lands. They use armed militias to create a truth war, that has killed hundreds and displaced thousands of indigenous peoples. These farmers (*latifundiarios*) deforest the Amazon rainforest for industrial agriculture and livestock, and the gold miners devastate the forest searching for gold and other minerals. The administration of Brazilian president Jair Bolsonaro has supported these actions against the forest and their peoples. COVID-19 seemed to be an opportunity to accelerate this process of the elimination of indigenous peoples, who were considered useless by Bolsonaro. According to him, they are lazy and unproductive people who prevent the country from development.[7] Using the theory of Achille Mbembe on necropolitics, Élio Gasda suggests that the Brazilian state has been dismantled by Bolsonaro with his neoliberal agenda and polices of death that gained an ally in the COVID-19 pandemic. Therefore, Bolsonaro used COVID-19 as an attempt to promote a genocide of the indigenous people.[8] Gasda stresses that the indigenous who were dying are not numbers, but rather, people with names and stories, such as the Yanomami mothers who lost their children from COVID-19 and the right to a funeral according to their traditions because the state was burying them in mass graves without reporting it to the family before the action was taken. The Yanomami do not bury their dead, but rather burn them in a communitarian ritual, an important ceremony of passage that is full of meaning.[9]

THE END OF LIFE OF THE POOR AND THE OPPRESSED

The three stories above reveal that the most urgent global health challenges for the end of life in low- and middle-income countries (LMIC) are far from discussions about euthanasia (intentional killing of a terminal patient or person with an incurable disease) and medical futility (the use of disproportional medical resources to prolong the life of a terminal patient). Their reality and the suffering of the poor in LMIC do not allow them to reach ethical concerns about an individual's autonomy to choose treatments or to refuse extraordinary measures of medical care to die with dignity. When we look at the realities where the poor and the oppressed die, meditate on their stories, and contemplate the faces of those who are suffering and dying because of injustice, oppression, exploitation, and lack of access to health care, we realize that the end of life in global health is challenged by the drama of injustice and premature death without dignity and an opportunity to flourish.

The development of modern medicine and the possibility of increasing human longevity and well-being are great achievements for humanity and yet, paradoxically, a failure because most of the world's population is kept far from this development. The benefits of modern medicine have not been available for all. Consequently, many people have been more vulnerable and have even suffered premature death at unacceptable levels despite our current medical progress. This fact challenges us to expand our theological bioethics when reflecting on end-of-life issues.

In recent documents, the Catholic Church teaching on the end of life has been limited to issues related to euthanasia, physician-assisted suicide, and palliative care. The Church aims to provide resources for a death with dignity and discernment about options of care without choosing euthanasia, which the magisterium considers a "grave violation of the law of God, since it is the deliberate and morally unacceptable killing of a human person" (*Evangelium Vitae* 65). The last document of the Congregation for Doctrine of the Faith (CDF) on the end of life clearly condemns euthanasia: "The church is convinced of the necessity to reaffirm as definitive teaching that euthanasia is a crime against human life because, in this act, one chooses directly to cause the death of another innocent human being."[10] This statement has a theological issue: whether or not a dicastery can affirm anything as "definitive teaching," but this is not the focus of our discussion. Instead, I want to show that this document illustrates that the Church's teaching on the end of life is limited to a first-world discussion about patient's autonomy and the use of medical technology to extend or abbreviate life. The document also states that the Church is against medical futility to prolong unnecessary suffering and supports palliative care to help people die at the right moment with dignity.

The CDF's document provides a great pastoral theology for end-of-life care, using the Good Samaritan to stress the Church's mission of care for those who are dying. However, this document does not address any issues related to death because of poverty and marginalization—social determinants that create disproportional vulnerability to fall sick—and lack of health care. *Evangelium Vitae* (1995) considers social injustice as threatening life: "Today this proclamation is especially pressing because of the extraordinary increase and gravity of threats to the life of individuals and peoples, especially where life is weak and defenseless. In addition to the ancient scourges of poverty, hunger, endemic diseases, violence and war, new threats are emerging on an alarmingly vast scale" (no. 3), but John Paul II failed to relate these threats to human life to health-care systems and the lack of medical assistance, especially in the LMIC. When addressing end-of-life issues, he also limited his approach to discuss euthanasia, medical futility, and palliative care, which is within a context where people have access to health care.

The approach of these documents emanates from a theoretical analysis. They do not include the voices and the experiences of people at the end of life, neither from rich countries, nor from the LMIC. Global health does not seem to be a concern and the discussion is narrowed to the physician-patient relationship.

The magisterium of Pope Francis provides a perspective that advances these documents and the discussion about the end of life, leading it to the reality of LMIC countries. However, it must be said that Francis, in the few occasions that he directly addresses end-of-life issues, did not make a link between bioethical challenges related to the end of life and the socioeconomic vulnerability of the poor, which makes them sick and prevents them from accessing health care. When Francis talks about the end of life, he focuses on traditional bioethical themes, such as euthanasia, palliative care, and decisions regarding therapies for the terminally ill.[11] Although end of life is not among the major focus of Francis's document, he offers a perspective that challenges traditional ways of seeing this topic by offering a theological foundation for an approach from the lens of the poor and the threats against their lives. Consistent in his major writings, Francis stresses the importance of listening to the poor in a posture open to learning from them. In his first document, Francis suggested, "I prefer a Church which is bruised, hurting, and dirty because it has been out on the streets, rather than a Church which is unhealthy from being confined and from clinging to its own security" (*Evangelii Gaudium* 49). This Church incarnates "the duty of hearing the cry of the poor" to "learn from them" (*Evangelii Gaudium* 193, 198). Thus, we can "properly accompany the poor in their path of liberation" (*Evangelii Gaudium* 199). In his encyclical *Laudato Si'*, Francis expanded this perspective by developing a theology of dialogical encounter with those who are at the bottom of society, in which he included the indigenous communities as "dialogical partners" from whom we have much to listen and learn (no. 196). The synod of bishops of the Amazon confirmed this view of encounter and dialogue with the reality of those who are at the bottom. Hence, Pope Francis talks about "places of encounter of mutual enrichment" with "a holiness born of encounter and engagement, contemplation and services, receptive solicitude and life in community, cheerful sobriety and the struggle for justice" (*Querida Amazonia* 30, 77).

Although Pope Francis does not address global health issues related to the end of life, he offers resources for us to engage with those suffering in local realities because of poverty, vulnerability to illness, lack of health care, and premature death. Francis's teaching leads us to engage with people like José, Michelin, and the Yanomami mothers to listen to their stories, contemplate their faces, and learn what is threating their lives. This engagement creates a path of liberation for justice in health care and has the support of the christological experience of an incarnate God who identifies with the suffering of the poor and the sick, to whom he brought the good news and healing.

In his last encyclical, *Fratelli Tutti*, Pope Francis continues the development of this theology of a culture that encounters and listens to the poor. He addresses the COVID-19 pandemic and, in doing so, global health, with his reflection against a culture of indifference and individualism that might foster a practice of "every man for himself" (no. 222) killing any opportunity to rebuild the human family. To rebuild this family in a globalized solidarity, Francis stresses the need of listening to others. "The ability to sit down and listen to others, typical or interpersonal encounters, is paradigmatic of the welcoming attitude shown by those who transcend narcissism and accept others, caring for them and welcoming them in their lives" (*Fratelli Tutti* 48). He then adds, "When one part of society exploits all that the world has to offer, acting as if the poor did not exist, there will eventually be consequences....Encounter cannot take place only between the holders of economic, political, or academic power. Genuine social encounter calls for a dialogue that engages the culture shared by the majority of the population" (*Fratelli Tutti* 219).

The poor are those who better embody and represent this population. They are those who are suffering most because of the poverty, oppression, and exploitation that make them disproportionally more vulnerable to illnesses, with no access to health care, and uncountable premature deaths. This context and approach are very relevant for the end of life in global health because they show the most challenging issues for people regarding life and death, and with a perspective that includes the voices of the poor and the oppressed.

THE END OF LIFE IN A BIOETHICS FROM THE POOR

Where you are when you look at something, impacts the way you understand the object of observation. This has significant methodological impact. In theology, this is called theological *locus*. In bioethics and global health, the *locus* from where you look at the challenges you want to address has great relevance. Furthermore, where you are and the experience you have tends to determine the issue on which you are going to focus. In this sense, it is not surprising nor bad that when bioethics in the United States looks at end-of-life issues, bioethicists see clinical challenges involving the terminally ill and their decisions. The problem begins when this prevents us from seeing other challenges related to the end-of-life in realities where people are dying because of lack of access to health care within a destitute situation of poverty and marginalization. The problem becomes bigger when the framework used in a context that has dominated bioethics discussion, since its origins is exported to another context, such as those local realities marked by poverty and "medical deserts"—an expression of Paul Farmer to refer to large regions in the global health scene lacking any health-care resource.[12]

Ethical discussions about the end of life are absent in global health debates. On the one hand, it is absent because the traditional, Western way of considering the end of life, such as euthanasia and physician-assisted suicide, do not seem to be a part of the health-care context in impoverished countries. Thus, this absence seems to make sense. On the other hand, ethical discussions surrounding global health fail to link the death of the poor, those premature deaths because of the lack of proper health care to end of life as a bioethical issue. It is a failure to see those unfair and avoidable deaths immorally resulting from the structures that sustain our world and its dominant economic system, and when most people are prevented from having access to the advancement of modern medicine and good living conditions because of their poverty and marginalization from opportunities to flourish.

I recognize that most people engaged in health-care delivery and research in global health stress the impact of poverty in people's health and the lack of access to health care. Poverty is considered a social determinant of health. Efforts to bring health care to the poor aims to address this challenge. However, the death of the poor tends to be joined to statistics that, hopefully, will be considered when global health strategies are developed. These deaths are rarely considered from a bioethical viewpoint as a key ethical challenge related to the end of life, even more urgent than any discussion about whether or not one should use the abundant health resources available in the United States for a wealthy patient. I am not diminishing the importance of this discussion, but rather the disproportional attention it receives in the field of bioethics. A change of *locus* might help us to reorient our bioethical priorities and perspectives.

The option for the poor, a christological concept with great ethical and social implications, helps us to create this movement of changing our locus to guide us to see the faces and the dramas of people like José Manuel, Michelin, and Yanomami mothers. Therefore, the preferential option for the poor is fundamental for theological bioethics and its attempt to offer a contribution to global health. This is especially the case in contexts where the end-of-life challenges are not yet within a clinic or an ICU with abundant medical technology available, but rather in the streets where people die in their vulnerability before having an opportunity to see a physician or a nurse. In a previous work, I suggested, "With the option for the poor, we do a bioethics incarnated in the reality of our people, we go beyond the defense of life only before the achievement of biomedical technology. We defend life in all its dimensions, from the basic needs—to meet a worthy life and care about our common home—to defending those excluded from information and access to quality health care services."[13] Theologically, this incarnation is an authentic manifestation of the christological mission of the Catholic Church, which is understood as the people of God, but this incarnation is a dialogical call, that is, its relevance goes beyond a particular religious community because it is an invitation for all who understand the unacceptable impact of poverty and injustice in the lives of fellow human beings to include the faces and voices of the poor in their efforts of promoting life and care for those who are sick in global health.

CONCLUSION

In 1989, the Brazilian theologian Márcio Fabri dos Anjos wrote a short essay for the newsletter *Boletim ICAPS* entitled "Eutanásia em chave de libertação" (Euthanasia from a liberating perspective). He argued that discussions about euthanasia was narrowed by biomedical ethics to focus on the physician-patient relationship and was not enough to understand end of life issues in countries marked by poverty, injustice, and oppression. Dos Anjos examined that the word *euthanasia* refers to a "good, happy death" for terminal patients. But it was also necessary to think about those "bad, unhappy deaths" because of lack of proper medical assistance and those deaths outside the hospital contexts. Those deaths cause us "to think about slow and quiet deaths created by systems and structures."[14] Hence, he coined the neologism *misthanasia* to incorporate these slow and quiet deaths in our discussion on the end of life and bioethics:

> Misthanasia makes us to think about those who died hungry...make us to think about the death of an impoverished person, embittered by abandonment, because the lack of the most basic resources. It also leads us to see the deaths because of torture by brutal political regimes and how these people disappeared.[15]

After this essay, *misthanasia* became part of the bioethical vocabulary in Brazil to represent those deaths due to injustice, oppression, and marginalization from access to health care.[16] Even today, the most urgent end-of-life issues in global health are not related to the autonomy of individuals to choose or refuse care while dying, but rather the daily risk of falling ill and dying without the ability to reach any proper health care. *Misthanasia*, and not euthanasia, is truly occurring every day among the poor, particularly in LMIC. Being with those at the bottom who experience this reality of the end of life seems an appropriate approach for global health to address the most urgent challenges toward life and death with dignity.

Conclusion

> *They [ten destitute and sick people] call out, saying, "Jesus, Master, have mercy on us!" When he saw them, he said to them, "Go and show yourselves to the priests." And as they went, they were made clean. Then one of them, when he saw that he was healed, turned back, praising God with a loud voice. He prostrated himself at Jesus' feet and thanked him. And he was a Samaritan.* (Luke 17:13–16)

We conclude this book with a biblical text showing the relationship between Jesus and the sick. The Gospels present so many interactions between Jesus and people who were poor and sick that it is not easy to pick only one. I chose this one that was suggested by a student who served in a project in Ecuador, caring for people with Hansen's disease, a skin disease that is related to leprosy that comes with much stigmatization. Lepers are present in many scriptural texts, and several of these texts include the mention of a cure by Jesus. In this text from Luke, I intentionally refer to "ten destitute and sick" and not "ten lepers," which is the traditional interpretation. Biblical leprosy has nothing to do with Hansen's disease, but the same destitute conditions of those with a skin disease are present, both then and now. Today, as in Jesus's time, poverty and illness have an intimate relationship. At that time, being sick was a reason for exclusion and marginalization: a sick individual was an unclean person, unworthy of participating in society, that is, unworthy of having opportunities and rights. Consequently, marginalization, suffering, and poverty were the inevitable consequences for a sick person, especially for those who were stigmatized for reasons such as skin diseases, visible and generally classified as leprosy. Even those who had economic resources experienced the same path until they became impoverished, for example, the bleeding woman who had a stable socioeconomic life, but lost everything with doctors and ended up on the streets as a poor person (Luke 8:43–48). Jesus's encounter with those who are destitute and sick was an act of recognition of the "other" who suffered, a movement of compassion.

The way that Jesus relates to the sick, caring for them beyond the physical illness, is a paradigm for approaching those who are suffering in their sickness, including everything that happens in their lives. Jesus offers the sick what they need and not what was assumed they would need, based on societal norms.

In the Gospels, Jesus always answered the cry of a destitute and sick person, caring and healing them, offering a form of best care and social reintegration, and not what someone decided was most cost-effective. Paul Farmer argues that the paradigm of cost-effectiveness and control-over-care creates a false conflict between epidemiological control and treatments for the sick and is a disgrace that has shaped health care in low-income countries.[1] In other words, the poor are prevented from receiving most of what they need, while the rich in affluent countries have the most advanced medical technology available.

The Gospels do not present Jesus—when dealing with a sick person—addressing health economic issues such as cost-effectiveness or any other paradigm in which the help for the destitute and the sick continues only until it becomes costly for the helper. The New Testament, however, offers values, principles, and virtues from Jesus and his relationship with the sick that can be used to shape health care and address the global health paradigm criticized by Farmer. The Gospels show Jesus providing the best medicine that one can ever provide: a care that heals the sick. Of course, we cannot perform miracles in a health-care setting like Jesus did, however, providing the best medicine and treatments available to relieve pain, to improve quality of life, and to heal when it is possible are the first teachings from Jesus's encounter with those who are destitute and sick. The preferential option for the poor that we have referred to many times throughout this book is also a christological option for the best medicine delivered to these people.

In Jesus's time, being sick meant carrying a double burden: suffering because of physical disease and spiritual impurity. Consequently, those who were sick were socially and religiously marginalized, and excluded from socioeconomic opportunities as well as from the love of God. Knowing this context helps us to understand how socially, religiously, and personally significant Jesus's encounters with the sick were. Jesus helped people whom mainstream societal and religious norms dictated were to be kept far away. Generally, those who were sick or destitute were or became poor and marginalized because of their condition. Thus, Jesus's encounter with these people was a revolutionary movement of compassion and care with socioeconomic and religious implications.

The brief passage of Luke's Gospel demonstrates Jesus's care for ten destitute and sick people with a skin disease. They were suffering because of their health status and social marginalization. Jesus's miracle was an act of healing that also offered them an opportunity of social inclusion. Only one returned to thank Jesus for this gift. Two elements of this story shine light on global health practice toward chronic, especially stigmatized noncommunicable and terminal diseases, areas that usually are neglected by global health initiatives because of the paradigm mentioned above. First, the ten sick people of the Gospel had been abandoned by society (including their religious community) because of a "chronic" and "incurable" (perhaps transmittable) disease for that time. This health status legitimatized the diminution of their dignity by society. They were not worthy of any care, so they should be placed apart from others to die without creating more trouble. Jesus broke this structural violence by showing that these people were worthy of care and reintegration into society. Here, one finds an ethical approach that highlights the dignity of the destitute and the sick: their lives matter! A new global health paradigm begins when we see the destitute and the sick as worthy of the best care available and not only as recipients of crumbs from the table of rich nations that maintain that treating certain chronic and noncommunicable diseases in low-income countries is not cost-effective.

Second, the one who went back to thank Jesus for the cure showed gratitude. Brazilian Bishop Hélder Câmara used to say that life "begins and ends with gratitude." For him, gratitude for being alive and for the life we have are the first revolutionary acts to protect the dignity of the life of the poor from conception to natural death. Regardless of health status, physical strength, mental ability, behavior, personal mistakes, individual accomplishments, and socioeconomic conditions, life is always a gift from God. Each of us must be thankful for her/his individual existence and the existence of all-fellow human beings. This gratitude recognizes the unique dignity of the human person and the commitment to those who have had their dignity hurt and diminished by structural violence. In the context of health care in impoverished regions, gratitude is the virtue of caring for a worthy life that is suffering, but this worthy life has a meaningful existence, despite the suffering, simply by the fact of its presence in the world. In global health, gratitude means an experience of companionship with the destitute and the sick who are worthy of receiving the best care available. It is also a journey to help patients and providers to recognize the value of their life, a unique gift for family, friends, community, and the world. When this unique gift is suffering, even in a context of a terminal illness, her/his dignity must guide our response through medical care, compassion, faith, and hope.

I chose Luke 17:14–17 to conclude this book because it shows Jesus going beyond the physical healing in caring for the sick. Jesus's actions toward those who were sick included a social dimension of care. He acted to promote quality of life and to reintegrate the marginalized-sick into social life. Jesus was not only worried about the biological aspect of these people, but also about promoting a life with dignity for the human being and his/her participation in social life. Based on this christological perspective, the Latin American bishops state,

> Health is a biographic experience covering the different dimensions of the human person; it has an intimate relationship with the particular experience that a person has with his/her own corporality, with his/her place in the world, and with the values on which he/she builds his/her existence. In short, we can say that health is a harmony between body and spirit, a harmony between person and environment, a harmony between character and responsibility.[2]

This harmony requires an approach that is able to integrate different social sectors and health-care actions targeting people's well-being, socioeconomic opportunities, and access to health care when needed. Care and justice must walk hand in hand. The parable of the good Samaritan (Luke 10:25–37) shows care and justice as active social principles that sustain a preferential option for the poor to be embraced by programs of health care. The action of the Samaritan toward the destitute and sick person embodies solidarity as a social principle that cares and promotes justice without distinction among people. Cost-effectiveness, conflict related to control over care, and making decisions about which lives matter more than others are not part of the Samaritan paradigm, but rather the dignity of the poor sick person who needs assistance. "This parable helps us think about solidarity and vulnerability"[3] inside the reality of the poor.

If there is no contemplation of the suffering face of the destitute and the sick, care and justice are mere abstractions. Many people and leaders in our contemporary society speak about poverty, marginalized people, lack of opportunities, and health inequalities. Everyone who is talking about this reality of poverty and suffering with millions of daily premature, avoidable deaths, has suggestions on how to address these issues. Many develop beautiful theories and systems to end poverty, showing data to support their claims. However, those who suffer are not mere numbers, statistics, nor a distant people who we do not know. In global health, the sick and the poor far from us are not anonymous subjects, without a face or voice. They are dying every day. Many people create "solutions" for them, but do not know who they are. These possible solutions are often arbitrary, nondemocratic, and elitist. These solutions come from people who are not victims of structural violence, who do not share the life of the victims, who do not listen to them.

Listening to the poor, engaging them in dialogue, and promoting their participation are essential to caring and promoting justice in any social context marked by poverty and oppression, and even health inequalities. This is one of the reasons this book did not focus on statistics of poverty, since they can be found in thousands of studies published in many journals, books, and institutional websites of organizations, such as the World Bank, the World Health Organization, and the Kaiser Foundation. My focus is on theological foundations that can lead us to engage with the poor in their realty, being their companion who see their faces, know their names, listen to their voices, and learn from them. I offer a christological reflection that shows a Jesus close to the poor, a Jesus who sent the Holy Spirt to guide the Church to continue his mission. Thus, I present stories of communities that read and interpreted the Gospel from their reality and the socioeconomic challenges they face. The Christology and global ethics offered in this book are no more than humble systematic theological reflections of an experience of faith and practice within communities that celebrate the Paschal Mystery of Jesus and struggle for liberation.

The preferential option for the poor was present as a principle grounded in the ministry of Jesus and offered to his followers to continue his mission in history, guided by the Holy Spirit. The christological foundation for the preferential option for the poor oriented to social ethics, in general, and to theological bioethics in global health, in particular, are perhaps the greatest resources developed in this book. The preferential option for the poor is a perspective that integrates care and justice with the active participation of impoverished communities in which their people are agents of transformation. As the destitute and sick Samaritan healed by Jesus returned to thank him, my final word is on gratitude. Thank you, God, for your grace that I have seen in the faith, love, and hope of communities that believe in your Son and walk with him in history guided by the Holy Spirit.

Notes

CHAPTER 1

1. J. Severino Croatto, "La Contribución de la Hermenéutica Bíblica a la Teología de la Liberación," *Cuadernos de Teología* 6, no. 4 (1985): 50. See also Tereza Cavalcanti, "Social Location and Biblical Interpretation: A Tropical Reading," in *Reading from This Place: Volume 2; Social Location and Biblical Interpretation*, ed. F. F. Segovia and M. A. Tolbert (Minneapolis, MN: Fortress Press, 1995), 201–18.

2. John Milbank, *Theology & Social Theory: Beyond Secular Reason*, 2nd ed. (Oxford: Blackwell Publishing, 2006), 206–54. Jorge Costadoat, "La Hermenéutica en las Teologías Contextuales de la Liberación," *Teología y Vida* XLVI (2005): 56–74, https://doi.org/10.4067/S0049-34492005000100003.

3. There are great works addressing this issue. See, e.g., The International Journal of Theology *Concilium* published two volumes on this subject: Hille Kaker, Luiz Carlo Susim, and Eloi Messi Metogo, eds., "Postcolonial Theology," *Concilium* 2 (London: SCM Press, 2013); Carlos Mendoza-Ávarez and Thierry-Marie Courau, eds., "Decolonial Theology: Violence, Resistance and Spiritualities," *Concilium* 1 (London: SCM Press, 2020). See also Jeseph Drexler-Dreis, "Latin American Liberation Theology as a Decolonial Project?: Considering the Theological Approaches of Clodovis Boff and Ignacio Ellacuría," *Louvain Studies* 39, no. 3 (2016): 218–39, https://doi.org/10.2143/LS.39.3.3170047.

4. Clodovis Boff, *Teoria do Método Teológico*, 4th ed. (Petrópolis: Vozes, 2009), 24–33.

5. Francisco Moreno Rejon, *Teologia Moral a partir dos Pobres: A Moral na Reflexão Teológica da América Latina* (Aparecida: Editora Santuário, 1987), 82–89.

6. Olga Consuelo Vélez Caro, *El Método Teológico: Fundamentos, Especializaciones, Enfoques* (Bogotá: Pontificia Universidad Javeriana Press, 2008), 172.

7. Clodovis Boff, *Teoria do Método Teológico*, 157–84.

8. Vélez Caro, *El Método Teológico*, 38–39; 166; David J. Bosch, *Missão Transformadora: Mudanças de Paradigma na Teologia da Missão*, 3rd ed. (São Leopoldo: Sinodal, 2002), 505.

9. *Contextual theology* is also a term to refer to same theological perspectives that emerged in the Global North to address specific issues related to injustice and marginalization, such as political theology in Germany and Black Theology in the United States. See Robert Schreiter, *Constructing Local Theologies*, 30th anniv. ed. (Maryknoll, NY: Orbis Books, 2015), 1–14; 20–44.

10. Olga Consuelo Vélez Caro, "El Quehacer Teológico y el Método de Investigación Acción Participativa: Una Reflexión Metodológica," *Theologica Xaveriana* 67, no. 183 (2017): 200, https://doi.org/10.11144/javeriana.tx67-183.qtmiap.

11. One criticism against liberation theology is that this perspective only focuses on the socioeconomic oppression of the poor, as the reality from which theology is developed. It is common to find this criticism especially coming from theologians of the Global North. It is fair, but this criticism might apply for the first liberation theologians in the 1970s and 1980s, who are the main liberation theologians read in the Global North because their books were translated into English. However, liberation theology did not stop in the 1980s. (In a conference with Latin American theologians, U.S. theologian M. Therese Lysaught recognized this limitation among many U.S. theologians. See her talk, "Ética Teológica en América: Avances y Desafíos," at https://www.polisandhope.org/post/ética-teológica-en-américa-avances-y-desafíos.) Although Latin American liberation theology does not have the publicity it had in the 1970s and 1980s, it continues its development, expanding its reflection to include other oppressed and marginalized groups. Brazilian theologian Elio Gasda, e.g., stresses, "The theological ethics of Latin America stands out because it includes the option of the discarded, those who are socially and culturally discriminated against....We are doing theological ethics in the face of world hunger, terroristic genocide toward the poor, the black, the female, the gay, the transexual, the indigenous, and the displaced populations." E. Gasda, "Theological Ethics from the Reality of the People," in *Building Bridges in Sarajevo: The Plenary Papers from CTEWC 2018*, eds. K. E. Heyer, L. R. Keenan, and A. Vicine (Maryknoll: Orbis Books, 2019), 87, 90.

12. CELAM, *Documento de Aparecida* (São Paulo; Brasília: Paulus; Edições CNBB, 2007), no. 303.

13. The help that these tools provide in support of theological endeavors is not structural, as suggested by Consuelo Vélez Caro: "In theological knowledge, all social scientific methods have supported contextual theologies, such as liberation theology, with an auxiliary service, but they are not structural in the theological endeavor." Vélez Caro, "El Quehacer Teológico y el Método de Investigación Acción Participativa," 190.

14. Marciano Vidal, "Gaudium et spes y Teología Moral: A los 50 Años del Concilio Vaticano II," *Moralia* 35, no. 134 (2012): 109.

15. Vidal, "Gaudium et spes y Teología Moral," 105.

16. CELAM, "Medellín," in *Documentos do Celam: Rio de Janeiro, Medellín, Puebla e Santo Domingo* (São Paulo: Paulus, 2005), 117, no. 4.8.

17. CELAM, "Puebla," in *Documentos do Celam: Rio de Janeiro, Medellín, Puebla e Santo Domingo* (São Paulo: Paulus, 2005), no. 1226.

18. CELAM, "Puebla," no. 1227.

19. CELAM, *Documento de Aparecida*, no. 97.

20. João Décio Passos, *A Igreja em Saída e a Casa Comum: Francisco e os Desafios da Renovação* (São Paulo: Paulinas, 2016), 67–69.

21. The initiative of the network of Catholic theological ethicists promoted by Catholic Theological Ethics in the World Church (CTEWC) is a great example of interaction and peer-dialogue between the Global North and South. CTEWC has promoted actions, events, publications, and other collaborative works with great international diversity, exchanging, and mutual support. See CTEWC mission, events, publications, and other initiatives at www.catholicethics.com.

22. Liberation from this colonial mentality, a colonizing one for the oppressor and a colonized one for the oppressed, is fundamental to the process of re-creating the world. This liberation impacts not only theology, but all aspects of our society. Paulo Freire deeply understood this oppression, this colonization of people's minds, by recognizing that for anyone to be free all must be free in order to create the ways of justice. Paulo Freire, *Pedagogy of the Oppressed*, 30th anniv. ed. (New York: Continuum, 2000), 50, 56, 71–72, 79; Paulo Freire, *Education for Critical Consciousness* (New York: Continuum, 2005), 15, 39–40.

23. Commonly, this contribution comes from narratives that express the experience of suffering of those who are victims of oppression and injustice. The contact with narratives and, at the same time, an experience of sharing lives once the theologian is a member of the same community, becomes a resource for the theologian to develop his or her reflection of the faith grounded on the reality. An example of this process is found in Maria Inês de Castro Millen's essay "Violence Against Women: The Macabre

Face of Every day." Castro Millen begins with a narrative from her community when she learned that a fifteen-year-old girl, leader of a Catholic youth group in the diocese, was a victim of femicide, killed by a man who did not accept she did not want to date him. The narrative of this death and the community's process of awareness and reconciliation made Castro Millen to rethink the theology she was developing about the experience of women in Brazil. She stresses that the poor include women victims of violence because the poor refer to those who are weak, the little ones of the gospel. She concludes by suggesting this exercise: "If we return to Pope Francis' words…and replace the words 'poor,' 'weak,' and 'little ones' by 'women,' we will be surprised. We will realize the urgent need to revise the Church's way of relationship with women." M. I. de Castro Millen, "Violência Contra as Mulheres: A Face Macabra do Cotidiano," in *A Moral do Papa Francisco: Um Projeto a partir dos Descartados*, ed. R. Zacharias and M. I. de Castro Millen (Aparecida: Editora Santuário, 2020), 166. The experience of women and their narratives challenge not only patriarchal societies, but also the structure of the Church in its ecclesial organization and in the way of doing theology.

24. Maria Clara L. Bingemer, "A Desventura e a Opção Pelos Pobres: Simone Weil e a Teologia da Libertação Latino-americana," *REB–Revista Eclesiástica Brasileira* 69, no. 276 (2009): 789, https://doi.org/10.29386/reb.v69i276.1251. New liberation theology approaches that reflect the concept of option for the poor described by Bingemer are found in a new generation of Latin American theologians who are engaged in the study of sexual ethics, gender studies, bioethics, race, ecology, and indigenous studies. See, e.g., Ronaldo Zacharias, *Ética e Direitos Sexuais* (São Paulo: Ideias & Letras, 2021); Cássia Quelho Tavares, "A Voz das Mulheres como Interpelação à Teologia Moral: A 'Igreja em Saída,'" in *Teologia Moral: Fundamentos, Desafios e Perspectivas*, ed. L. Pessini and R. Zacharias (Aparecida: Editora Santuário, 2015), 223–50; Luiz A. de Mattos, "O Cuidado da Casa Comum: Os desafios éticos e Espirituais de uma Ecologia Integral," in *A Moral do Papa Francisco: Um Projeto a partir dos Descartados*, ed. R. Zacharias and M. I. de Castro Millen (Aparecida: Editora Santuário, 2020), 229–56; Marilú Rojas Salazar, "Tendências Interculturais para uma Espiritualidade Ecofeminista Libertadora" and Carlos Mendoza-Álvarez, "*Extra Victimas Salus Non Est* ou da Vigência da Teologia da Libertação em Tempos Pós Modernos," in *A Teologia da Libertação em Prospectiva*, ed. A. Brighenti and R. Hermano (São Paulo: Paulus/Paulinas, 2013), 313–21; 323–41; Alejandro Castillo Morga, "Ante la Pandemia: Pensar los Desequilibrios Ambientales como Reacción Ética ante la Acción Humana," *Journal of Moral Theology* 10, Special Issue (Spring 2021): 52–66.

25. Alexandre A. Martins, *The Cry of the Poor: Liberation Ethics and Justice in Health Care* (Lanham: Lexington Books, 2020). In this book, I present the knowledge of the poor from their narratives as partners of my dialogue to develop a theological ethics toward justice in health care. Vélez Caro, "El Quehacer Teológico y el Método de Investigación Acción Participativa," 59–72.

26. Leonardo Boff and Clodovis Boff, *Como Fazer Teologia da Libertação*, 8th ed. (Petrópolis: Vozes, 2001), 41–42. They suggest that the novelty of liberation theology is the root of its theological act. According to them, the first step is something "pre-theological," that is, the encounter with the poor and its implications.

27. I am not claiming that other liberating perspectives historically originated from Latin American liberation theology. Many other liberating perspectives emerged organically within the same period of the 1960s (e.g., Black liberation theology in the United States and protestant contextual theologies in the Global South), and in some cases earlier. Sidney M Sanches, "A Contextualização da Teologia: Conceitos, História, Tensões, Métodos e Possibilidades," *Revista Tecer* 2, no. 3 (2019): 1–20, https://doi.org/10.15601/1983-7631/rt.v2n3p1-20. My point here is that liberation theology has expanded to use the same liberation method to address other situations of oppression beyond socioeconomic injustice. Maria Clara Bingemer argues that today the concept of poor in liberation theology is understood in a broad, inclusive category that includes not only the socioeconomic poor, but also other people and groups who are victims of oppression and injustice. Maria Clara L. Bingemer, "A Desventura e a Opção Pelos Pobres: Simone Weil e a Teologia da Libertação Latinoamericana," 772–91.

28. Vélez Caro, "El Quehacer Teológico y el Método de Investigación Acción Participativa," 200. Vélez Caro affirms that liberation theology is plural, that is, liberation theologies use liberating approaches in different contexts of oppression. This has led to new theological developments, such as: feminist theology, Black and African-American theology, Amerindian theology, ecological and holistic theology, postcolonial theology, and religious pluralist theology. Vélez Caro, "El Quehacer Teológico y el Método de Investigación Acción Participativa," 200–201.

29. See the work of Brazilian theologian Elio Gasda from his engagement with the Amazon indigenous group Yanomami, especially with the Yanomami mothers and their experience losing their children to COVID-19. Gasda considers their experience of suffering because of children's deaths and their cultural tradition related to funerals, a narrative that interacts with Gasda's Catholic social theology. E. Gasda, "Los Muertos No

Son Números: Gestión Política de la Muerte en Tiempos de Pandemia," *Jornal of Moral Theology* 10, Special Issue (Spring 2021): 22–32.

30. On the relation between theology and social science in liberation theology, see Francisco de Aquino Júnior, "Teologia e Ciências Sociais," *Horizonte* 10, no. 28 (2012): 1324–49, https://doi.org/10.5752/P.2175-5841.2012v10n28p1324.

31. Gustavo Gutiérrez, *Teologia da Libertação*, 4th ed. (Petrópolis: Vozes, 1983), 98–99.

32. Alexandre A. Martins, *The Cry of the Poor: Liberation Ethics and Justice in Health Care* (Lanham: Lexington Books, 2020). See particularly the first chapter of the book, titled "Prolegomenon of a Project: Hermeneutical and Methodological Lines."

33. The philosophy of Simone Weil on affliction and the liberation theology perspective of the suffering of the poor provide foundations for the development of an anthropology of suffering that is able to respond to the deepest questions of our societies marked by the unfair suffering of the marginalized. Considering global health challenges, this articulation has been developed in Alexandre A. Martins, *The Cry of the Poor*, 1–98. See the works of Simone Weil where she develops her account of affliction (*malheur*) and the suffering of the unfortunate (*malheureux*): "L'Amour de Dieu et le Malheur" in *Œuvres* (Paris: Quarto Gallimard, 1999), 693–715; *Œuvres Complètes V 2: L'Enracinement* (Paris: Gallimard, 2013).

34. The systematic basis for a liberation ethics was developed by: Francisco Moreno Rejon, *Teologia Moral a partir dos Pobres: A Moral na Reflexão Teológica da América Latina* (Aparecida: Editora Santuário, 1987), 121–39.

35. Boff and Boff, *Como Fazer Teologia da Libertação*, 26–26; 41–42.

36. A clarification: I am not yet using "acting morally" in the narrow sense of good acts based on principles and values. There is no implication or judgment of good and evil in moral acts of the poor. I am using this expression in a simple and preliminary sense that all action is a matter of ethical reflection. I clarify this point so as to avoid a common critique that liberation theology makes the poor a moral option in the sense of "being poor" necessarily means to perform good moral acts. In Puebla, the poor are defined from their history of deprivation of basic needs for their flourishing. This situation is a scandal of structural factors (CELAM, "Puebla," nos. 1135, 1159–60, 1209). See also Rejon, *Teologia Moral a partir dos Pobres*, 140–50. Rejon examines the social aspect of the option for the poor and its ethical implication.

37. James H. Cone, *The Cross and The Lynching Tree* (Maryknoll, NY: Orbis Books, 2013), 2–3.

38. Cone, *The Cross and The Lynching Tree*, 151.

39. Cone, *The Cross and The Lynching Tree*, 132. Catholic theologian Bryan N. Massingale expands Cone's reflection by applying it in the context of the Catholic Church in the United States and its struggle to assume an antiracism agenda that is, according to him, indispensable for social justice in the United States. See Bryan N. Massingale, *Racial Justice and the Catholic Church* (Maryknoll, NY: Orbis Books, 2010).

40. Emilce Cuda, "Theology of the People as Theological Ethics," in *Building Bridges in Sarajevo: The Plenary Papers from CTEWC 2018*, ed. K. E. Heyer, L. R. Keenan, and A. Vicine (Maryknoll, NY: Orbis Books, 2019), 83.

41. Cuda, "Theology of the People as Theological Ethics," 85.

42. Henrique C. de Lima Vaz, *Escritos de Filosofia II: Ética e Cultura* (São Paulo: Loyola, 1998), 13.

43. Vaz, *Escritos de Filosofia II*, 14.

44. Antonio Gramsci, "Problems of History and Cultures," in *Selections from the Prison Notebooks of Antonio Gramsci*, ed. and trans. Quintin Hoare and Geoffrey N. Smith (New York: International Publishers, 1971), 3–43.

45. João B. Libanio, *Cenários da Igreja*, 2nd ed. (São Paulo: Loyola, 2000), 111–25. See also José Comblin who presents the development of the Catholic communities in Latin American as an embodiment of the Vatican II's concept of Church as the people of God. This perspective gained an expression in Latin American ecclesiology of a horizontal community of faith in a praxis of liberation. Part of this experience as the intentional communities where Catholic leaders, numbers of the clergy, religious man and women, and theologians were to live in communities marked by poverty, experiencing the struggle of the poor and their liberation praxis. José Comblin, *O Povo de Deus*, 3rd ed. (São Paulo: Paulus), 2011.

46. In the United States, Marcus Mescher develops an approach that favors this dialogical method of theology in ethics from a theological ethics approach grounded on the theology of encounter promoted by Pope Francis. M. Mescher, *The Ethics Encounter: Christian Neighbor Love as a Practice of Solidarity* (Maryknoll, NY: Orbis Books, 2020).

47. Leonardo Boff and Clodovis Boff, *Introducing Liberation Theology* (Maryknoll, NY:1987), 22–23.

CHAPTER 2

1. María Teresa Davila, "The Political Anthropology of *Fratelli Tutti*: The Transcendent Nature of People's Political Projects Grounded in History," *Journal of Catholic Social Thought* 19, no. 1 (2022): 89–103, https://

doi.org/10.5840/jcathsoc20221917. Pope Francis presents this perspective several times in his Encyclical Letter *Fratelli Tutti*, when he talks about the relation between the universal and the local, considering that it is in the local reality where the encounter of fraternity and solidarity occurs. See, e.g., *Fratelli Tutti*, nos. 06, 83, 142–53.

2. Carlos Mesters, "The Liberating Reading of the Bible," *SEDOS Bulletin* 28 (1996): 164–70.

3. John D. Crossan and Jonathan L. Reed, *Excavating Jesus: Beneath the Stones, Behind the Texts* (New York: HarperSanFrancisco, 2001), 28.

4. Pablo O. Richard, "Evangelho de Lucas: Estrutura e Chaves para uma interpretação global do Evangelho," *RIBLA* 44, no. 1 (2003): 8.

5. François Bovon, "Evangelho de Lucas e Atos dos Apóstolos," in *Os Evangelhos Sinóticos e Atos dos Apóstolos*, ed. J. Auneau et al. (São Paulo: Ed. Paulinas, 1985), 271.

6. Bovon, "Evangelho de Lucas e Atos dos Apóstolos," 204.

7. José L. Sicre, *O Quadrante: Introdução aos Evangelhos*, vol. 1 (São Paulo: Paulinas, 1999), 250–51.

8. Bovon, "Evangelho de Lucas e Atos dos Apóstolos," 212.

9. Bovon, "Evangelho de Lucas e Atos dos Apóstolos," 281–83.

10. Sicre, *O Quadrante: Introdução aos Evangelhos*, 249.

11. Bovon, "Evangelho de Lucas e Atos dos Apóstolos," 271.

12. Richard, "Evangelho de Lucas," 8.

13. As said earlier, Luke's concern is historical and apologetic, but with great missionary and pastoral zeal. That is why he does not write a doctrinal treatise or essay, but it is a text that seeks to carry out a theological project. In the prologue (Luke 1:1–4), Luke himself presents the purpose of his project, which is not a work of the first proclamation or *kerygma*, even though this aspect frequently appears in Acts of Apostles. Rather it is a work to catechize, to deepen the faith of those who have already accepted the good news, that is, Jesus Christ. This is clear in the conclusion of the prologue: "so that you may verify the solidity of the teachings you have received." On this, see Sicre, *O Quadrante: Introdução aos Evangelhos*, 250–51. François Bovon, "Evangelho de Lucas e Atos dos Apóstolos," 273.

14. François Bovon, *L'Œuvre de Luc: Études d'Exégèse et de Théologie* (Paris: du Cerf, 1987), 19–23.

15. Luke's Gospel is the one that speaks most of the Holy Spirit acting in the life of Jesus and the journey of the Christian Community. See Sicre, *O Quadrante: Introdução aos Evangelhos*, 243–44.

16. Sicre, *O Quadrante: Introdução aos Evangelhos*, 228; J. Kodell, "Lucas," in *Comentário bíblico.* vol. 3. 3, ed. R. Bergant and R. J. Karris (São Paulo: Loyola, 2001), 74.

17. Kodell, "Lucas," 74–75.

18. José L. Sicre, *O Quadrante: O Mundo de Jesus*, vol. 2 (São Paulo: Paulinas, 1999), 238–39.

19. I use the original text in Koiné Greek as it is offered at *The Greek New Testament*, ed. Kurt Aland et al. (New York: American Bible Society; Wüttermberg Bible Society, 1966).

20. They say, "Then Jesus, filled with the power of the Spirit, returned to Galilee, and a report about him spread through all the surrounding country. He began to teach in their synagogues and was praised by everyone."

21. Alexander C. Loney, "Narrative structure and verbal aspect choice in Luke," in: *Filología Neotestamentaria*, vol. 18, ed. Jesús Peláez (Faculdade de Filosofia y Letras–Universidad de Córdoba: Espanha, 2005), 24.

22. They say, "But he passed through the midst of them and went on his way. He went down to Capernaum, a city in Galilee, and was teaching them on the Sabbath."

23. Richard, "O Evangelho de Lucas," 13.

24. Sicre, *O Quadrante: Introdução aos Evangelhos*, 226. On the same thesis, also see Crossan and Reed, *Excavating Jesus*, 28.

25. Sicre, *O Quadrante: Introdução aos Evangelhos*, 226.

26. Archeological findings suggest that there were still no copies of the Scriptures on papyrus, but on scrolls, so the verb "unroll" is more appropriate. Although copyists may have introduced *anaptúxas* as a pedantic correlative of *ptúxas*—in verse 20, it is more likely that, being accustomed to books in codex form or sheets like ours, they introduced the often-used verb *anoigin*, "to open," as an explanatory replacement for *anaptúxas* (what only happens here in the New Testament). Russel N. Champlin, *O Novo Testamento Interpretado: Versículo por Versículo*, vol. 2 (São Paulo: Cadeia, 1998), 49.

27. Brendan Byrne, *The Hospitality of God: A Reading of Luke's Gospel* (Collegeville, MN: Liturgical Press, 2000), 46.

28. In many translations of the Bible, when we read the quote from Luke and then we read the same text in Isaiah, we find different texts in their language. This is because both translations come from different texts and original languages. Luke's text is translated from Greek, and Isaiah's, from Hebrew, a text that Luke did not use. This difference is easily seen in the Jerusalem Bible translation.

29. There are those who interpret that when Jesus reads Isaiah, when he speaks of liberation, he does not speak of an earthly, social, and material liberation, but of an interior liberation from the chains of sin, that is, of a spiritual liberation. On this perspective, see Champlin, *O Novo Testamento*

Interpretado, 50. Following the perspective of other biblical scholars, I interpret it from socioeconomic lens. Throughout Luke's Gospel, one finds a concern for the poor and a contempt for the rich, as it would interfere with the experience of the Gospel. Crossan and Reed, *Excavating Jesus*, 51–97.

30. Champlin, *O Novo Testamento Interpretado*, 50.

31. Anyone who reads the entire Gospel knows that Jesus is not the son of Joseph, but of God through the work of the Holy Spirit and that Jesus has been concerned about his Father's house since he was a boy (Luke 2:48–49). On this statement, see Byrne, *The Hospitality of God*, 51.

32. Sicre, *O Quadrante: Introdução aos Evangelhos*, 236.

33. Byrne, *The Hospitality of God*, 52.

34. Champlin, *O Novo Testamento Interpretado*, 50.

35. Crossan and Reed, *Excavating Jesus*, 1–14.

36. There are New Testament scholars who support the hypothesis of the existence of a synagogue in Nazareth and it was destroyed by the Romans around the year AD 70. On this hypothesis, see Champlis, *O Novo Testamento Interpretado*, 49. However, archaeological excavations and more recent historical studies do not support this hypothesis.

37. Nazareth was an insignificant village that does not appear even once in the Old Testament. The Jewish historian of the first century of the Christian era, Flavius Josephus, often mentions the region of Galilee, but he never talks about Nazareth, which further demonstrates the neglect of this village and its obscurity. On more information concerning the village of Nazareth, see Champlin, *O Novo Testamento Interpretado*, 49. On the Flavius Josephus, see *Josephus: The Essential Work*, ed. Paul L. Maier (Grand Rapids, MI: Kregel Academic & Professional, 1995).

38. Crossan and Reed, *Excavating Jesus*, 25–26. On the same matter, see also André Myre, "Jesus e seu Movimento," in *Escritos e Ambiente do Novo Testamento: Uma Introdução*, ed. Odotte Mainville (Petrópolis: Vozes, 2002), 74.

39. Crossan and Reed, *Excavating Jesus*, 31–36.

40. Jean-Paul Michaud, "Palestina do primeiro século," in *Escritos e ambiente do Novo Testamento, Escritos e Ambiente do Novo Testamento: Uma Introdução*, ed. Odette Mainville (Petrópolis: Vozes, 2002), 29. Also see Sean Freyne, *A Galileia, Jesus e os Evangelhos: Enfoques Literários e Investigações Históricas* (São Paulo: Loyola, 1996), 87.

41. Helmut Koester, *Introduction to the New Testament: History and Literature of Early Christianity*, vol. 2 (Philadelphia: Fortress Press, 1982), 86–94.

42. Champlin, *O Novo Testamento Interpretado*, 49.

43. Champlin, *O Novo Testamento Interpretado*, 49.

44. Whether Jesus could read or not is an unresolved controversy. Those who defend that Jesus was not literate rely on historical knowledge of this period—that presents a region of poor peasants little concerned with the literacy of their children—and on other New Testament writings that do not imply that Jesus knew how to read and write. Only Luke 4:16–30 offers something related to Jesus's literacy. More on this issue, see Crossan and Reed, *Excavating Jesus*, 30–31. Myre, "Jesus e seu Movimento," 84. However, some argue the opposite, that Jesus was literate, based on ancient traditions of the disciples that demonstrate that Jesus had significant knowledge of the Scriptures, suggesting his literacy. See Koester, *Introduction to the New Testament*, 73–74.

45. Byrne, *The Hospitality of God*, 47–48.

46. It is the case of all Sacred Scripture's texts, in which God speaks through people and in human ways, that those who wrote the sacred texts did so because they were inspired by the Holy Spirit. *Dei Verbum*, no. 11–12.

47. Crossan and Reed, *Excavating Jesus*, 28–39.

48. Crossan and Reed, *Excavating Jesus*, 29.

49. Considering this similarity, Crossan and Reed say, [Luke 4:15–30] "is, as presented, not history from Jesus' past in Jewish homeland in the late 20s, but as a parable about Paul's future in the Jewish diaspora of the early 50s" (Crossan and Reed, *Excavating Jesus*, 31). But the rejection of Jesus in the synagogue at Nazareth may foreshadow the rejection in Jerusalem by the Jewish authorities.

50. Crossan and Reed, *Excavating Jesus*, 29.

51. Crossan and Reed, *Excavating Jesus*, 27.

52. As for the book of Isaiah, after questioning its internal historical, theological, and literary differences, it was concluded that the entire writing of the book could not be attributed to a single person known as the prophet Isaiah, born around 750 BC. Therefore, this book is divided into three parts, writing in different occasions and possible by different people: Proto-Isaiah (chaps. 1—39); Deutro-Isaiah (chaps. 40—55) and Trito-Isaiah (chaps. 56—66). On details about this division and why, see José L. Sicre, *Profetismo em Israel: O Profeta: os Profetas: A Mensagem* (Petrópolis: Vozes, 1996), 182–83; 264–66.

53. Byrne, *The Hospitality of God*, 49.

54. Ivo Storniolo, *Como Ler o Evangelho de Lucas: Os Pobres Constroem a Nova História*, 3rd ed. (São Paulo: Paulus, 1992), 46.

55. Byrne, *The Hospitality of God*, 50.

56. José L. Sicre, *O Quadrante: O Mundo de Jesus*, 317.

57. Jacques Dupuis, *Who Do You Say I Am? Introduction to Christology* (Maryknoll, NY: Orbis Books, 1994), 41–43.

58. Champlin, *O Novo Testamento Interpretado*, 49–50.

59. In Leonardo Boff's words, "The kingdom of God that Christ announces is not a liberation from this or that evil, from the political oppression of the Romans, from the economic difficulties of the people, or from sins alone. The kingdom of God cannot be narrowed down to any particular aspect. It embraces all, the world, the human person, and society; the totality of reality is to be transformed by God." Leonardo Boff, *Jesus Christ Liberator: A Critical Christology for Our Time* (Maryknoll, NY: Orbis Books, 1978), 55.

60. Sicre, *O Quadrante: Introdução aos Evangelhos*, 239.

61. Byrne, *The Hospitality of God*, 48.

62. Storniolo, *Como Ler o Evangelho de Lucas*, 46.

63. Sicre, *O Quadrante: O Mundo de Jesus*, 309–24.

64. Sicre, *O Quadrante: O Mundo de Jesus*, 316.

CHAPTER 3

1. Juan Carlos Scannone, *Theology of the People: The Pastoral and Theological Roots of Pope Francis* (New York: Paulist Press, 2021).

2. On theology of people in Francis's thought, see Massimo Borghesi, *The Mind of Pope Francis: Jorge Mario Bergoglio's Intellectual Journey* (Collegeville, MN: Liturgical Press Academic, 2017), 44–55.

3. Pope Francis said at beginning of his pontificate during the first general audience with about 5,000 journalists. Joshua J. McElwee, "Pope Francis: 'I would love a church that is poor,'" *National Catholic Report*, March 16, 2013, https://www.ncronline.org/blogs/francis-chronicles/pope-francis-i-would-love-church-poor. Care for the poor has been a mark of Francis's pontificate. This is very clear in his documents, such as *Evangelli Gaudium*, *Laudato Si'*, and *Fratelli Tutti*. He also has promoted meeting with impoverished peoples and communities, exemplified in what occurred during the World Day of the Poor. For him, "the poor are treasures of the Church." Vatican News Staff Writer, "Pope on World Day of Poor: the poor are treasure of the Church," *Vatican News*, November 14, 2021, https://www.vaticannews.va/en/pope/news/2021-11/pope-on-world-day-of-poor-the-poor-are-treasure-of-the-church.html.

4. José Comblin, *O Povo de Deus*, 3rd ed. (São Paulo: Paulinas, 2011), 106. In the *Evangelii Gaudium*, Francis affirms, "The people of God is incarnate in the people of the earth, each of which has its own culture" (no. 115).

5. Jon Sobrino, *Jesus the Liberation: A Historical-Theological Reading of Jesus of Nazareth* (Maryknoll, NY: Orbis Books, 1993), 33.

6. Jacques Dupuis, *Who Do You Say I Am? Introduction to Christology* (Maryknoll, NY: Orbis Books, 1994), 39–41.

7. Dupuis, *Who Do You Say I Am*, 41–42.

8. Roger Haight, "Scripture: A Pluralistic Norm for Understanding our Salvation in Jesus Christ," *Concilium* 326, no. 3 (2008): 11–23.

9. Raymond E. Brown, *The Community of the Beloved Disciple: The Life, Loves and Hates of an Individual Church in New Testament Times* (New York: Paulist Press, 1979), 40–41.

10. Roger Haight, *The Future of Christology* (New York: Continuum, 2005), 13–15.

11. This theological conception of Jesus alive and present in history is also offered by Vatican II Dogmatic Constitution *Dei Verbum*. It says that God is present in history and reveals himself through words and actions (*Dei Verbum* 2). The encounter with Christ takes place in the reality in which a person and/or a community is historically inserted. Hence, Christ becomes alive in the concrete existence of human beings, in the dilemmas and challenges of their life.

12. Haight, *The Future of Christology*, 45.

13. Our faith is apostolic because we believe that the witness of the apostles is truth. On this, see the *Catechism of the Catholic Church*, nos. 857–65.

14. Concept developed by Ignacio Ellacuría to designate the Latin American people marked by poverty, exploitation, and oppression. I. Ellacuría, "The Crucified People: Na Essay in Historical Soteriology," in *Ignacio Ellacuría: Essays on History, Liberation, and Salvation*, ed. Michael E. Lee (Maryknoll, NY: Orbis Books, 2013), 195–224.

15. Sobrino, *Jesus the Liberator*, 30.

16. See the discussion of liberation ethics in the session on "Methodological Framework for Theology" in chapter 1.

17. On a discussion about *Christology from above* and *Christology from below*, and their differences, see Dupuis, *Who Do You Say I Am?*, 22–27; Haight, *The Future of Christology*, 32–43; Maria Clara Bingemer, *Jesus Cristo: Servo de Deus e Messias Glorioso* (São Paulo: Paulinas; Valência: Siquem, 2008), 11–25.

18. Among other books, see Sobrino's Christology in two volumes, published in English as *Jesus the Liberation: A Historical-Theological Reading of Jesus of Nazareth* (Maryknoll, NY: Orbis Books, 1993) and *Christ the Liberator: A View from the Victims* (Maryknoll, NY: Orbis Books, 2001); see also *Christology at the Crossroads: A Latin American Approach* (Eugene, OR: Wipf and Stock, 2002).

19. The main books of Boff's Christology published in English are *Jesus Christ Liberator: A Critical Christology for Our Time* (Maryknoll, NY:

Orbis Books, 1978) and *Passion of Christ, Passion of the World* (Maryknoll, NY: Orbis Book, 2011).

20. Sobrino, *Jesus the Liberator*, 79–82.

21. Albert Nolan, *Jesus before Christianity*, 25th anniv. ed. (Maryknoll, NY: Orbis Books, 2001), 28.

22. Nolan, *Jesus Before Christianity*, 28–29.

23. Maria Clara Bingemer, *Jesus Cristo: Servo de Deus e Messias Glorioso* (São Paulo: Paulinas; Valência: Siquem, 2008), 44.

24. The reality of religious exclusion does not necessarily lead a person to socioeconomic oppression. This was the case with many tax collectors (the publicans), people who were considered sinners, but were rich. See, e.g., Zacchaeus in Luke 19:1–10.

25. Bingemer, *Jesus Cristo*, 44–45.

26. Leonardo Boff, *Jesus Christ Liberator: A Critical Christology for Our Time* (Maryknoll, NY: Orbis Books, 1978), 282.

27. Sobrino, *Jesus the Liberator*, 82–83.

28. *Catechism of Catholic Church*, no. 516.

29. Dupuis, *Who Do You Say I Am?*, 44.

30. Dupuis, *Who Do You Say I Am?*, 43.

31. "As an eschatological reality, the kingdom of God is universal, everyone can enter it, although not everyone in the same way. But, directly, the kingdom of God belongs only to the poor. And if this is so, the kingdom is essentially 'partial.'" Sobrino, *Jesus the Liberator*, 82–84.

32. On Jesus as a prophet, see José Comblin, *A Profecia na Igreja* (São Paulo: Paulus, 2008), 51–72. Comblin suggests that Jesus was a prophet, but he was also more than a prophet. He did not announce something in the future but made the future to be at the present. His gestures were signs of anticipation of the kingdom of God. After the resurrection, the disciples, with the lens of faith, reinterpreted the life of Jesus and realized that he was more than a prophet. During this historical life, Jesus was recognized as a prophet, but after the experience of his resurrection, he was announced as the Messiah and Son of God.

33. Boff, *Jesus Christ Liberator*, 61.

34. *Catechism of the Catholic Church*, no. 544.

35. Bingemer, *Jesus Cristo*, 45.

36. *Catechism of the Catholic Church*, no. 2444. The *Catechism* is an example of magisterial teaching emphasizing the poor as privileged recipients of the gospel, but this is present in many other teachings coming from the magisterium. In the most recent teaching from the magisterium, this centrality of the poor in the mission of the Catholic Church is constantly highlighted by Pope Francis, who speaks about a poor Church for the poor (*Evangelii Gaudium* 198).

37. Comblin, *A Profecia na Igreja*, 109.

38. John Chrysostom, *On the Incomprehensible Nature of God* (Washington, DC: The Catholic University of America Press, 1984), 70–71.

39. Comblin, *A Profecia na Igreja*, 111.

40. John Chrysostom quoted in the *Catechism of the Catholic Church*, no. 2446.

41. João Crisóstomo [John Chrysostom], *Da Providência de Deus* (São Paulo: Paulus, 2007), 195.

42. Comblin, *A Profecia na Igreja*, 113.

43. See Basil's homilies on "Luke 12," "On the Rich," and "On Time of Famine and Thirst" that are in *Defensor Pauperum: Los Pobres en Basílio de Cesareia (homilías VI, VII, VIII y XIVB)*, ed. Fernando Rivas Rebaque (Madrid: BAC, 2005), 591–667.

44. Fernando Rivas Rebaque, *Defensor Pauperum: Los Pobres en Basilio de Cesarea* (Madrid: BAC, 2005), 41–54.

45. Basilio de Cesarea [Basil of Caesarea], "Homilía Dicha en Tiempos de Hambre y Sed," in Rebaque, *Defensor Pauperum*, 591–605.

46. Basil was a great defender of the faith proclaimed at the Council of Nicaea (325), so much so that he strongly faced the Arian bishops who exercised a significant presence in the Cappadocian region. Basil also faced the problem of the heresy of the *pneumatomachus*, those who denied the equal glorification of the Holy Spirit with the Father and the Son. He was the first to write a treatise on the nature of the Holy Spirit, which served as basis for the Council of Constantinople (391) to proclaim the equality of natures between the Holy Spirit, the Father, and the Son. Basil, The Great, *On the Holy Spirit* (Yonkers, NY: St. Vladimir's Seminary Press, 2011).

47. Basilio de Cesarea [Basil of Caesarea], "Homilía Dicha en Tiempos de Hambre y Sed," in Rebaque, *Defensor Pauperum*, 53.

48. Basil of Caesarea, "Homily 6, On Greed," in *Basil of Caesarea*, ed. Stephen Hildebrand (New York: Routledge, 2018), 125.

49. Basil of Caesarea, "Homily 6, On Greed," 128–29.

50. Basilio de Cesarea [Basil of Caesarea], "Homilía sobre los Ricos," in Rebaque, *Defensor Pauperum*, 575–90.

51. Basilio de Cesarea [Basil of Caesarea], "Homilía sobre los Ricos," in Rebaque, *Defensor Pauperum*, 587.

52. Basilio de Cesarea [Basil of Caesarea], "Homilía sobre los Ricos," in Rebaque, *Defensor Pauperum*, 583–84.

53. Basilio de Cesareia [Basil of Caesarea], "Homilía sobre los Ricos," in Rebaque, *Defensor Pauperum*, 592–96.

54. Basilio de Cesareia [Basil of Caesarea], "Homilía sobre los Ricos," in Rebaque, *Defensor Pauperum*, 661.

55. One of the key perspectives of the Document of Aparecida from the CELAM (Episcopal Conference of Latin American and Caribbean) is that the entire Catholic community is formed by disciples and missionaries of Jesus Christ wherever they live. It shows a perspective of being a missionary in your own land, community, and home. See, e.g., CELAM, *Documento de Aparecida*, no. 31–33.

56. Antonio Spadaro, "A Big Heart Open to God: A Conversation with Pope Francis," *America: The Jesuit Review* 209, no. 8 (September 30, 2013), https://www.americamagazine.org/faith/2013/09/30/big-heart-open-god-interview-pope-francis.

57. *Lumen Gentium*, no. 8; *Sacrosanctum Concilium*, no. 526; *Ad gents*, no. 868; *Presbyterorum Ordinis*, no.1157, 1202.

58. *Lumen Gentium*, no. 9.

59. *Dei Verbum*, no. 2.

60. *Gaudium et Spes*, no. 4.

61. Comblin, *A Profecia na Igreja*, 203–7.

62. José O. Beozzo, *Pacto das Catacumbas: Por Uma Igreja Servidora e Pobre* (São Paulo: Paulinas, 2015).

63. Comblin, *A Profecia na Igreja*, 207.

64. CELAM, "Conclusões de Medellín," in *Documentos do Celam: Rio de Janeiro, Medellín, Puebla e Santo Domingo* (São Paulo: Paulus, 2005), no. 5.

65. CELAM, "Conclusões de Medellín," no. 7.

66. CELAM, "Conclusões de Medellín," no. 9.

67. José O. Beozzo, "Medellín: Quarenta Anos," *Concilium* 328, no. 5 (2008): 127.

68. Sobrino, *Jesus the Liberator*, 80.

69. CELAM, "Conclusões de Puebla," in *Documentos do Celam: Rio de Janeiro, Medellín, Puebla e Santo Domingo* (São Paulo: Paulus, 2005), no. 1134.

70. CELAM, "Conclusões de Puebla," no. 31.

71. CELAM, "Conclusões de Puebla," no. 1142.

72. CELAM, "Conclusões de Santo Domingo," no. 302.

73. Although I think this criticism was fair in the months following the publication of the Document of Aparecida given that it suffered some editorial work in the Vatican, who published a version with differences from the text approved by the CELAM bishops, the reception of a text and development of its interpretation influence its impact. In the case of Aparecida, its reception recused the prophetic emphasis of the preferential option of the poor presented in Medellín and Puebla, grounding it in a christological understanding of this option. The Document of Aparecida and its reception have fostered the development of the preferential

option for the poor with a dynamism able to respond to the challenge of today's world and its new mechanisms of oppression and impoverishment of vulnerable people in Latin America and elsewhere. This development and dynamism of the preferential option for the poor are present in Pope Francis's texts who talks about the option for the poor as the resource for responding to the cry of the earth, the cry of the poor, and many other current challenges.

74. Conferência Episcopal Latino Americana—CELAM. *Documento de Aparecida* (São Paulo; Brasília: Paulus; Edições CNBB, 2007), no. 392. The highlighted sentences are words of Pope Benedict XVI in the opening address of the Conference of Aparecida on March 13, 2007. It was the first time that a CELAM's document included the option for the poor as a christological option. However, christological foundations for the option for the poor were present in Medellín and Puebla. Moreover, liberation theologians have affirmed this since the 1970s, e.g., in Leonardo Boff's book *Jesus Christ Liberator* published in 1972. Boff, *Jesus Christ Liberator*, 6, 26, 36–37, 52, 224–27.

75. CELAM, *Documento de Aparecida*, no. 392.

76. CELAM, *Documento de Aparecida*, no. 402.

77. Jon Sobrino, *No Salvation Outside the Poor: Prophetic-Utopian Essays* (Maryknoll, NY: Orbis Books, 2008), xii.

78. John Chrysostom, *On the Incomprehensible Nature of God*, 102–3.

79. Francisco Catão, *Falar de Deus* (São Paulo: Paulinas, 2001), 7–21.

80. On a theological account about the immanent and economic dimensions of God's revelation, see Karl Rahner, *Foundations of Christian Faith: An Introduction to the Ideal of Christianity* (New York: Crossroad, 1997), 133–37.

81. Joaquim Severino Croatto, "La Contribución de la Hermenéutica Bíblica a la Teología de la Liberación" *Cuadernos de Teología* 6, no. 4 (1985): 45–69.

82. Luke mentions the Holy Spirit seventeen times in his Gospel. Key moments of the presence of the Holy Spirit in Jesus's life are: Jesus is conceived by the Holy Spirit (Luke 1:26–36); Jesus is led by the Spirit into the desert (Luke 4:1); he walks to Galilee moved by the Spirit (Luke 4: 18); he inaugurates his mission anointed by the Spirit (Luke 4:18); Jesus is filled with joy in the Spirit (Luke 10: 21); the Father gives the Spirit to Jesus through prayer (Luke 11:13). José L. Sicre, *O Quadrante: Introdução aos Evangelhos*, vol. 1 (São Paulo: Paulinas, 1999): 243–44.

83. The Council of Chalcedon (451) defined that Jesus Christ is perfect in terms of his divinity and his humanity, two natures without confusion, without change, without division and without separation. Heinrich

Denzinger, *Compendium of Creed, Definitions, and Declarations of the Catholic Church* (San Francisco: Ignatius Press, 2012), no. 302.

84. Catão, *Falar de Deus*, 103.

85. Catão, *Falar de Deus*, 100.

86. St. Irenaeus, Adv. haeres. 3,18,3: PG 7/1, 934, quoted in *Catechism of the Catholic Church*, no. 438.

87. Francisco Catão, *Trindade: Uma Aventura Teológica* (São Paulo: Paulinas, 2000), 18.

88. Catão, *Trindade*, 32.

89. *Catechism of the Catholic Church*, no. 247–48, shortly addresses the problem between the Greek and Latin traditions about the origin of the Holy Spirit. The Greek confesses that the Spirit proceeds from the Father through the Son and the Latin confesses that the Spirit proceeds from the Father and the Son (*filioque*). This controversy was among the reasons (certainly the main theological reason) for the first schism of the Church in the eleventh century. The *Catechism* does not provide a comprehensive explanation on these two theological perspectives but says that there is a legitimate complementarity between the two theologies of the Holy Spirit if they are not radicalized.

90. Leonardo Boff, *Trinity and Society* (Maryknoll, NY: Orbis Books, 1988), 25.

91. Nolan, *Jesus Before Christianity*, 37–44.

92. Boff, *Trinity and Society*, 31.

93. Catão, *Falar de Deus*, 107.

94. Boff, *Trinity and Society*, 33.

95. Catão, *Falar de Deus*, 108.

96. Catão, *Falar de Deus*, 74.

97. Boff, *Trinity and Society*, 34.

98. Haight, *The Future of Christology*, 49.

99. Haight, *The Future of Christology*, 50.

100. Haight, "Scripture: A Pluralistic Norm for Understanding our Salvation in Jesus Christ," 20.

101. Sobrino, *No Salvation Outside the Poor*, 49.

102. Sobrino, *No Salvation Outside the Poor*, 19.

103. Boff, *Jesus Christ Liberator*, 2–5.

104. Basilio de Cesarea [Basil of Caesarea], "Homília VI y VII," in Rebaque, *Defensor Pauperum*, 591–605.

CHAPTER 4

1. Brian P. Flanagan, "Can the Church Be Both Holy and Sinful?" *America Magazine*, October 22, 2018, https://www.americamagazine.org/faith/2018/10/22/can-church-be-both-holy-and-sinful.

2. Mário de França Miranda, "O Desafio de Aparecida: Uma Configuração Eclesial para a América Latina," *Revista Eclesiástica Brasileira* 69, no. 273 (January 2009): 81–83, https://doi.org/10.29386/reb.v69i273.1372.

3. José Comblin, *A Profecia na Igreja* (São Paulo: Paulus, 2008), 123–64.

4. Miranda, "O Desafio de Aparecida," 80–84.

5. João Batista Libano, *Cenários de Igreja*, 2nd ed. (São Paulo: Loyola, 2000).

6. Libano, *Cenários de Igreja*, 69.

7. Libano, *Cenários de Igreja*, 91–130.

8. CELAM, *Documento de Aparecida* (São Paulo; Brasília: Paulus; Edições CNBB, 2007), no. 393.

9. D. Joel Portella Amado, "O Documento de Aparecida e sua Proposta para toda a Igreja," *Atualidade Teológica* 22, no. 58 (Jan/Apr 2018): 65–90, https://doi.org/10.17771/PUCRio.ATeo.32793.

10. Examples of Francis's references to Aparecida can be found at *Evangelii Gaudium*, nos. 15, 21, 124, and 181; *Laudato Si'*, no. 54; and *Fratelli Tutti*, no. 234.

11. *Gaudium et Spes*, no. 4. CELAM, *Documento de Aparecida*, no. 33.

12. CELAM, *Documento de Aparecida*, no. 366.

13. CELAM, *Documento de Aparecida*, no. 367.

14. Miranda, "O Desafio de Aparecida," 80.

15. Pope Francis says, "The Holy Spirit is the soul of the Church. He gives life, he brings forth different charisms which enrich the people of God and, above all, he creates unity among believers: from the many he makes one body, the Body of Christ. The Church's whole life and mission depend on the Holy Spirit; he fulfils all things." Homily of His Holiness Pope Francis at the Catholic Cathedral of the Holy Spirit, Istanbul, November 29, 2014, https://www.vatican.va/content/francesco/en/homilies/2014/documents/papa-francesco_20141129_omelia-turchia.html.

16. Alexandre A. Martins, *The Cry of the Poor: Liberation Ethics and Justice in Health Care* (Lanham: Lexington Books, 2020), 59–60.

17. José Comblin, *The Holy Spirit and Liberation* (Eugene, OR: Wipf & Stock Publishers, 2004).

18. Comblin, *The Holy Spirit and Liberation*, 89–92.

19. Comblin, *The Holy Spirit and Liberation*, 94–95.

20. Vatican II presents the Catholic Church as the people of God, a priestly people: *Lumen Gentium*, nos. 9–10.

21. Comblin, *The Holy Spirit and Liberation*, 106.

22. On the experience of the Spirit in the Scriptures, see Yves Congar, *Creio no Espírito Santo 1: Revelação e Experiência do Espírito* (Paulinas: São Paulo, 2005), 17–88.

23. Santo Irineu, "Contra as Heresias," in *Antologia dos Santos Padres*, ed. C. F. Gomes (São Paulo: Edições Paulinas, 1979), 124.

24. José Comblin, *O Espírito Santo e a Libertação* (Petrópolis: Vozes, 1987), 108.

25. Francisco Catão, *Falar de Deus* (São Paulo: Paulinas, 2001), 99.

26. Comblin, *O Espírito Santo e a Libertação*, 115.

27. Comblin, *O Espírito Santo e a Libertação*, 154.

28. Comblin, *O Espírito Santo e a Libertação*, 157.

29. Comblin, *O Espírito Santo e a Libertação*, 158.

30. Leonardo Boff, *Church, Charism and Power: Liberation Theology and The Institutional Church* (London: SCM Press, 2011).

31. Jon Sobrino, *Spirituality of Liberation: Toward Political Holiness* (Maryknoll, NY: Orbis Books, 1985), 13–22.

32. Catão, *Falar de Deus*, 146.

33. Comblin, *O Espírito Santo e a Libertação*, 166.

34. In his encyclical *Laudato Si'*, Pope Francis is very clear in his presentation of an integral ecology from the Catholic tradition as a proposal for dialogue with all to develop collaborative ways to care for the earth and for the poor, those who most suffer the impact from the ecological crisis.

35. Miranda, "O Desafio de Aparecida," 100.

36. Sobrino, *Spirituality of Liberation*, 167.

37. José Comblin, *A Profecia na Igreja* (São Paulo: Paulus, 2008), 277–78.

38. Bishop Hélder Câmara was certainly one of the main organizers of the so-called Church of the poor and of the meeting that brought together thirty-nine bishops in the Catacomb of St. Domitila on November 16, 1965, when the Pact of the Catacombs was signed. He was probably one of the main drafters of the text of this pact. His letters from that time have phrases and ideas present in the text from catacombs. To verify this, one can compare the letter that Bishop Câmara wrote on November 30, 1965, addressed to *Família Mecejanense* with the text of the Pact of the Catacombs. In that letter, Câmara even suggested that he wished to pres-

ent the Pact in a session of the Second Vatican Council. The Letter can be found at Hélder Câmara, *Circulares Conciliares: de 10/11 de setembro a 7/8 de dezembro de 1965*, vol. I, Tomo III (Recife: CEPE, 2009), 300–303.

39. The text of the Pact of the Catacombs can be found at José Oscar Beozzo, *Pacto da Catacumbas: Por uma Igreja Servidora e Pobre* (São Paulo: Paulinas, 2015), 29–49. The Church historian Beozzo offers the original text with commentaries. An English Version of the text, translated by Francis McDonagh, is published as *The Pact of the Catacombs: The Mission of the Poor in the Church*, ed. Zabier Pikaz and José Antunes da Silva (Navarra, Spain: Editorial Verbo Divino, 2015), 14–17.

40. Comblin, *A Profecia na Igreja*, 268.

41. CELAM, *Documento de Aparecida*, nos. 8 and 520.

42. CELAM, *Documento de Aparecida*, no. 540.

43. CELAM, *Documento de Aparecida*, no. 397.

44. CELAM, *Documento de Aparecida*, no. 94.

45. CELAM, *Documento de Aparecida*, nos. 98 and 396.

46. CELAM, *Documento de Aparecida*, no. 379.

47. CELAM, *Documento de Aparecida*, no. 550.

48. CELAM, *Documento de Aparecida*, no. 383.

49. For more on the Pact of Catacombs, the bishops who signed it, and theological reflection and commentaries on the Pact and its relevance for the Catholic Church, see Zabier Pikaz and José Antunes da Silva, eds., *The Pact of the Catacombs: The Mission of the Poor in the Church* (Navarra, Spain: Editorial Verbo Divino, 2015) and José Oscar Beozzo, *Pacto da Catacumbas: Por uma Igreja Servidora e Pobre* (São Paulo: Paulinas, 2015).

50. Comblin, *A Profecia na Igreja*, 203–43.

51. Sobrino, *Spirituality of Liberation*, 129.

52. Jon Sobrino, *No Salvation Outside the Poor: Prophetic-Utopia Essays* (Maryknoll, NY: Orbis Books, 2008), 52.

53. Sobrino, *No Salvation Outside the Poor*, 9.

54. Pope Francis, "Homily of Holy Father Francis: Visit to Lampedusa," July 8, 2013, http://w2.vatican.va/content/francesco/en/homilies/2013/documents/papa-francesco_20130708_omelia-lampedusa.html. See also *Laudato Si'*, no. 52; *Fratelli Tutti*, no. 138.

55. Albert Nolan, *Jesus Before Christianity*, 25th anniv. ed. (Maryknoll, NY: Orbis Books, 2011), 35.

56. Calisto Vendrame, *A Cura dos Doentes na Bíblia* (São Paulo: Loyola, 2001), 61–62. The text of Luke in Greek used is from *The Greek New Testament*, ed. Kurt Aland et al. (New York: American Bible Society, 1966).

57. Gustavo Gutiérrez, "Seguimiento de Jesús y Opción por el Pobre," *Religião e Cultura* 6, no. 12 (2007): 139.

58. Pontifical Council for Justice and Peace, *Compendium of the Social Doctrine of the Church* (Vatican: Libreria Editrice Vaticana, 2005), no. 96, https://www.vatican.va/roman_curia/pontifical_councils/justpeace/documents/rc_pc_justpeace_doc_20060526_compendio-dott-soc_en.html.

59. Pontifical Council for Justice and Peace, *Compendium of the Social Doctrine of the Church*, no. 203.

60. Pontifical Council for Justice and Peace, *Compendium of the Social Doctrine of the Church*, 2005, no. 208.

61. Alexandre A. Martins, "Preferential Option for the Poor and Equity in Health," *Rivista Camillianum* 40 (2014): 31–48.

62. The concept of *equity* is widely used in current ethical and bioethical debates around the world, but especially in low and middle-income countries. Considering a context marked by poverty and inequalities, the concept of *equity* is fundamental for any action that seeks to fight for justice in health care and other social challenges. Volnei Garrafa and Dora Porto, "Bioética, Poder e Injustiça: Por uma Ética de Intervenção," in *Bioética: Poder e Injustiça*, ed. V. Garrada and L. Pessini (São Paulo: Loyola, 2003), 38–40.

63. World Health Organization, *World Health Report 2008: Primary Health Care* (2008), 12, http://www.who.int/whr/2008/en/index.html.

64. World Health Organization, *World Health Report 2008*, 12.

65. Alexandre A. Martins, *The Cry of the Poor: Liberation Ethics and Justice in Health Care* (Lanham, MD: Lexington Books, 2020).

66. Todd A. Salzman and Michael G. Lawler, "Solidarity and Catholic Social Thought: Confronting the Globalization of Indifference," *Journal of Religion & Society*, Supplement 16 (2018): 125–49, http://hdl.handle.net/10504/116861.

67. Comblin, *Profecia na Igreja*, 273.

68. Sobrino, *No Salvation Outside the Poor*, 12.

69. *Gaudium et Spes*, no. 53.

70. Andrés Torres Queiruga, "Jesus: Genuinely Human," *Concilium* 326, no. 3 (2008): 36.

71. Queiruga, "Jesus: Genuinely Human," 36 (emphasis in the original).

72. On the conflict between the community of Matthew and the Pharisees, J. Andrew Overman, *Matthew's Gospel and Formative Judaism: The Social World of the Matthean Community* (Minneapolis: Fortress Press, 1990).

73. Roger Haight, "Scripture: A Pluralistic Norm for Understanding our Salvation in Jesus Christ," *Concilium* 326, no. 3 (2008): 21.

74. Haight, "Scripture," 22.

75. Felix Wilfred, "Christological Pluralism: Some Reflections," *Concilium* 326, no. 3 (2008): 86.

76. CELAM, *Documento de Aparecida*, no. 56.

77. CELAM, *Documento de Aparecida,* no. 57.

78. This is present throughout the whole of Francis's encyclical *Fratelli Tutti*, but I highlight numbers 77, 94, 106, 154, and 271. They offer a great sense of Francis's Christology to ground this social teaching on fraternity as essential for social justice.

79. Roger Haight, *The Future of Christology* (New York: Continuum, 2005), 126–27.

80. Pontifical Council for Justice and Peace, *Compendium of the Social Doctrine of the Church*, nos. 334–35.

81. Haight, *The Future of Christology*, 137.

82. Haight, *The Future of Christology*, 141–43.

83. Ivone Gebara and Maria Clara Bingemer, *Mary, Mother of God, Mother of the Poor* (Maryknoll, NY: Orbis Books, 1989).

84. On the Guadalupe event and the message of the Virgin of Guadalupe, see Richard Nebel, *Santa Maria Tonantzin Virgen de Guadalupe* (México: Fondo de Cultura Económica, 1995).

85. Nebel, *Santa Maria Tonantzin Virgen de Guadalupe*, 290–300.

86. Nebel, *Santa Maria Tonantzin Virgen de Guadalupe*, 301–4.

87. Pope Francis even affirms that all must learn from the popular faith of the poor. *Evangelii Gaudium*, no. 198.

88. *Sacrosantum Concilium*, nos. 37–40.

89. *Sacrosantum Concilium*, no. 54.

90. Leonardo Boff, *Sacraments of Life, Life of the Sacraments* (Washington, DC: The Pastoral Press, 1987), 58.

91. Matias Augé, *Espiritualidade Litúrgica* (Aparecida: Ave Maria, 2002), 25–37.

92. Ione Buyst, "Em Minha Memória," in *O Mistério Celebrado: Memória e Compromisso I*, ed. I. Buyst and J. A. da Silva (São Paulo: Paulinas; Valência: Siquem, 2006), 77–91.

93. Buyst, "Em Minha Memória," 84.

94. Augé, *Espiritualidade Litúrgica*, 26.

95. Augé, *Espiritualidade Litúrgica*, 31.

96. Boff, *Sacraments of Life, Life of the Sacraments*, 77–79.

97. I see it, e.g., in the experience of the Black Christian communities in the United States. James Cone, *The Cross and the Lynching Tree* (Maryknoll, NY: Orbis Books, 2013).

98. Buyst, "Em Minha Memória," 85.

CHAPTER 5

1. Although the preferential option for the poor was discussed in the previous chapter, I want to add that it is a principle of the Catholic social teaching that appeared for the first time in a Church document in 1987 (*Sollicitudo rei socialis* 39) by John Paul II. He incorporated this principle in the official magisterium after its development in Latin American theology. Pope Francis continued this tradition of developing the meaning of the preferential option for the poor as a choice from christological faith (*Evangelii Gaudium* 198) and an ethical imperative (*Laudato Si'* 158). Although the preferential option for the poor has been broadly accepted in theological cycles around the world, this understanding has a more conceptual-theoretical aspect than its practical implication, as a way of life and perspective for building justice. This practical implication is in the first writing about this option, which only expressed theologically an experience embodied by Latin American communities in the 1950s, 1960s, and 1970s. To understand this process, see "The Preferential Option for the Poor as an Existential Commitment" in Alexandre A. Martins, *The Cry of the Poor: Liberation Ethics and Justice in Health Care* (Lanham: Lexington, 2020), 59–75.

2. There are many comprehensive reports with studies showing the connection between poverty and illness. These reports are promoted by organizations, such as WHO, World Bank and The Lancet works teams, and can be found on their websites. See also Nazim Habibov, Alena Auchynnikava, and Rong Lou, "Poverty Does Make Us Sick," *Annals of Global Health* 85, no. 1 (2019): 1–12, https://doi.org/10.5334/aogh.2357.

3. Norman Daniels et al. speak of a cycle in which poverty causes bad health, which makes vulnerable people even poorer, and thus produces a lower health status for this population. Norman Daniels et al., "Health and Inequality, or, Why Justice Is good for Our Health," in *Public Health, Ethics, and Equity*, ed. S. Anand, F. Peter, and A. Sen (New York: Oxford University Press, 2004), 65–66.

4. Christus Health, "Our Mission and Values," accessed November 12, 2022, https://christushealth.org/about/our-mission-values-and-vision.

5. Catholic Health Association of the United States of America, "About," accessed November 12, 2022, https://www.chausa.org/about/about.

6. Calisto Vendrame, *A Cura dos Doentes na Bíblia* (São Paulo: Loyola, 2001).

7. Ascension Health, "Mission, Vision and Values," accessed November 12, 2022, https://www.ascension.org/Our-Mission/Mission-Vision-Values.

8. John Paul II affirms, "When interdependence becomes recognized in this way, the correlative response as a moral and social attitude, as a 'virtue,' is solidarity. This then is not a feeling of vague compassion or shallow distress at the misfortunes of so many people, both near and far. On the contrary, it is a firm and persevering determination to commit oneself to the common good" (*Sollicitudo rei socialis* 38).

9. CELAM, *Documento de Aparecida* (São Paulo; Brasília: Paulus; Edições CNBB, 2007), no. 353.

10. CELAM, *Documento de Aparecida*, no. 112.

11. CELAM, *Documento de Aparecida*, no. 392.

12. This liberating approach in health care is developed from a liberation ethics: "an exercise of the transcendental spirit in the midst of the historical praxis of the poor. It is a dialogical movement of listening to the poor and being open to learn from them. Far from a romantic vision of the poor, liberation ethics is the fruit of a practical engagement in the life, suffering, faith, hope, and struggle of the poor." Martins, *The Cry of the Poor*, xxxiv.

13. Hélder Câmara, *Essential Writings*, ed. F. McDonagh (Maryknoll, NY: Orbis Books, 2009), back cover page.

14. Paul Farmer, *Pathologies of Power: Health, Human Rights, and the New War on the Poor* (Berkeley: University of California Press, 2003), 127.

15. Paulo Freire, *Pedagogy of the Oppressed*, 30th anniv. ed. (New York: Continuum, 2000), 43–45.

16. Gustavo Gutiérrez, *La Fuerza Histórica de los Pobres*, 2nd ed. (Lima CEP, 1980). Gustavo Gutiérrez, "The Irruption of the Poor in Latin American and the Christian Communities of the Common People," in *The Challenge of Basic Christian Communities*, ed. S. Torres and J. Eagleson (Maryknoll, NY: Orbis Books, 1981), 107–23.

17. Paulo Freire, *Pedagogy of the Oppressed*, 44.

18. Leonardo Boff, *Jesus Christ Liberator: A Critical Christology for Our Time* (Maryknoll, NY: Orbis Books, 1978), 264–68.

CHAPTER 6

1. Some versions translate: "Your faith has saved you." The original text in Greek is *sésokén* that can be translated as "has saved" or "has healed." In *koiné* Greek and the use of this language in the context of the New Testament, there is not a clear distinction between being healed as a

physical cure and being saved as an eschatological reality since physical diseases and spiritual forces are related.

2. The entire narratives of these two scriptural scenes are in Luke 8:40–56 and 18:35–43.

3. Sonja Myhre et al., "Bridging Global Health Actors and Agendas: The Role of National Public Health Institutes," *Journal of Public Health Policy* 43, no. 2 (2022): 251–65, https://doi.org/10.1057/s41271-022-00342-0.

4. Thana Cristina de Campos, "A European Take on Global Public Health: Applying the Catholic Principle of Subsidiarity to Global Health Governance," in *Ethical Challenges in Global Public Health: Climate Change, Pollution, and the Health of the Poor*, ed. Philip J. Landrigan and Andrea Vicini (Eugene, OR: Wipf and Stock Publishers, 2021), 143.

5. Lawrence O. Gostin, Dave Sridhar, and Daniel Hougendobler, "The Normative Authority of the World Health Organization," *Public Health* 129, no. 7 (2015): 854–63, https://doi.org/10.1016/j.puhe.2015.05.002.

6. Boaventura de Sousa Santos, *Epistemologies of the South: Justice against Epistemicide* (New York: Routledge, 2014), 108.

7. Eugene T. Richardson, *Epidemic Illusions: And the Coloniality of Global Public Health* (Cambridge, MA: The MIT Press, 2020), 1.

8. Coloniality is a concept created by Anibal Quijano to express the mentality of people from former-colonies and from former colonial powers that reproduces, respectively, the colonial and colonized mindset that functions as a *modus operandi* in the world. One of its manifestations is the understanding that the European culture and epistemology are superior. Anibal Quijano, "Colonialidad y modernidad-racionalidad," *Perú Indígena* 13, no. 29 (1992): 11–20.

9. Richardson, *Epidemic Illusions*, 32–55.

10. Pope Francis presents the preferential option for the poor as an ethical imperative (*Laudato Si'* 158). This is discussed in chapter 5.

11. Nurith Aizenman and Malaka Gharib, "American with No Medical Training Ran Center for Malnourished Ugandan Kids. 105 Died," *National Public Radio: Special Report*, August 9, 2019, https://www.npr.org/sections/goatsandsoda/2019/08/09/749005287/american-with-no-medical-training-ran-center-for-malnourished-ugandan-kids-105-d.

12. Baganda is one of the several ethnical people of a traditional Bantu kingdom that is in today's country Uganda. This country has its origin as a modern state in a territorial definition determined by English colonization that did not respect the previous divisions of the original people of the land. Uganda achieved independency only in 1962. Although there is a national identity whereby all see themselves as part of the nation,

Uganda, they also preserve an ethnic identity in which people recognize themselves as part of an ancestral people, cultivating their own traditions and languages.

13. African novelist, *Ngũgĩ* Wa Thiong'o says that "most important area of domination [of colonialism] was the mental universe of the colonized, the control, through culture, of how people perceived themselves and their relationship to the world." He points out the urgent need of the liberation of the mind of former colonized people in the Global South. *Ngũgĩ* Wa Thiong'o, *Decolonizing the Mind: The Politics of Language in African Literature* (Nairobi: James Currey, 1986), 17.

14. Boaventura de Sousa Santos, *Epistemologies of the South: Justice Against Epistemicide* (New York: Routledge, 2014), 49.

15. Simone Weil, "L'amour de Diieu el la malheur," in *Œuvres* (Paris: Quarto Gallimard, 1999), 693–715.

16. Simone Weil, *Œuvres Complètes VI 4: La Connaissance Surnaturelle* (Paris: Gallimard, 2006), 122–23.

17. For a study on the concepts of *malheur* and grace in Simone Weil, see Alexandre A. Martins, *A Pobreza e a Graça: Experiência de Deus em Meio ao Sofrimento em Simone Weil* (São Paulo: Paulus, 2013).

18. Simone Weil, "Réflexions sur les causes de la liberté et de l'oppression social," in *Œuvres* (Paris: Quarto Gallimard, 1999), 275–340.

19. Paulo Freire, *Pedagogy of the Oppressed*, 30th anniv. ed. (New York: Continuum, 2000), 50–53.

20. On this issue, see my article: "The Leftist Political Parties in Light of Simone Weil's Criticism: The Workers' Party Care," *Síntese: Revista de Filosofia* 46, no. 145 (2019): 283–300, https://doi.org/10.20911/21769389v46n145p47/2019.

21. Paulo Freire, *Education for Critical Consciousness* (New York: Continuum, 2005), 13–16.

22. Elisabeth Rosenthal, *An American Sickness: How Healthcare Became Big Business and How You Can Take It Back* (New York: Penguin Books, 2017).

23. Paul Farmer, *Pathologies of Power: Health, Human Rights, and the New War on the Poor* (Berkeley: University of California Press, 2003), 201.

24. Historical determinism was discussed in the previous chapter.

25. Sousa Santos, *Epistemologies of the South*, 106.

26. Sousa Santos, *Epistemologies of the South*, 42.

27. Gustavo Gutiérrez, "The Irruption of the Poor in Latin American and the Christian Communities of the Common People," in *The Challenge of Basic Christian Communities*, ed. S. Torres and J. Eagleson (Maryknoll, NY: Orbis Books, 1981), 107–23.

28. Paulo Freire, *Pedagogy of the Oppressed*, 41.

29. There are many comprehensive reports with studies showing the connection between poverty and illness. These reports are promoted by organizations, such as WHO, World Bank, and The Lancet works teams, and can be found on their websites. See also Nazim Habibov, Alena Auchynnikava, and Rong Luo, "Poverty Does Make Us Sick," in *Annals of Global Health* 85, no. 1 (2019): 1–12, https://doi.org/10.5334/aogh.2357. This vicious cycle, that is, poverty, vulnerability to be sick, lack of health care, premature death, is discussed in chapter 5.

30. Other Catholic social principles also contribute to the development of the perspective and model I emphasize in this chapter, such as the principle of solidarity, subsidiarity, participation, and the common good. For more on the contribution of these principles to global health governance, see Michael D. Rozier, "Global Public Health and Catholic Insights: Collaboration on Enduring Challenges"; Lisa S. Cahill, "Social Justice and the Common Good: Improving the Catholic Social Teaching Framework"; Thana Cristina de Campos, "A European Take on Global Public Health: Applying the Catholic Principle of Subsidiarity to Global Health Governance," in *Ethical Challenges in Global Public Health: Climate Change, Pollution, and the Health of the Poor*, ed. Philip J. Landrigan and Andrea Vicini (Eugene, OR: Wipf and Stock Publishers, 2021), 63–79, 106–18, 141–52.

31. María T. Davila, "The Political Anthropology of *Fratelli Tutti*: The Transcendent Nature of People's Political Projects Grounded in History," *Journal of Catholic Social Thought* 19, no. 1 (2022): 101, https://doi.org/10.5840/jcathsoc20221917.

32. Massimo Faggioli, "From Collegiality to Synodality: Promise and Limits of Francis's 'Listening Primacy,'" *Irish Theological Quarterly* 85, no. 4 (2020): 353, https://doi.org/10.1177/0021140020916034.

33. Vincent J. Miller, "Synodality and the Sacramental Mission of the Church: The Struggle for Communion in a World Divided by Colonialism and Neoliberal Globalization," *Theological Studies* 83, no. 1 (2022): 9, https://doi.org/10.1177/00405639221076556.

34. International Theological Commission, "Synodality in the Life and Mission of the Church," March 2, 2018, no. 118, https://www.vatican.va/roman_curia/congregations/cfaith/cti_documents/rc_cti_20180302_sinodalita_en.html.

35. International Theological Commission, "Synodality in the Life and Mission of the Church," no. 103.

36. International Theological Commission, "Synodality in the Life and Mission of the Church," no. 119.

37. Agenor Brighenti and Stefano Raschietti, "O Sínodo para a Amazônia em Perspectiva Decolonial," *REB–Revista Eclesiástica Brasileira* 82, no. 321 (2022): 74, https://doi.org/10.29386/reb.v82i321.3936.

38. João Nunes, "A Pandemia de COVID-19: Securitização, Crise Neoliberal e a Vulnerabilização Global," *Cadernos de Saúde Pública* 36, no. 4 (2020): 1–4, https://doi.org/10.1590/0102-311X00063120.

39. Alexandre A. Martins, "Desafios éticos de uma crise mundial: Uma crise latente, sua manifestação (Covid-19) e confrontos a partir da ética social católica," *Ephata* 3, no. 2 (2021): 13–37, https://doi.org/10.34632/ephata.2021.9709.

40. Pope Francis, *Let Us Dream: The Path to a Better Future* (New York: Simon & Schuster, 2020), 1.

CHAPTER 7

1. Norman Daniels et al., speak of tragic sequences of events in terms of a cycle that poverty causes, resulting in bad health that makes vulnerable people even poorer, and thus produces a lower health status. Norman Daniels et al., "Health and Inequality, or, Why Justice Is good for Our Health," in *Public Health, Ethics, and Equity*, ed. S. Anand, F. Peter, and A. Sen (New York: Oxford University Press, 2004), 65–66.

2. There are many comprehensive reports with studies showing the connection between poverty and illness. These reports are promoted by organizations, such as WHO, World Bank, and The Lancet and can be found on their websites. See also Nazim Habibov, Alena Auchynnikava, and Rong Luo, "Poverty Does Make Us Sick," *Annals of Global Health* 85, no. 1 (2019): 1–12, https://doi.org/10.5334/aogh.2357.

3. Instituto Socioambiental, "Povos indígenas nos Brasil," accessed November 12, 2022, https://pib.socioambiental.org/pt/página_principal.

4. Carlos Fausto, "O Sarampo do Tempo de Meu Avô: Memórias do Etnocídio na Pandemia," *Nexo Jornal*, April 24, 2020, https://www.nexojornal.com.br/ensaio/debate/2020/O-sarampo-do-tempo-de-meu-av%C3%B4-mem%C3%B3rias-do-etnoc%C3%ADdio-na-pandemia.

5. Ministério da Saúde, Secretaria Especial de Saúde Indígena—SESAI, "Boletim Epidemiológico da SESAI," accessed November 12, 2022, https://saudeindigena.saude.gov.br/corona.

6. Ricardo V. Santos et al., "Um Fato Social Total: COVID-19 e Povos Indígenas no Brasil," *Cadernos de Saúde Pública* 36, no. 10 (2020): 2, https://doi.org/10.1590/0102-311X00268220.

7. Redação, "Veja 10 Declarações Racistas de Bolsonaro Sobre os Indígenas," *Esquerda Diário*, August 27, 2019, http://www.esquerdadiario.com.br/Veja-10-declaracoes-racistas-de-Bolsonaro-sobre-os-indigenas.

8. Élio Gasda, "Os Mortos Não São Números: Gerenciamento Político da Morte em Tempos de Pandemia," *Annales FAJE* 5, no. 4 (2020): 43.

9. Gasda, "Os Mortos Não São Números," 45–46.

10. Congregation for the Doctrine of the Faith, *Letter Samaritanus Bonus: On the Care of Persons in the Critical and Terminal Phases of Life*, July 14, 2020, https://www.vatican.va/roman_curia/congregations/cfaith/documents/rc_con_cfaith_doc_20200714_samaritanus-bonus_en.html.

11. Some examples of these messages of Pope Francis's are "Message of His Holiness Pope Francis to the Participants in the European Regional Meeting of the World Medical Association," November 7, 2017. https://www.vatican.va/content/francesco/en/messages/pont-messages/2017/documents/papa-francesco_20171107_messaggio-monspaglia.html. "Pope Francis: The Dying Need Palliative Care, Not Euthanasia or Assisted Suicide," *Catholic Agency News*, February 9, 2022, https://www.catholicnewsagency.com/news/250333/at-general-audience-pope-francis-says-the-dying-need-palliative-care-not-euthanasia-or-assisted-suicide.

12. Paul Farmer, *Fevers, Feuds, and Diamonds: Ebola and the Ravages of History* (New York: Farrar, Straus and Giroux, 2020), 3–4.

13. Alexandre A. Martins, *Bioética, Saúde e Vulnerabilidade: Em Defesa da Vida da Dignidade dos Vulneráveis* (São Paulo: Paulus, 2011), 96.

14. Márcio Fabri dos Anjos, "Eutanásia em Chave de Libertação," *Boletim ICAPS* 7, no. 57 (1989): 6.

15. Dos Anjos, "Eutanasia em Chave de Libertação," 7.

16. Luiz Antonio Lopes Ricci, *A Morte Social: Mistanásia e Bioética* (São Paulo: Paulus, 2017). Ricci argues that the concept of *misthanasia* allows us to include a prophetic dimension to bioethics, leading this discipline to think and act against structures that create social vulnerability and prevents marginalized people from access to health care (Ricci, *A Morte Social*, 20).

CONCLUSION

1. Paul Farmer, *Fevers, Feuds, and Diamonds: Ebola and the Ravages of History* (New York: Farrar. Straus and Giroux, 2020), 12.

2. Conselho Episcopal Latino-Americano, *Discípulos Missionários no Mundo da Saúde: Guia para a Pastoral da Saúde na América Latina e no Caribe* (São Paulo: Centro Universitário São Camilo Press, 2010), no. 8.

3. Conferência Nacional dos Bispos do Brasil, *Campanha da Fraternidade 2012*, no. 186.

Bibliography

Aizenman, Nurith, and Malaka Gharib. "American with No Medical Training Ran Center for Malnourished Ugandan Kids. 105 Died." *National Public Radio: Special Report*, August 9, 2019. https://www.npr.org/sections/goatsandsoda/2019/08/09/749005287/american-with-no-medical-training-ran-center-for-malnourished-ugandan-kids-105-d.

Aland, Kurt, et al., eds. *The Greek New Testament*. New York: American Bible Society; Wüttermberg Bible Society, 1966.

Amado, D. Joel Portella. "O Documento de Aparecida e sua Proposta para Toda a Igreja." *Atualidade Teológica* 22, no. 58 (2018): 65–90. https://doi.org/10.17771/PUCRio.ATeo.32793.

Ascension Health, "Mission, Vision and Values." Accessed November 12, 2022. https://www.ascension.org/Our-Mission/Mission-Vision-Values.

Augé, Matias. *Espiritualidade Litúrgica*. Aparecida: Ave Maria, 2002.

Basil of Ceasariea. *Basil of Ceasareia*. Edited by Stephen Hildebrand. New York: Routledge, 2018.

Basílio de Cesareia. *Defensor Pauperum: Los Pobres en Basílio de Cesareia (homilías VI, VII, VIII y XIVB)*. Edited by Fernando Rivas Rebaque. Madrid: BAC, 2005.

Basil the Great. *On the Holy Spirit*. Yonkers, NY: St. Vladimir's Seminary Press, 2011.

Benedict XVI, pope. *Encyclical Letter Deus Caritas Est*. December 25, 2005. https://www.vatican.va/content/benedict-xvi/en/encyclicals/documents/hf_ben-xvi_enc_20051225_deus-caritas-est.html.

Beozzo, José O. "Medellín: Quarenta Anos." *Concilium* 328, no. 5 (2008): 124–36.

———. *Pacto da Catacumbas: Por uma Igreja Servidora e Pobre*. São Paulo: Paulinas, 2015.

Bingemer, Maria Clara L. "A Desventura e a Opção Pelos Pobres: Simone Weil e a Teologia da Libertação Latino-americana." *REB–Revista Eclesiástica Brasileira* 69, no. 276 (2009): 772–91. https://doi.org/10.29386/reb.v69i276.1251.

———. *Jesus Cristo: Servo de Deus e Messias Glorioso.* São Paulo: Paulinas; Valência: Siquem, 2008.

Boff, Clodovis. *Teoria do Método Teológico*, 4th ed. Petrópolis: Vozes, 2009.

Boff, Leonardo. *Church, Charism and Power: Liberation Theology and The Institutional Church*. London: SCM Press, 2011.

———. *Jesus Christ Liberator: A Critical Christology for Our Time.* Maryknoll, NY: Orbis Books, 1978.

———. *Jesus Cristo Libertador: Ensaio de Cristologia Crítica para o Nosso Tempo.* Petrópolis: Vozes, 2012.

———. *Passion of Christ, Passion of the World.* Maryknoll, NY: Orbis Book, 2011.

———. *Sacraments of Life, Life of the Sacraments.* Washington, DC: The Pastoral Press, 1987.

———. *Trinity and Society*. Maryknoll, NY: Orbis Books, 1988.

Boff, Leonardo, and Clodovis Boff. *Como Fazer Teologia da Libertação*, 8th ed. Petrópolis: Vozes, 2001.

———. *Introducing Liberation Theology.* Maryknoll, NY: Orbis Books, 1987.

Borghesi, Massimo. *The Mind of Pope Francis: Jorge Mario Bergoglio's Intellectual Journey.* Collegeville, MN: Liturgical Press Academic, 2017.

Bosch, David J. *Missão Transformadora: Mudanças de Paradigma na Teologia da Missão*, 3rd ed. São Leopoldo: Sinodal, 2002.

Bovon, François. "Evangelho de Lucas e Atos dos Apóstolos." In *Os Evangelhos Sinóticos e Atos dos Apóstolos*, edited by J. Auneau et al., 265–89. São Paulo: Ed. Paulinas, 1985.

———. *L'Œuvre de Luc: Études d'Exégèse et de Théologie.* Paris: Editions du Cerf, 1987.

Brighenti, Agenor, and Stefano Raschietti, "O Sínodo para a Amazônia em Perspectiva Decolonial." *REB–Revista Eclesiástica Brasileira* 82, no. 321 (January/April 2022): 66–91. https://doi.org/10.29386/reb.v82i321.3936.

Brown, Raymond E. *The Community of the Beloved Disciple: The Life, Loves and Hates of an Individual Church in New Testament Times.* New York: Paulist Press, 1979.

Buyst, Ione, and J. A. da Silva, eds. *O Mistério Celebrado: Memória e Compromisso I.* São Paulo: Paulinas; Valência: Siquem, 2006.

Byrne, Brendan. *The Hospitality of God: A Reading of Luke's Gospel.* Collegeville, MN: Liturgical Press, 2000.

Cahill, Lisa S. "Social Justice and the Common Good: Improving the Catholic Social Teaching Framework." In *Ethical Challenges in Global Public Health: Climate Change, Pollution, and the Health of the Poor*, edited by Philip J. Landrigan and Andrea Vicini, 106–18. Eugene, OR: Wipf and Stock Publishers, 2021.

Câmara, Hélder. *Circulares Conciliares: de 10/11 de setembro a 7/8 de dezembro de 1965*. Vol. I, Tomo III. Recife: CEPE, 2009.

———. *Essential Writings*. Edited by F. McDonagh. Maryknoll, NY: Orbis Books, 2009.

CAN Staff. "Pope Francis: The dying Need Palliative Care, Not Euthanasia or Assisted Suicide." *Catholic Agency News*, February 9, 2022. https://www.catholicnewsagency.com/news/250333/at-general-audience-pope-francis-says-the-dying-need-palliative-care-not-euthanasia-or-assisted-suicide.

Catão, Francisco. *Falar de Deus*. São Paulo: Paulinas, 2001.

———. *Trindade: Uma Aventura Teológica*. São Paulo: Paulinas, 2000.

Catholic Church. *Catechism of the Catholic Church: Revised in Accordance with the Official Latin Text Promulgated by Pope John Paul II*. Vatican City: Libreria Editrice Vaticana, 1997. https://www.vatican.va/archive/ENG0015/_INDEX.HTM.

———. *Documents of the Second Vatican Council*. Vatican. Accessed November 22, 2022. https://www.vatican.va/archive/hist_councils/ii_vatican_council/index.htm.

Catholic Health Association of the United States of America. "About." Accessed November 12, 2022. https://www.chausa.org/about/about.

Cavalcanti, Tereza. "Social Location and Biblical Interpretation: A Tropical Reading." In *Reading from This Place. Volume 2: Social Location and Biblical Interpretation*, edited by F. F. Segovia and M. A. Tolbert, 201–18. Minneapolis, MN: Fortress Press, 1995.

Champlin, Russel N. *O Novo Testamento Interpretado: Versículo por Versículo*. Vol. 2. São Paulo: Cadeia, 1998.

Christus Health, "Our Mission and Values." Accessed November 12, 2022. https://christushealth.org/about/our-mission-values-and-vision.

Chrysostom, John. *On the Incomprehensible Nature of God*. Washington, DC: The Catholic University of America Press, 1984.

———. *On the Providence of God*. Platina, CA: St. Herman Press, 2015.

Comblin, José. *A Profecia na Igreja*. São Paulo: Paulus, 2008.

———. *O Espírito Santo e a Libertação*. Petrópolis: Vozes, 1987 (*The Holy Spirit and Liberation*. Eugene, OR: Wipf & Stock Publishers, 2004).

———. *O Povo de Deus*. 3rd ed. São Paulo: Paulinas, 2011 (*People of God*. Maryknoll, NY: 2004).

Cone, James. *The Cross and the Lynching Tree.* Maryknoll, NY: Orbis Books, 2013.

Conferência Episcopal Latino Americana–CELAM. *Documento de Aparecida.* São Paulo; Brasília: Paulus; Edições CNBB, 2007.

———. *Documentos do Celam: Rio de Janeiro, Medellín, Puebla e Santo Domingo.* São Paulo: Paulus, 2005.

Congar, Yves. *Creio no Espírito Santo 1: Revelação e Experiência do Espírito.* Paulinas: São Paulo, 2005.

Congregation for the Doctrine of the Faith. *Letter Samaritanus Bonus: On the Care of Persons in the Critical and Terminal Phases of Life*, July 14, 2020. https://www.vatican.va/roman_curia/congregations/cfaith/documents/rc_con_cfaith_doc_20200714_samaritanus-bonus_en.html.

Costadoat, Jorge. "La Hermenéutica en las Teologías Contextuales de la Liberación." *Teología y Vida* XLVI (2005): 56–74. https://doi.org/10.4067/S0049-34492005000100003.

Crisóstomo, João. *Da Providência de Deus.* São Paulo: Paulus, 2007 (John Chrysostom, *On the Providence of God.* Platina, CA: St. Herman Press, 2015).

Croatto, J. Severino. "La Contribución de la Hermenéutica Bíblica a la Teología de la Liberación." *Cuadernos de Teología* 6, no. 4 (1985): 45–59.

Crossan, John D., and Jonathan L. Reed. *Excavating Jesus: Beneath the Stones, Behind the Texts.* New York: HarperSanFrancisco, 2001.

Cuda, Emilce. "Theology of the People as Theological Ethics." In *Building Bridges in Sarajevo: The Plenary Papers from CTEWC 2018*, edited by K. E. Heyer, L. R. Keenan, and A. Vicine, 83–86. Maryknoll, NY: Orbis Books, 2019.

Daniels, Norman, et al. "Health and Inequality, or, Why Justice Is good for Our Health." In *Public Health, Ethics, and Equity*, edited by S. Anand, F. Peter, and A. Sen, 64–78. New York: Oxford University, 2004.

Davila, María Teresa. "The Political Anthropology of *Fratelli tutti*: The Transcendent Nature of People's Political Projects Grounded in History." *Journal of Catholic Social Thought* 19, no. 1 (2022): 89–103. https://doi.org/10.5840/jcathsoc20221917.

de Aquino Júnior, Francisco. "Teologia e Ciências Sociais." *Horizonte* 10, no. 28 (2012): 1324–49. https://doi.org/10.5752/P.2175-5841.2012v10n28p1324.

de Campos, Thana Cristina. "A European Take on Global Public Health: Applying the Catholic Principle of Subsidiarity to Global Health Governance." In *Ethical Challenges in Global Public Health: Climate Change, Pollution, and the Health of the Poor*, edited by Philip J. Landrigan and Andrea Vicini, 141–52. Eugene, OR: Wipf and Stock Publishers, 2021.

de Mattos, Luiz A. "O Cuidado da Casa Comum: Os desafios éticos e Espirituais de uma Ecologia Integral." In *A Moral do Papa Francisco: Um Projeto a partir dos Descartados*, edited by R. Zacharias and M. I. de Castro Millen, 229–56. Aparecida: Editora Santuário, 2020.

Denzinger, Heinrich. *Compendium of Creed, Definitions, and Declarations of the Catholic Church.* San Francisco: Ignatius Press, 2012.

dos Anjos, Márcio Fabri. "Eutanásia em Chave de Libertação." *Boletim ICAPS* 7, no. 57 (1989): 6–9.

Drexler-Dreis, Jeseph. "Latin American Liberation Theology as a Decolonial Project?: Considering the Theological Approaches of Clodovis Boff and Ignacio Ellacuría." *Louvain Studies* 39, no. 3 (2016): 218–39. https://doi.org/10.2143/LS.39.3.3170047.

Dupuis, Jacques. *Who Do You Say I Am? Introduction to Christology.* Maryknoll, NY: Orbis Books, 1994.

Ellacuría, I. *Ignacio Ellacuría: Essays on History, Liberation, and Salvation.* Edited by Michael E. Lee. Maryknoll, NY: Orbis Books, 2013.

Faggioli, Massimo. "From Collegiality to Synodality: Promise and Limits of Francis's 'Listening Primacy.'" *Irish Theological Quarterly* 85, no. 4 (2020): 352–69. https://doi.org/10.1177/0021140020916034.

Farmer, Paul. *Fevers, Feuds, and Diamonds: Ebola and the Ravages of History.* New York: Farrar. Straus and Giroux, 2020.

———. *Pathologies of Power: Health, Human Rights, and the New War on the Poor.* Berkeley: University of California Press, 2003.

Fausto, Carlos. "O Sarampo do Tempo de Meu Avô: Memórias do Etnocídio na Pandemia." *Nexo Jornal*, April 24, 2020. https://www.nexojornal.com.br/ensaio/debate/2020/O-sarampo-do-tempo-de-meu-av%C3%B4-mem%C3%B3rias-do-etnoc%C3%ADdio-na-pandemia.

Flanagan, Brian P. "Can the Church Be Both Holy and Sinful?" *America Magazine*, October 22, 2018. https://www.americamagazine.org/faith/2018/10/22/can-church-be-both-holy-and-sinful.

Francis, Pope. Apostolic Exhortation *Evangelii Gaudium.* November 24, 2013. http://www.vatican.va/holy_father/francesco/apost_exhortations/documents/papa-francesco_esortazione-ap_20131124_evangelii-gaudium_en.html.

———. Encyclical Letter *Fratelli Tutti.* October 03, 2021. https://www.vatican.va/content/francesco/en/encyclicals/documents/papa-francesco_20201003_enciclica-fratelli-tutti.html.

———. Encyclical Letter *Laudato Si'*. May 25, 2015. http://w2.vatican.va/content/francesco/en/encyclicals/documents/papa-francesco_20150524_enciclica-laudato-si.html.

———. Homily of His Holiness Pope Francis at the Catholic Cathedral of the Holy Spirit, Istanbul, November 29, 2014. https://www.vatican.va/content/francesco/en/homilies/2014/documents/papa-francesco_20141129_omelia-turchia.html.

———. "Homily of Holy Father Francis: Visit to Lampedusa." July 8, 2013. http://w2.vatican.va/content/francesco/en/homilies/2013/documents/pap a-francesco_20130708_omelia-lampedusa.html.

———. *Let Us Dream: The Path to a Better Future.* New York: Simon & Schuster, 2020.

———. "Message of His Holiness Pope Francis to the Participants in the European Regional Meeting of the World Medical Association." November 7, 2017. https://www.vatican.va/content/francesco/en/messages/pont-messages/2017/documents/papa-francesco_20171107_messaggio-monspaglia.html.

———. Post-Synodal Apostolic Exhortation *Querida Amazonia.* February 20, 2020. https://www.vatican.va/content/francesco/en/apost_exhortations/documents/papa-francesco_esortazione-ap_20200202_querida-amazonia.html.

Freire, Paulo. *Education for Critical Consciousness.* New York: Continuum, 2005.

———. *Pedagogia do Oprimido*. 59th ed. Rio de Janeiro: Paz & Terra.

———. *Pedagogy of the Oppressed*. 30th anniv. ed. New York: Continuum, 2000.

Freyne, Sean. *A Galileia, Jesus e os Evangelhos: Enfoques Literários e Investigações Históricas.* São Paulo: Loyola, 1996 (*Galilee, Jesus and the Gospels: Literary Approaches and Historical Investigations*. Minneapolis: Fortress Press, 1988).

Garrafa, Volnei, and Dora Porto. "Bioética, Poder e Injustiça: Por uma Ética de Intervenção." In *Bioética: Poder e Injustiça*, edited by V. Garrada and L. Pessini, 35–40. São Paulo: Loyola, 2003).

Gasda, Élio. "Los Muertos No Son Números: Gestión Política de la Muerte en Tiempos de Pandemia." *Journal of Moral Theology* 10, Special Issue (Spring 2021): 22–32.

———. "Os Mortos Não São Números: Gerenciamento Político da Morte em Tempos de Pandemia." *Annales FAJE* 5, no. 4 (2020): 40–49.

———. "Theological Ethics from the Reality of the People." In *Building Bridges in Sarajevo: The Plenary Papers from CTEWC 2018*, edited by K.

E. Heyer, L. R. Keenan, and A. Vicine, 87–90. Maryknoll, NY: Orbis Books, 2019.

Gebara, Ivone, and Maria Clara Bingemer. *Mary, Mother of God, Mother of the Poor.* Maryknoll, NY: Orbis Books, 1989.

Gostin, Lawrence O., Dave Sridhar, and Daniel Hougendobler, "The Normative Authority of the World Health Organization." *Public Health* 129, no. 7 (2015): 854–63. https://doi.org/10.1016/j.puhe.2015.05.002.

Gramsci, Antonio. *Selections from the Prison Notebooks of Antonio Gramsci.* Edited and translated by Quintin Hoare and Geoffrey N. Smith. New York: International Publishers, 1971.

Gutiérrez, Gustavo. *La Fuerza Histórica de los Pobres.* 2nd ed. Lima CEP, 1980.

———. "Seguimiento de Jesús y Opción por el Pobre." *Religião e Cultura* 6, no. 12 (2007): 137–51.

———. *Teologia da Libertação.* 4th ed. Petrópolis: Vozes, 1983 (*A Theology of Liberation.* Maryknoll, NY: Orbis Books, 1973).

———. "The Irruption of the Poor in Latin American and the Christian Communities of the Common People." In *The Challenge of Basic Christian Communities,* edited by S. Torres and J. Eagleson, 107–23. Maryknoll, NY: Orbis Books, 1981.

Habibov, Nazim, Alena Auchynnikava, and Rong Lou. "Poverty Does Make Us Sick." *Annals of Global Health* 85, no. 1 (2019): 1–12. https://doi.org/10.5334/aogh.2357.

Haight, Roger. *The Future of Christology.* New York: Continnum, 2005.

———. "Scripture: A Pluralistic Norm for Understanding Our Salvation in Jesus Christ." *Concilium* 326, no. 3 (2008): 11–23.

Instituto Socioambiental. "Povos indígenas nos Brasil." Accessed November 12, 2022. https://pib.socioambiental.org/pt/página_principal.

International Theological Commission. "Synodality in the Life and Mission of the Church," March 2, 2018. https://www.vatican.va/roman_curia/congregations/cfaith/cti_documents/rc_cti_20180302_sinodalita_en.html.

Irineu, Santo. "Contra as Heresias." In *Antologia dos Santos Padres,* edited by C. F. Gomes, 115–35. São Paulo: Edições Paulinas, 1979.

John Paul II, Pope. Encyclical Letter *Evangelium vitae.* March 25, 1995. https://www.vatican.va/content/john-paul-ii/en/encyclicals/documents/hf_jp-ii_enc_25031995_evangelium-vitae.html.

———. Encyclical Letter *Sollicitudo rei socialis.* December 30, 1987. https://www.vatican.va/content/john-paul-ii/en/encyclicals/documents/hf_jp-ii_enc_30121987_sollicitudo-rei-socialis.html.

Josephus, Flavius. *Josephus: The Essential Work*, edited by Paul L. Maier. Grand Rapids, MI: Kregel Academic & Professional, 1995.

Kaker, Hille, Luiz Carlo Susim, and Eloi Messi Metogo, eds. "Postcolonial Theolog." *Concilium* 2. London: SCM Press, 2013.

Kodell, Jerome. "Lucas." In *Comentário bíblico*. Vol. 3. 3. Edited by R. Bergant and R. J. Karris, 73–108. São Paulo: Loyola, 2001.

Koester, Helmut. *Introduction to the New Testament: History and Literature of Early Christianity*. Vol. 2. Philadelphia: Fortress Press, 1982.

Libano, João Batista. *Cenários de Igreja*. 2nd ed. São Paulo: Loyola, 2000.

Loney, Alexandre C. "Narrative Structure and Verbal Aspect Choice in Luke." In *Filología Neotestamentaria*. Vol. 18, edited by Jesús Peláez, 3–31. Faculdade de Filosofia y Letras–Universidad de Córdoba: Espanha, 2005.

Martins, Alexandre A. *Bioética, Saúde e Vulnerabilidade: Em Defesa da Vida da Dignidade dos Vulneráveis.* São Paulo: Paulus, 2011.

———. *The Cry of the Poor: Liberation Ethics and Justice in Health Care.* Lanham: Lexington, 2020.

———. *Introdução à Cristologia Latino-americana: Cristologia no Encontro com a Realidade Pobre e Plural da América Latina.* São Paulo: Paulus, 2014.

———. "The Leftist Political Parties in Light of Simone Weil's Criticism: The Workers' Party Care." *Síntese: Revista de Filosofia* 46, no. 145 (2019): 283–300. https://doi.org/10.20911/21769389v46n145p47/2019.

———. *A Pobreza e a Graça: Experiência de Deus em Meio ao Sofrimento em Simone Weil.* São Paulo: Paulus, 2013.

———. "Preferential Option for the Poor and Equity in Health." *Rivista Camillianum* 40 (2014): 31–48.

Massingale, Bryan N. *Racial Justice and the Catholic Church.* Maryknoll, NY: Orbis Books, 2010.

McElwee, Joshua J. "Pope Francis: 'I would love a church that is poor.'" *National Catholic Report*, March 16, 2013. https://www.ncronline.org/blogs/francis-chronicles/pope-francis-i-would-love-church-poor.

Mendoza-Álvarez, Carlos. "*Extra Victimas Salus Non Est* ou da Vigência da Teologia da Libertação em Tempos Pós Modernos." In *A Teologia da Libertação em Prospectiva*, edited by Agenor Brighenti and Rosário Hermano, 323–41. São Paulo: Paulus/Paulinas, 2013.

Mendoza-Ávarez, Carlos, and Thierry-Marie Courau, eds. "Decolonial Theology: Violence, Resistance and Spiritualities." *Concilium* 1. London: SCM Press, 2020.

Mescher, Marcus. *The Ethics Encounter: Christian Neighbor Love as a Practice of Solidarity.* Maryknoll, NY: Orbis Books, 2020.

Mesters, Carlos. "The Liberating Reading of the Bible." *SEDOS Bulletin* 28 (1996): 164–70.

Michaud, Jean-Paul. "Palestina do primeiro século." In *Escritos e ambiente do Novo Testamento, Escritos e Ambiente do Novo Testamento: Uma Introdução*, edited by Odette Mainville, 15–67. Petrópolis: Vozes, 2002.

Milbank, John. *Theology & Social Theory: Beyond Secular Reason*, 2nd ed. Oxford: Blackwell Publishing, 2006.

Millen, Maria Inês de Castro. "Violência Contra as Mulheres: A Face Macabra do Cotidiano." In *A Moral do Papa Francisco: Um Projeto a partir dos Descartados*, edited by R. Zacharias and M. I. de Castro Millen, 149–71. Aparecida: Editora Santuário, 2020.

Miller, Vincent J. "Synodality and the Sacramental Mission of the Church: The Struggle for Communion in a World Divided by Colonialism and Neoliberal Globalization." *Theological Studies* 83, no. 1 (2022): 8–24. https://doi.org/10.1177/00405639221076556.

Ministério da Saúde, Secretaria Especial de Saúde Indígena–SESAI. "Boletim Epidemiológico da SESA." Accessed November 12, 2022. https://saudeindigena.saude.gov.br/corona.

Miranda, Mário de França. "O Desafio de Aparecida: Uma Configuração Eclesial para a América Latina." *Revista Eclesiástica Brasileira* 69, no. 273 (January 2009): 77–102. https://doi.org/10.29386/reb.v69i273.1372.

Moreno Rejon, Francisco. *Teologia Moral a partir dos Pobres: A Moral na Reflexão Teológica da América Latina.* Aparecida: Editora Santuário, 1987.

Morga, Alejandro Castillo. "Ante la Pandemia: Pensar los Desequilibrios Ambientales como Reacción Ética ante la Acción Humana." *Journal of Moral Theology* 10, Special Issue (Spring 2021): 52–66.

Myhre, Sonja, et al. "Bridging Global Health Actors and Agendas: The Role of National Public Health Institutes." *Journal of Public Health Policy* 43, no 2 (June 2022): 251–65. https://doi.org/10.1057/s41271-022-00342-0.

Myre, André. "Jesus e seu Movimento." In *Escritos e Ambiente do Novo Testamento: Uma Introdução*, edited by Odette Mainville, 69–110. Petrópolis: Vozes, 2002.

Nebel, Richard. *Santa Maria Tonantzin Virgen de Guadalupe.* México: Fondo de Cultura Económica, 1995.

Nolan, Albert. *Jesus Before Christianity.* Twenty-fifth Anniversary Edition. Maryknoll, NY: Orbis Books, 2011.

Nunes, João. "A Pandemia de COVID-19: Securitização, Crise Neoliberal e a Vulnerabilização Global." *Cadernos de Saúde Pública* 36, no. 4 (2020): 1–4. https://doi.org/10.1590/0102-311X00063120.

Overman, J. Andrew. *Matthew's Gospel and Formative Judaism: The Social World of the Matthean Community.* Minneapolis: Fortress Press, 1990.

Passos, João Décio. *A Igreja em Saída e a Casa Comum: Francisco e os Desafios da Renovação.* São Paulo: Paulinas, 2016.

Paul VI, Pope. Encyclical Letter *Ecclesiam Suam.* August 6, 1964. https://www.vatican.va/content/paul-vi/en/encyclicals/documents/hf_p-vi_enc_06081964_ecclesiam.html.

———. Encyclical Letter *Populorum Progressio.* March 26, 1967. https://www.vatican.va/content/paul-vi/en/encyclicals/documents/hf_p-vi_enc_26031967_populorum.html.

Pikaz, Zabier, and José Antunes da Silva, eds. *The Pact of the Catacombs: The Mission of the Poor in the Church.* Translated by Francis McDonagh. Navarra, Spain: Editorial Verbo Divino, 2015.

Pontifical Council for Justice and Peace. *Compendium of the Social Doctrine of the Church.* Vatican: Libreria Editrice Vaticana, 2005. https://www.vatican.va/roman_curia/pontifical_councils/justpeace/documents/rc_pc_justpeace_doc_20060526_compendio-dott-soc_en.html.

Queiruga, Andrés Torres. "Jesus: Genuinely Human." *Concilium* 326, no. 3 (2008): 33–43.

Quijano, Anibal. "Colonialidad y modernidad-racionalidad." *Perú Indígena* 13, no. 29 (1992): 11–20.

Rahner, Karl. *Foundations of Christian Faith: An Introduction to the Ideal of Christianity.* New York: Crossroad, 1997.

Rebaque, Fernando Rivas. *Defensor Pauperum*: *Los Pobres en Basilio de Cesarea*. Madrid: BAC, 2005.

Redação. "Veja 10 Declarações Racistas de Bolsonaro Sobre os Indígenas." *Esquerda Diário,* August 27, 2019. http://www.esquerdadiario.com.br/Veja-10-declaracoes-racistas-de-Bolsonaro-sobre-os-indigenas.

Ricci, Luiz Antonio Lopes. *A Morte Social: Mistanásia e Bioética.* São Paulo: Paulus, 2017.

Richard, Pablo O. "Evangelho de Lucas: Estrutura e Chaves para uma interpretação global do Evangelho." *RIBLA* 44, no. 1 (2003): 7–35.

Richardson, Eugene T. *Epidemic Illusions: And the Coloniality of Global Public Health.* Cambridge, MA: MIT Press, 2020.

Rosenthal, Elisabeth. *An American Sickness: How Healthcare Became Big Business and How You Can Take It Back.* New York: Pinguin Books, 2017.

Rozier, Michael D. "Global Public Health and Catholic Insights: Collaboration on Enduring Challenges." In *Ethical Challenges in Global Public*

Health: Climate Change, Pollution, and the Health of the Poor, edited by Philip J. Landrigan and Andrea Vicini, 63–79. Eugene, OR: Wipf and Stock Publishers, 2021.

Salazar, Marilú Rojas. "Tendências Interculturais para uma Espiritualidade Ecofeminista Libertadora." In *A Teologia da Libertação em Prospectiva*, edited by A. Brighenti and R. Hermano, 313–21. São Paulo: Paulus/Paulinas, 2013.

Salzman, Todd A., and Michael G. Lawler. "Solidarity and Catholic Social Thought: Confronting the Globalization of Indifference." *Journal of Religion & Society*, Supplement 16 (2018): 125–49. http://hdl.handle.net/10504/116861.

Sanches, Sidney M. "A Contextualização da Teologia: Conceitos, História, Tensões, Métodos e Possibilidades." *Revista Tecer* 2, no. 3 (2019): 1–20. https://doi.org/10.15601/1983-7631/rt.v2n3p1-20.

Santos, Boaventura de Sousa. *Epistemologies of the South: Justice Against Epistemicide.* New York: Routledge, 2014.

Santos, Ricardo, V., Ana Lúcia Pontes, and Carlos E. A. Coimbra Jr. "Um Fato Social Total: COVID-19 e Povos Indígenas no Brasil." *Cadernos de Saúde Pública* 36, no. 10 (2020): 1–5. https://doi.org/10.1590/0102-311X00268220.

Scannone, Juan Carlos. *Theology of the People: The Pastoral and Theological Roots of Pope Francis.* Mahwah, NJ: Paulist Press, 2021.

Schreiter, Robert. *Constructing Local Theologies*. 30th anniversary ed. Maryknoll, NY: Orbis Books, 2015.

Sicre, José L. *O Quadrante: Introdução aos Evangelhos*. Vol. 1. São Paulo: Paulinas, 1999.

———. *O Quadrante: O Mundo de Jesus*. Vol. 2. São Paulo: Paulinas, 1999.

———. *Profetismo em Israel: O Profeta: os Profetas: A Mensagem.* Petrópolis: Vozes, 1996.

Sobrino, Jon. *Christology at the Crossroads: A Latin American Approach.* Eugene, OR: Wipf and Stock, 2002.

———. *Christ the Liberator: A View from the Victims.* Maryknoll, NY: Orbis Books, 2001.

———. *Jesus the Liberation: A Historical-Theological Reading of Jesus of Nazareth.* Maryknoll, NY: Orbis Books, 1993.

———. *No Salvation outside the Poor: Prophetic-Utopia Essays.* Maryknoll, NY: Orbis Books, 2008.

———. *Spirituality of Liberation: Toward Political Holiness.* Maryknoll, NY: Orbis Books, 1985.

Spadaro, Antonio. "A Big Heart Open to God: A Conversation with Pope Francis." *America: The Jesuit Review* 209, no. 8, September 30, 2013.

https://www.americamagazine.org/faith/2013/09/30/big-heart-open-god-interview-pope-francis.

Storniolo, Ivo. *Como Ler o Evangelho de Lucas: Os Pobres Constroem a Nova História*. 3rd ed. São Paulo: Paulus, 1992.

Tavares, Cássia Quelho. "A Voz das Mulheres como Interpelação à Teologia Moral: A 'Igreja em Saída.'" In *Teologia Moral: Fundamentos, Desafios e Perspectivas*, edited by L. Pessini and R. Zacharias, 223–50. Aparecida: Editora Santuário, 2015.

Thiong'o, Ngũgĩ Wa. *Decolonizing the Mind: The Politics of Language in African Literature*. Nairobi: James Currey, 1986.

Vatican News Staff Writer. "Pope on World Day of Poor: The Poor Are Treasure of the Church," *Vatican News*, November 14, 2021. https://www.vaticannews.va/en/pope/news/2021-11/pope-on-world-day-of-poor-the-poor-are-treasure-of-the-church.html.

Vaz, Henrique C. de Lima. *Escritos de Filosofia II: Ética e Cultura*. São Paulo: Loyola, 1998.

Vélez Caro, Olga Consuelo. *El Método Teológico: Fundamentos, Especializaciones, Enfoques.* Bogotá: Pontificia Universidad Javeriana Press, 2008.

———. "El Quehacer Teológico y el Método de Investigación Acción Participativa: Una Reflexión Metodológica." *Theologica Xaveriana* 67, no. 183 (2017): 197–208. https://doi.org/10.11144/javeriana.tx67-183.qtmiap.

Vendrame, Calisto. *A Cura dos Doentes na Bíblia.* São Paulo: Loyola, 2001.

Vidal, Marciano. "*Gaudium et spes* y Teología Moral: A los 50 Años del Concilio Vaticano II." *Moralia* 35, no. 134 (2012): 103–53.

Weil, Simone. *Œuvres*, Edited by Florence de Lussy. Paris: Quarto Gallimard, 1999.

———. *Œuvres Complètes V 2: L'Enracinement.* Paris: Gallimard, 2013.

———. *Œuvres Complètes VI 4: La Connaissance Surnaturelle.* Paris: Gallimard, 2006.

Wilfred, Felix. "Christological Pluralism: Some Reflections." *Concilium* 326, no. 3 (2008): 84–94.

World Health Organization. *World Health Report 2008: Primary Health Care.* 2008. http://www.who.int/whr/2008/en/index.html.

Zacharias, Ronaldo. *Ética e Direitos Sexuais.* São Paulo: Ideias & Letras, 2021.

Index